TAKARAZUKA

Sexual Politics
and Popular Culture
in Modern Japan

JENNIFER ROBERTSON

University of California Press
Berkeley · Los Angeles · London

The costs of publishing this book have been supported in part by an award from the Hiromi Arisawa Memorial Fund (named in honor of the renowned economist and the first chairman of the board of the University of Tokyo Press) and financed by the generosity of Japanese citizens and Japanese corporations to recognize excellence in scholarship on Japan.

University of California Press
Berkeley and Los Angeles, California

University of California Press, Ltd.
London, England

Chapters 2 and 3 are reprinted by permission of the American Anthropological Association from *American Ethnologist* 19:3, August 1992, and *American Ethnologist* 22:4, November 1995, respectively. Not for further reproduction.

Library of Congress Cataloging-in-Publication Data

Robertson, Jennifer Ellen.
    Takarazuka : sexual politics and popular culture in modern Japan / Jennifer Robertson.
        p.   cm.
        Includes bibliographical references and index.
        ISBN 0–520-21150-2 (alk. paper). —ISBN 0-520-21151-0 (pbk. : alk. paper)
        1. Takarazuka Kagekidan.   2. Ethnology—Japan.
3. Theater—Japan.   4. Musicals—Japan.   5. Popular culture—Japan.   6. Sex role—Japan.   7. Social structure—Japan.   8. Japan—Social life and customs.
I. Title.
GN635.J2R62   1998
306'.0952—dc21   97-38671
                                                                                  CIP

Printed in the United States of America
9 8 7 6 5 4 3 2 1

The paper used in this publication meets the minimum requirements of American National Standards for Information Sciences—Permanence of Paper for Printed Library Materials, ANSI Z39.48–1984.

For Celeste

7/018

Contents

Illustrations

Preface

The establishment of the all-female Takarazuka Revue in 1913 sparked a heated debate in Japan on the relationship of gender, sexuality, popular culture, and national identity. Since a substantial part of my book focuses on prewar and wartime developments in the Revue and Japanese society at large, I have prepared a brief sketch of key historical periods and institutions for readers unfamiliar with Japan.

The Edo (or Tokugawa) period (1603–1867) was distinguished by an agrarian-based social and political order unified under a hereditary succession of generals (shogun) from the Tokugawa clan, which was based in the capital city of Edo. Their ruling power was valorized by a hereditary succession of emperors based in Kyoto. *Bakufu* was the term for the military government. A Confucian social hierarchy adapted from China divided the population into four unequal classes of people: samurai, farmers, artisans, and merchants, in that order. Each class was further bifurcated by a patriarchal sex/gender hierarchy. There were several categories of "nonpeople" as well, including outcastes and itinerants, such as Kabuki actors. Commoners developed a vigorous urban culture in the late seventeenth century, out of which emerged several genres of fine and performing arts that are today regarded as "traditional"—for example, puppet theater, Kabuki, woodblock printing, and haiku. A policy of seclusion kept the country more or less closed to foreign contact and exchange for 250 years.

Victorious antishogun forces restored the emperor to a ruling position in 1868, marking the beginning of the Meiji period (1868–1912). The social changes of this period are conveyed by the slogans "civilization and enlightenment" and "rich country, strong army." Agrarianism gave way to industrialization, and the seclusion policy to imperialism. Japan's first constitution, civil code, and elected assembly were selectively adapted from European forms of government. The occupational hierarchy of the Edo social system was replaced by a class system premised on economic stratification and noble lineage. Strict distinctions between female and male, both in division of labor and deportment, were codified in the Meiji Civil Code, operative until 1947. Generally speaking, the industrialization, militarization, and imperialist claims of the Meiji period escalated during the succeeding Taishō (1912–26) and Shōwa (1926–89) periods. (Heisei [1989–] is the name of the current reign.) The late 1930s and 1940s in particular were marked by Japan's intensified imperialist aggression in Asia and the Pacific and by the military mobilization of the population, in part through the state's appropriation of the Shinto religion as a national cult.

Universal male suffrage was inaugurated in 1925, but women could not vote or be elected until 1945; they first exercised that right in April 1946. In addition to women's suffrage, the political reforms initiated during the Allied (American) Occupation (1945–52) following World War II included an equal rights amendment. The present constitution, which renounces war and (theoretically) the right to possess military potential, became effective in May 1947. The emperor is recognized as a symbol of the state; sovereignty rests with the people, and the Diet is the highest organ of the state.

Throughout the book, Japanese names are presented family name first unless the person has published in English, in which case the given name appears first. All translations from Japanese to English are mine unless otherwise indicated.

Acknowledgments

A cast almost as big as Takarazuka's helped bring this book to press. I should start at the beginning with thanks to my parents, Helen and Ron Robertson, who took me to Japan when I was three years old and raised me and my three younger siblings, Dan, Sarah and Edie, as bilingual, cultural hybrids in the rural outskirts of Tokyo. According to my parents and Japanese family friends, I was exposed to Takarazuka during those initial ten years—we even had a Takarazuka "music album" record in our collection—and those first but forgotten impressions likely influenced in a subliminal way my later scholarly interest in the Revue.

Serena Tennekoon saw nearly as many Takarazuka dress rehearsals and stage shows as I did before her death in 1989, and our lively discussions helped shape the first papers I wrote on the Revue. The sacred memory of her love, courage, and intelligence continues to inspire me in all ways.

There are many friends, colleagues, and acquaintances whose assistance, expertise, and goodwill greatly facilitated both my research and this manuscript at various stages. I owe thanks to Anne Allison, Ruth Behar, Gunhild Borggreen, Donald Brenneis, Norman Bryson, Chino Kaori, Michael Cooper, Eileen Elliott, Ezoe Midori, Thomas Fricke, Sabine Frühstück, Funasaka Osamu and Funasaka Mizuho, Alvia Golden, Gotō Yumiko, Stephen Greenblatt, Arthur Groos, Jean Grossholtz, Hagiwara Hiroko, Helen Hardacre, Hayashi Chiaki, Michael Herzfeld, Irmela Hijiya-Kirschnereit, Hosokawa Shūhei, Ikeda Shinobu, Stephanie Jed, Rebecca Jennison, Laurel Kendall, Maria Teresa Koreck, Conrad Kottak, Renate Lachmann, Takie Sugiyama Lebra, Ming-Cheng Lo, Lisa Lowe, Maho Shibuki, Liisa Malkki, Minoura Yasuko, Muro Nobuko, Nakao Katsumi, Nakao Michiko, Yōichi Nagashima, Bea Nergaard, Vivien Ng, Marie Rosegaard, Deepthi Senanayake, Sharon Sievers, Eric Jan Sluijter and Nicolette Sluijter-Seiffert, Robert Smith and Kazuko Smith, Carroll Smith-Rosenberg, Suemoto Yōko, Sugiura Noriyuki, Sunada Toshiko, Tada Eiko, Hope Tennekoon and Quintus Tennekoon, Yohko Tsuji, Umehara Riko, and Martha Vicinus. I am also grateful to Wolf Lepenies and Joachim Nettelbeck, the rector and secretary, respectively, of the Wissenschaftskolleg zu Berlin, and to the administration, staff, and fellows of the Wissenschaftskolleg.

I wish to thank Takarazuka director Hashimoto Masao for his energetic assistance in the early stages of this project. He introduced me to the administrators, staff, actors, and students of the Revue and Takarazuka Music Academy and arranged for me to attend numerous rehearsals. I hope that Hashimoto-*san* and the rest of the Revue administration will appreciate my efforts to represent the colorful history of Takarazuka in a responsible and scholarly manner.

I must thank the many Takarazuka fans who befriended me and trusted me to represent them in an honest way. As promised, I am obliged to safeguard their identities and thus unfortunately cannot thank them individually. Their enthusiastic responses to the questions informing this project were an invaluable resource.

My thanks also to the staffs of the various libraries and archives listed below for helping to track down obscure documents on the revue theater, fan clubs, wartime recreations, colonial policies, and related subjects. In Japan: Ikeda Bunko, Keio University Library, National Diet Library, Ōya Sōichi Bunko, Self-Defense Force Reading Room Library, and the Waseda University Theater Arts Library. I especially wish to thank the staff of Shōchiku's Ōtani Bunko for so generously allowing me to peruse and photocopy uncatalogued archival material on the revue theater and fan clubs. In the Netherlands: the Film Archive of the National Information Service, Leiden University Asia Library, the Netherlands State Institute for War Documentation (RIOD), and the Film and Science Foundation. I owe special thanks to Elly Touwen-Bouwsma, a director at the RIOD, and to her staff for their kind assistance and hospitality. I also wish to thank Gesine Bottomley and the library staff of the Wissenschaftskolleg zu Berlin for their gracious assistance in gaining access to German libraries. Finally, I must thank Yasuko Matsudo of the Japan Collection, University of Michigan Graduate Library, for her assistance in procuring important Japanese texts for me.

I must also give my thanks for their helpful feedback to my colleagues and their students in the anthropology, Asian/Japanese studies, and women's studies departments, institutes, and programs at the different universities where over the past decade I have presented work related to this book. These include the University of California, Berkeley, Irvine, Los Angeles, San Diego, and Santa Barbara; Cambridge University; the University of Chicago; the University of Copenhagen; Cornell University; Duke University; Free University, Berlin; Harvard University; Hebrew University, Jerusalem; Johns Hopkins University; Kalamazoo College; the University of Kansas; the School of Oriental and African Studies, University of London; the University of Michigan; Occidental College; the University of Oklahoma; Oxford Brookes University; Oxford University; Seika University, Kyoto; Sophia University, Tokyo; Technical University, Berlin; the University of Texas; and Yale University. I am similarly indebted to colleagues and scholars taking part in the many symposia and conferences where I have presented related work. These include the annual meetings of the American Anthropological Association, the American Ethnological Society, the Association for Asian Studies, and the Semiotic Society of America, as well as the international symposia at the University of Colorado, the Einstein Forum (Potsdam), the University of Iowa, the Japan Society (New York), the Japan Foundation (Tokyo), Leiden University, the University of Montreal, and the University of Vienna.

I would like to use this opportunity to thank the graduate students who have shared my interest in exploring the murkier strata of Japanese society and cultural history. Ian Condry, Katarzyna Cwiertka, Elise Edwards, Elyssa Faison, Bethany Grenald, Adrienne Hurley, Gretchen Jones, Kim Kono, Chris Nelson, Beth Notar, Eric Rath, Joshua Roth, and Tomomi Yamaguchi have contributed panel papers and translations related to the different projects represented in this book.

I owe special thanks to Sheila Levine, an exceptional sponsoring editor, for her encouragement and patience, and also to Laura Driussi for her editorial assistance. I am indebted to Sue Heinemann, who, as project editor, expertly shepherded this book through the complicated production process, and wish to express my gratitude to Alice Falk, a brilliant copyeditor. I also wish to express my thanks to Kikuchi Yasuhiro, Murai Mitsuo, and Yoshida Hideto of Gendai Shokan for their interest in publishing my work in Japanese.

Celeste Brusati has shared with me the pleasures and pains of researching and writing. Her acute observations and critical comments, contributed so generously despite her own demanding schedule, were crucial to the realization of this book. It is with love, admiration, and grateful thanks that I dedicate my book to Celeste.

Chapters 2 and 3 are significantly reworked and expanded versions of my articles "The Politics of Androgyny in Japan: Sexuality and Subversion in the Theater and Beyond," *American Ethnologist* 19, no. 3 (1992):419–42, and "Mon Japon: The Revue Theater as a Technology of Japanese Imperialism," *American Ethnologist* 22, no. 4 (1995):970–96, respectively.

Fieldwork and archival research in Japan, the Netherlands, and Germany were funded by the following institutions, fellowships, and grants: the Japan Foundation, Professional Fellowship (1987); the Northeast Asia Council of the Association for Asian Studies, Research Grant (1987); the Social Science Research Council and the American Council of Learned Societies, Advanced Research Grants (1987, 1995); the University of California, San Diego, Affirmative Action Faculty Career Development Grant (1990); Fulbright, Research Scholar Grant (1990 and 1991); Rackham School of Graduate Studies, University of Michigan Research Grants (1992, 1996); the Center for International Business Education, University of Michigan, Faculty Research Grant (1992); the Center for Japanese Studies, University of Michigan, Faculty Grant (1994); Wenner-Gren Foundation for Anthropological Research, Regular Grant (1995); International Institute, University of Michigan, Faculty Grant (1996); Wissenschaftskolleg zu Berlin, Invited Fellow (1996–97).

Introduction

Spectators come to the theater to hear the subtext. They can read the text at home.

Konstantin Stanislavski,
quoted in Moore 1988 (1960):28

When [Takarazuka] "stars" embody song-and-dance artifacts from America, they preserve the surface but change
the context. . . . Old schmaltz become new and transcends
its banality. . . . You don't notice the spin you spin with. You
can only see theirs. They can only see yours.

Carr 1989:48

FIRST IMPRESSIONS

I first saw them on Japanese television in 1976: tall, handsome women with short, slick hair and husky voices—cool, confident, and dashing in their chic suits.[1] They were the players of men's roles in the all-female Takarazuka Revue (figure 1). Intrigued by these most unstereo-typic women, I began to collect sundry information on Takarazuka and its cross-dressed stars, and gradually, I became aware of the high profile the Revue had occupied in Japanese popular culture ever since its inaugural performance in 1914. Revue posters brighten the interiors of trains and railroad stations; its shows and stars are featured in popular magazines; the splashy trailers for the latest Takarazuka spectacle appear regularly on television; and the actors are frequent guests on talk and game shows.

The Golden Wings (*Habatake ōgon no tsubasa yo*) was my initiation into the rococo world of the Takarazuka Revue. The musical opened in Tokyo in April 1985, after a two-month run at the Revue's home theater in Takarazuka city near Osaka. It was billed as the "*sayonara* performance" of Asami Rei, a leading "man" who was retiring that month after fifteen years with the company to pursue a career in the wider world of show business. Set in northern Italy in the thirteenth century, *The Golden Wings* revolves around the antics of a ruthless lord,

1

Figure 1.   Takarazuka today: The Snow Troupe in the finale of *La Passion* (*Ra passhon*, 1989). The beplumed cast—the leading actors are wearing white—stand in front of and on the Revue's trademark giant, illuminated staircase. From Hashimoto (1994:138).

Vittorio Ala d'Oro, "who is in truth a peace-loving man" (*Habatake ōgon no tsubasa yo*, 1985:49). He forces his deceased rival's daughter Clarice into marriage and then attempts to seduce (or rape?) her on their wedding night—earlier that day, she had tried to stab him. The seduction scene was executed onstage in a bizarre way: as Vittorio climbed into Clarice's canopy bed, the stage blackened and an illuminated, rotating mirror ball splattered the audience with colorful dots. As the dots swirled around the auditorium, the anxious woman's feverish thoughts were "heard" over the loudspeakers: "Stop it! Stop it! I don't want to think about anything anymore. I don't want to feel anything. . . . Ahh, that's so cool and nice. Someone's cool hands are gently caressing my forehead. Who is it? Whose are they, those gentle hands" (38). A frisson pulsed through the audience. Clarice subsequently falls in love with Vittorio, and, dodging assassination attempts and other nefarious intrigues, they live happily ever after (figure 2).

I was hooked—not by the retrograde, if steamy, sexual politics of

Figure 2. *The Golden Wings*. Asami Rei as Vittorio Ala d'Oro and Ichiro Maki as Clarice. From Hashimoto (1994:130).

the story, but by the mostly female audience whose intense absorption in the wrenching action onstage made the auditorium sizzle with eroticized energy. During the intermission, I chatted with the "old girl" fans sitting next to me and exchanged comments with other spectators milling about the refreshment stands, all of whom had expert opinions about Asami Rei, *The Golden Wings,* and the Revue in general. I bought all the official fan magazines and photograph albums on display in the main lobby, and after the show, I tucked myself into the crowd of fans waiting for their favorite actors to emerge from the dressing room before vanishing into the mysterious night. My first impressions of the Takarazuka Revue convinced me that there was a very interesting story to be found behind the glitter in the complex relationships interweaving the actors, the fans, the administration, and other parties, including media critics. An exploration and analysis of these intricate relationships forms one of the repeating, looping themes of my book, which is thus not a sustained piece of theater criticism.

In the following brief history of the Takarazuka Revue I emphasize those features central to my general subject of sexual politics and popular culture in modern Japan. This introduction to the theater frames and contextualizes a summary of the chapters.

REVIEWING THE REVUE

The all-female Takarazuka Revue (Takarazuka kagekidan) was founded in 1913 in the hot springs resort of Takarazuka by Kobayashi Ichizō (1873–1957), the Hankyū railroad and department store tycoon, impresario, and two-time cabinet minister.[2] Kobayashi was motivated to create an all-female revue in part as a novel solution to his financial woes. Two years earlier in the village of Takarazuka, west of Osaka, he had opened and then quickly closed a spa that included Japan's first indoor swimming pool. He was keen to develop the area to increase traffic on the new railroad line he had established. The spa, a Victorian-orientalist structure named Paradise (Paradaisu), attracted few guests. Kobayashi's failure to proscribe mixed bathing and the lack of heaters to warm the icy water contributed to its lack of success. Following the precedent set by the Mitsukoshi Dry Goods Store (now Department Store) in Osaka, which had established a Western-style band of boy sopranos and instrumentalists in 1911 to entertain customers, Kobayashi recruited twenty girls, trained them to sing and dance, gave them each a stage name, and scheduled their first public performance in April 1914 (Kobayashi 1961b:445–52).[3] Converting the pool into the Paradise Theater "made good business sense," and the Revue was promoted as "wholesome family entertainment." Originally called the Takarazuka Choir (Takarazuka shōkatai), Kobayashi changed the name within five months to the Takarazuka Girls' Opera Training Association (Takarazuka shōjokageki yōseikai).[4] This modification, and specifically the addition of *shōjo* (girl), set the enduring public image of the Revue, even though *shōjo* was removed when the name was changed one last time in 1940. Since the 1920s, the Revue's actors have been called "Takarasiennes" (*Takarajiennu*), after Parisiennes, in recognition of the early influence of the French revue. They include *otokoyaku*, who play the roles of men, and *musumeyaku*, who play the roles of women. Approximately 700 people at present enable Takarazuka to function. These include 350–400 performers and 300 specialists, including producers, directors, writers, costumers, set designers, instructors, and two thirty-five-piece orchestras.

The 3,000-seat Takarazuka Grand Theater was completed in 1924, the largest Japanese theater of its kind at the time.[5] It remains one component of an expansive entertainment complex—the name was changed from Paradise to Familyland (Fuamirirando) in 1960—that comprises a library, theater arts museum, botanical garden, entomology museum, amusement park, and zoo noted for its white tiger, together with the spa. A similarly large theater was opened in Tokyo in 1934. In 1919 Kobayashi established the forerunner of the present-day Takarazuka Music Academy. Originally an integral part of the Revue, whose actors were Academy students, the two were divided into autonomous institutions in 1939. Kobayashi required that all Takarasiennes must be graduates of the two-year Academy.[6] Today, with two huge theaters in Takarazuka and Tokyo and regularly scheduled regional and international tours, not to mention television and radio broadcasts, the Revue remains one of the most widely recognized and watched of the so-called theaters for the masses (*taishū engeki*) that were created in the early twentieth century.

The widespread popularity and social impact of the Revue is evident in the hundreds of articles that have appeared in a wide range of publications since its founding. Kobayashi, with his entrepreneurial zeal, and the flashy revue theaters that mushroomed in the late teens and early 1920s in Japan were representative of the volatile, Janus-faced culture of consumption described so richly by Edward Seidensticker (1990) and Miriam Silverberg (1990, 1991, 1992, 1993). The emergence of "a middle-class culture organized around new conceptions of family life and leisure activities" clashed with the expansion and politicization of the Japanese industrial workforce (Silverberg 1990:225; see also Gordon 1991). My focus will be the ambivalence that characterized the discourse of gender and sexuality then and continues to the present day, revealed in public debates about the meaning and significance of women—as revue actors, as fans, as delinquents, as wives and mothers, as workers, as consumers.

Takarazuka spawned over a dozen copycat all-female revues in the 1920s, as reported in the mainstream press ("Karakuri no ōi shōjo-kagekidan" 1925; "Nisemono Takarazuka kageki" 1923). The Tokyo Girls' Revue (Tōkyō shōjokagekidan), established in 1917, was modeled after Takarazuka and plagiarized from the premier revue (Ōzasa 1986:73; Aoyagi 1924:26–28). Most notable was the Shōchiku Revue founded in 1928 in Asakusa, a major working-class theater district in Tokyo, which quickly became Takarazuka's main rival in every respect. An Osaka branch of the Shōchiku Revue had been founded eight years earlier in 1920 to compete with Takarazuka on the older troupe's home turf; it broke with the Tokyo company after World War II. Both were formally disbanded in 1990, although special performances are scheduled occasionally.[7] From the start, the Shōchiku Revue was cast as the opposite of Takarazuka. For example, while Takarazuka productions were stereotyped as naive and romantic, the Shōchiku actors performed allegedly more mature and erotic revues. Fans partial to one revue rarely attended performances staged by the rival troupe. Moreover, after the Tokyo Takarazuka Theater was established in 1934, their regional and class distinctions were emphasized. Takarazuka was cast as an "uptown" theater attractive to girls from wealthy households, and Shōchiku as a "lowtown" theater appealing to a blue-collar clientele. Other, much smaller, Tokyo revues included the Casino Follies (opened in 1929) in Asakusa and the Moulin Rouge (opened in 1931) in Shinjuku, a student and intellectual center at the time (see Seidensticker 1990:68–87). The Nichigeki Dancing Team was established under Shōchiku's auspices in 1936 as a revue more overtly erotic than either Shōchiku or Takarazuka ("Adeyū NDT 'hanseiki'" 1977). These theaters and cabarets, along with cafés and coffee shops, were known generically as "revues," although theater critics drew distinctions between grand revues, operetta revues, variety shows, and grand operettas (Ashihara E. 1936:6). Practically speaking, the Takarazuka Revue was an eclectic mix of all these types.

Takarazuka productions include Japanese-style classical dramas and historical subjects, such as the *Tale of Genji*; European-style and Broadway-based performances, such as *Mon Paris* and *West Side Story*; and folk dances from all over the world. Kobayashi, a prolific essayist, wrote many of the earliest scripts under the pen name Ikeda Hatao. The first stage shows were based on folktales and children's stories, and reviewers found them to be above all "cute" (*kawaii*) (e.g., Nishimura 1916). Within five years, Takarazuka was producing more mature musicals with a romantic twist. *Parisette*, staged in 1930, a year after the first Western talkie was shown in Japan,[8] marked the Revue's transition to a modern and erotic style that, with the exception of the martial dramas of the late 1930s and early 1940s, has persisted to the present day. From this production onward, the actors ceased to apply the traditional whiteface (*oshiroi*), wearing instead modern greasepaint that accentuated their own features, distinguished skin colors, and demarcated more clearly a character's gender and ethnicity (figure 3). Most Takarazuka performances today consist of a musical drama, followed by a revue with quick changes of scene and subject, and ending in a finale featuring the Revue's trademark—the entire cast cascades down a giant illuminated staircase in glittering tuxedos and gowns, from which sprout huge ostrich plumes, for a final bow (see figure 1). Generally speaking, with the exception of wartime revues, contemporary Japan and Japanese were not and are not now represented on the Takarazuka stage, which instead offers audiences a chance to dream of other lives in other worlds.

THE CALL OF DUTY

The Takarazuka Revue was among the modern theaters that marked the return of women to a major public stage after being banned from public (i.e., Kabuki) performances in 1629 by the Confucian-oriented Tokugawa Shogunate.[9] At the time the Revue was founded, actresses (*joyū*) were still publicly denounced as "defiled women" who led profligate lives. For example, Mori Ritsuko (1890–1961), one of the best known Shinpa (New School) actresses, was erased from the graduation register of the girls' school she had attended when the administrators discovered that she had pursued a career in theater (Ozaki 1986:14–15).[10] Theater critics proclaimed the new coinage *joyū*, with its connotations of superiority and excellence, preferable to the older

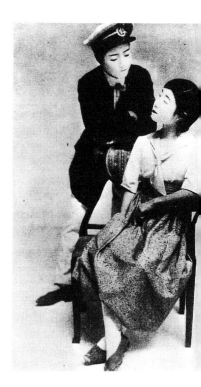

Figure 3.   The early Revue with and without whiteface. *Right*, a scene from *Five Daughters* (*Gonin musume*, 1920) with the childlike actors in whiteface. *Opposite*, in 1930 the application of whiteface was discontinued, and the Revue's cast appeared more adult, as evident in the scene from *Rosarita* (*Rosariita*, 1936). From *The Takarazuka: Takarazuka kageki 8oshūnen kinen* (1994:84) and Hagiwara (1954:13).

term *onnayakusha*, with its historical connotations of itinerant actresses who were associated with unlicensed prostitution (Asagawa 1921). It seems that Kobayashi founded the Takarazuka Music Academy not only to train students in the Western and Japanese theatrical arts, but also to reassure parents that their daughters were under the constant supervision of Academy officials who took responsibility for preventing the young women from falling into a decadent lifestyle (see his essay on the lifestyle of actresses in Kobayashi 1961a:370–73).

The Academy solicits applications from females between the ages of fifteen and twenty-four. Although those in the first group of performers were barely in their teens, the average age of entry-level students was soon increased and today most applicants are nineteen years old. As required, they are either junior high or high school graduates, or they are enrolled in high school. Academy officials continue to claim that the young women are from "good families," and although detailed information about their socioeconomic status is kept confidential, "good" is widely understood as "affluent." Students and Academy of-

ficials alike acknowledge that without the generous support of their parents, the aspiring Takarasiennes would be unable to attend the private singing and dance lessons necessary to keep them competitive.[11] According to statistical data provided to me by the principal's office, 75 percent of the students recruited between 1983 and 1987 reside in Tokyo, Osaka, and Hyōgo prefectures. That percentage has shrunk to about 50 percent today (*Fushigi no kuni no Takarazuka* 1993:101). Graduation from the Academy marks a Takarasienne's public debut as a specialist in one gender and enables her to perform onstage as a bona fide member of one of the five troupes constituting the Revue.

The five troupes are Flower (*hana*), Moon (*tsuki*), Snow (*yuki*), Star (*hoshi*), and Sky (*sora*). The Flower and Moon Troupes, established in 1921, are the oldest. The Snow Troupe was formed in 1924, and the Star Troupe in 1933. Each of these troupes possesses a distinctive character: the Flower Troupe is known for its florid but elegant style; the Moon Troupe for its exquisite charm; the Snow Troupe for its restrained grace; and the Star Troupe for its showiness (Hashimoto 1984:48; Takagi Shimei 1976:65–67). Dividing the actors into troupes and sometimes rotating them helped organize the growing number of applicants and meet the growing demand for Takarazuka performances.[12] This demand prompted the company to create a fifth troupe, whose name, Sky (*sora*), was selected from those submitted in a public competition in the fall of 1996. The new troupe debuted in Hong Kong in January 1998 and in March at the main theater. A third Takarazuka Theater is reportedly under construction near Tokyo Disneyland, and the art deco Tokyo Takarazuka Theater will be replaced by a futuristic high rise scheduled to open in January 2001 ("Takarazuka ni dai 5 no kumi" 1997; "Takarazuka to Get New Tokyo Theater" 1996).[13]

Each troupe is overseen by a (male) member of the Revue administration appointed to that post. The internal hierarchy consists of a troupe manager (*kumichō*) and a vice-manager (*fukukumichō*), drawn from the ranks of the senior actors, and several chairpersons (*zachō*) who include the leading romantic man (*nimaime*),[14] the leading woman (*musumeyaku*), the leading comic man (*sanmaime*), and the supporting actors (*wakiyaku*). Each troupe has a leading man and woman, often paired as a "golden combination" (*goruden combi*), making it easier to satisfy more fans and their diverse tastes than if only one leading star or couple represented the Revue as a whole.

The Takarazuka Music Academy presently provides a two-year curriculum designed to teach the students ensemble playing and to equip them with the skills necessary to play a variety of roles. Forty hours a week during the first year are devoted to lessons in voice, musical instruments, music history, Japanese, Western, and modern dance, acting and theater theory, cultural history, and etiquette. The second-year curriculum is essentially the same (Ueda 1986 [1976]:48). During a three-month-long field trip in 1987, I was invited to attend several classes and to join the students for their weekly tea ceremony lesson at a nearby tea house. The young women are also drilled in the proper manner of walking and bowing by local Self-Defense Force personnel, whose presence helps clinch the overwhelmingly martial tenor of everyday life in the Academy.

The Academy, widely acknowledged as one of the best performing arts schools in Japan, is very competitive: of the 734 applicants in 1985, only 42 (or one in 17.5) were accepted. Since then, the number of applications has nearly tripled; consequently, the chance of acceptance was far lower in 1993, when 1,839 young women applied for

40 openings—one place for every 46 applicants (*Fushigi no kuni no Takarazuka* 1993:102). Aspiring students are judged on the basis of their overall physique and musical talents, in addition to their academic achievements. Rumors that some parents buy their daughter's enrollment are commonplace. The annual tuition averages nearly 300,000 yen (about $3,000 at the current exchange rate), and the students must themselves purchase the school's gray, military-style uniform (Ueda 1986 [1976]:33). The switch from *hakama*, Japanese formal wear, to Western, military-style outfits was made in 1939.

Most of the students live with one or two roommates in the Violet (*sumire*) Dormitories,[15] where the administration seeks to socialize the young women into a life of discipline and hierarchical relationships. All of the residents are required to clean the dorms, but the first-year or junior (*kōhai*) students are also responsible for cleaning the classrooms and rehearsal studios under the watchful eyes of the second-year or senior (*senpai*) students. The cleaning is done by hand without the benefit of vacuum cleaners, for Academy officials are convinced that a labor-intensive cleaning regimen builds character, ensures humility, and boosts stamina in their young charges.[16] The junior-senior relationships formed at this time are maintained throughout and even beyond the young women's tenure in the Takarazuka Revue. A 10:00 P.M. curfew is strictly maintained, and first-year students are not allowed to venture outside the campus itself. Males are scrupulously forbidden from the premises with the exception of fathers and brothers, who, like all guests, are limited to the lobbies (Ueda 1986 [1976]:118–19). Although the attrition rate is not publicized, a number of students drop out midway through the spartan regimen. Many of the young women continue to live in the dormitory after they join the Revue proper, although some—leading Takarasiennes in particular— are able to maintain their own apartments and houses, sometimes with the financial support of affluent fans.

GENDERING PERFORMANCE

Upon their successful application to the Takarazuka Music Academy, the student actors are assigned what I refer to as their "secondary" genders. Unlike "primary" gender, which is assigned at birth on the basis of an infant's genitalia, secondary gender is based on both physical (but not genital) and sociopsychological criteria: namely, height, physique, facial shape, voice, personality, and, to a certain extent, personal preference. Secondary gender attributes or markers are premised on contrastive gender stereotypes themselves; for example, men ideally should be taller than women; should have a longer, more rectangular face, a broader forehead, thicker eyebrows and lips, a higher bridged nose, darker skin, straighter shoulders, narrower hips, and a lower voice than women; and should exude charisma (*kosei*), which is disparaged in women. The assignment of gender involves the selection and cosmetic exaggeration of perceived nongenital physical differences between females and males, and it reinforces socially prescribed behavioral differences. An actor's inherited features became especially central to the process of gender assignment with the shift in 1930 from the traditional whiteface to modern greasepaint. Ironically, in the Takarazuka Revue, gender(ed) differences that are popularly perceived as inherent in female and male bodies are embodied by females alone. Personal motivations and desires aside, both *musumeyaku* and *otokoyaku* are products of a dominant social ideology that privileges masculinity and men.

The femininity embodied and enacted by the player of women's roles serves as a foil for the masculinity of the player of men's roles.[17] Much of the training of the Revue actors focuses on learning *kata*, which refers collectively to technologies of gender, including form, posture, sign, code, gesture, and choreography. The *kata* learned by the Takarasiennes specifically involve stylized gestures, movements, intonations, and speech patterns that signify gender. A player of men's roles, for example, must stride forthrightly across the stage, her arms held stiffly away from her body, her fingers curled around her thumbs to form a fist. Her arm and hand gestures are expansive and bold; when she stands still, her legs are apart, with feet firmly planted and pelvis pushed slightly forward, Elvis style. Trousers, which are pulled over an *otokoyaku*'s elevator boots with cuff straps, help accentuate the length of her legs. In contrast, a player of women's roles pivots her forearms from the elbows, which are kept pinned against her side, constraining her freedom of movement and consequently making her appear more "feminine." The *otokoyaku* are actively encouraged to study the behavior and actions, or *kata*, of male celebrities in order to more effectively represent ideal men onstage, be they samurai or cowboys. Among the popular Japanese and foreign stars whose acting style is emulated are Ishihara Yūjirō, Ichikawa Ennosuke, Hasegawa Ichio,

Alain Delon, Maurice Chevalier, Clark Gable, James Dean, Elvis Presley, Marlon Brando, and Jack Nicholson.

Masculinity *kata* comprise attributes that may be grouped into three basic categories: physical appearance, voice and gesture, and temperament. In addition to the physical characteristics influencing her secondary-gender attribution, an actor's natural endowments are often augmented with the liberal use of makeup and hairpieces. Until Kadota Ashiko cut off her hair in 1932, *otokoyaku* either pulled their hair back into a flat chignon or stuffed it into hats but not wigs, which were deemed "too realistic" ("Takarazuka ihen" 1932). Kadota was possibly imitating the Shōchiku Revue's leading *otokoyaku*, Mizunoe Takiko, better known as Tākii, although "Modern Girls" (*modan gāru*, or *moga*) had sported short hair since the 1920s (Bollinger 1994; Silverberg 1991). Before then, short hair announced a woman's withdrawal from secular and sexual affairs; the *moga* turned hair symbolism on its head, and short hair became the hallmark of the extroverted, maverick, sexually active woman. Ever since Kadota's act, short hair, often peroxided in recent years, has remained an essential component of masculinity *kata*. A student assigned to specialize in men's roles is required to cut her hair short by the end of her first semester at the Academy. All other junior students are required to wear their hair in shoulder-length braids, until ordered to do otherwise.

Only since the premier production of *Gone with the Wind* in 1977 have leading *otokoyaku* also added mustaches and beards to their *kata*—previously, only minor characters sometimes had facial hair. In fact, Haruna Yuri, who was the first to play Rhett Butler in 1977, caused a stir when she wore her mustache offstage during the play's months-long run, ostensibly to feel more "natural" and convincing in the role (Haruna 1979:78; Hashimoto 1984:92; "Kaze to tomo ni hige ka" 1977). Clothing *kata* run the gamut from the chic kimono of an Edo-period dandy to the blue jeans of a *West Side Story* delinquent, to the boas and sequined tuxedos associated with Liberace. Yellows, browns, blues, greens, and black are considered appropriate *otokoyaku* colors; pink is the paramount color for *musumeyaku*. A white outfit denotes the star of the show (Ueda 1974:97–99).

Many *otokoyaku* have naturally low—as opposed to a *musumeyaku*'s unnaturally high—voices, although others "crush" (*tsubusu*) theirs, often by chain-smoking, to attain the requisite huskiness. Breathing must be from the stomach and not the chest. Speech *kata* include the use of *boku*, a masculine self-referent, and the masculine *nu* (as opposed to the feminine *wa*) in the sentence-final position (Ueda 1974:62). Each Takarazuka man creates a distinct charismatic persona, amplifying and extending her individuality through her expert interpretation, combination, and manipulation of masculinity *kata* (see Robertson 1987; see also Yano 1995). She does not merely imitate or mimic actual males. Fans describe an *otokoyaku* whose masculine posturing is especially compelling as *kizatte-iru*, or "camping it up"; here "camp" is defined in a serious sense as "actions and gestures of exaggerated emphasis," rather than as a system of humor (Meyer 1994b:75; Newton 1972:107; Tanabe and Sasaki 1983:135).[18]

NOMENCLATURE

Kobayashi conceived of Takarazuka as Kabuki's complement but not its equal in historical prestige. The asymmetrical relationship between the two same-sex theaters is evident in their respective nomenclature. The Kabuki player of women's roles, or *onnagata*, is regarded as an exemplary model (*kata*) of "female" (*onna*) gender, and actual women have been encouraged to emulate the feminine mannerisms of the male actor (figure 4). Neither *otokoyaku* nor *musumeyaku* are terms used in the Kabuki theater. *Yaku*, unlike *kata*, connotes serviceability and dutifulness. An *otokoyaku* thus is an actor whose theatrical duty is to showcase masculinity; she is not, however, promoted as a model for males offstage to imitate.

Kobayashi resorted to the terminology of kinship in naming the Takarazuka player of women's roles *musume*, or "daughter," instead of *onna*, or "woman." The conflation of gender and kinship attribution in the vocabulary of the Takarazuka Revue reflects their mutual construction: "Neither can be treated as analytically prior to the other, because they are realized together in particular cultural, economic, and political systems" (Collier and Yanagisako 1987:7). Kobayashi's choice of nomenclature was informed by the Good Wife, Wise Mother (*ryōsai kenbo*) model of female subjectivity and femininity codified in the Meiji Civil Code (operative from 1898 to 1947), as well as by the primacy of the patriarchal, conjugal household. Females acting on their own behalf outside of the household were regarded by the state as socially disruptive and dangerously anomalous[19]—social disorder,

Figure 4.   Kabuki *onnagata*. Hanayagi Shōtarō in the role of a young woman. From *Engei Gahō* (1942:n.p.).

in other words, was a "woman problem" (Nolte 1983:3). Note, in this connection, that Good Husband, Wise Father was never employed as a trope for social order, nor was social disorder ever linked to a "man problem." The public vocation of the actor, however, reversed the usual association of females with the private domain; consequently, distinctions between "private" and "public" were neither incumbent upon nor possible for Takarasiennes. As Juliet Blair has pointed out, "One result of this is that although [the actor] is aware of the dominant rules governing the society of which her small dramatic world is a part, her experience permits her to fuse the value-systems, and to bring the . . . private interpersonal sphere of women in the home into the light of public scrutiny" (1981:205). The fusion was manipulated in a number of ways. Whereas Kobayashi sought to use the actor as a vehicle for introducing the artistry of the theater into the home (Kobayashi 1961b:460, 499, 509–10), some Takarasiennes and their fans used the theater as a starting point for an opposing strategy, rejecting gender roles associated with the patriarchal household and constructing alternative styles or modes of sexuality.

Kobayashi tempered the revolutionary potential of the actor by denying them maturity. Whether Academy students or Revue actors, all Takarasiennes continue to be referred to as students (*seito*), partly to create an aura of innocence and amateurism to minimize the distance between stage and spectator, and partly to keep their wages low relative to those of professional actors.[20] More important, he relegated the players of women's roles to the status of daughter, with its attendant connotations of filial piety, youthfulness, pedigree, virginity, and being unmarried. These were precisely the characteristics that Kobayashi sought in the young recruits and that marked the makings of a Good Wife, Wise Mother. To clinch the filial and paternal symbolism, he encouraged all Takarasiennes to call him Father (*otōsan*) and regarded them as members of his extended family. Gender assignment notwithstanding, all the actors thereby were daughters. Many Takarasiennes and their fans eventually appropriated kinship terminology, effectively subverting Father's filial symbolism and asserting their own.

The deployment of kinship terminology in the Takarazuka Revue recalls the parent- (father-)child (*oyabun-kobun*) type of group formation, whereby a patriarch controls a tightly knit, hierarchical following of "children"—in this case, daughters. When kinship terminology is used to denote relationships between individual Takarasiennes, it is based both on age or seniority, as "elder sister" (*onēsan* or *ane*) and "younger sister" (*imōto*), and on gender, as "older brother" (*aniki*) and "younger sister," without regard, necessarily, to literal age or seniority. Both sets of kinship terms are applied by Takarasiennes and their fans to identify both homosocial and homosexual relations between females.

The representational inequality between the Kabuki *onnagata* and the Takarazuka *otokoyaku* is paralleled by the inequality between the player of men's roles and the player of women's roles. The naive and compliant daughter represents not only femininity but also the female subject in a patriarchal society who is excluded from participating in discourses about gender ideology and sexuality. Kobayashi, as the privileged father, invested much energy in advocating arranged marriages both for the 3,000 female clerks employed by Hankyū and for those Takarasiennes scheduled to retire (Kobayashi 1961b:465–67, 531–32; 1962:70–75). Moreover, Kobayashi argued, the *otokoyaku* participates not in the construction of alternative gender roles for females but in the glorification of men and masculinity. He even proclaimed that the *otokoyaku* is more suave, more affectionate, more courageous, more charming, more handsome, and more fascinating than actual males (1961b:467–68). Kobayashi perhaps was implying that "real" (that is, anatomically correct) males need not be suave and charming in the real world, where patriarchal privilege compensates for aesthetic deficiencies.

This introduction to the Takarazuka Revue would not be complete without a brief discussion of the relationship of sex, gender, and sexuality, which sets the stage for an exploration and analysis of the politics of sexuality in modern Japan. Theoretically, the three terms signify different things, although they are often conflated in popular discourse. "Sex," as I use it here, denotes both a physical act (not limited to heterosexual intercourse) and the physical body distinguished by either "female" or "male" genitalia—or both, to varying degrees, in the case of intersexed persons—and by their usual capabilities, such as menstruation, seminal ejaculation, and orgasm. "Gender" refers to sociocultural and historical conventions of deportment, costume, voice, gesture, and so on, attributed and ascribed to females and males. By the same token, gender stereotypes enable people to perceive otherwise clothed bodies as either "female" or "male," a practice that has prompted some scholars to refer to gender as "cultural genitals": "The relationship between cultural genitals and gender attribution is reflexive. The reality of a gender is 'proved' by the genital which is attributed, and, at the same time, the attributed genital only has meaning through the socially shared construction of the gender attribution process" (Kessler and McKenna 1985 [1978]:155; see 153–55).

"Sexuality" may overlap with sex and gender, but it pertains specifically to a domain of desire and erotic pleasure more complex and varied than the hegemonic construction of reproductive heterosexuality (see Kessler and McKenna 1985 [1978]:1–12; Vance 1985:9). Sex, gender, and sexuality may be related but they are not synonymous; the pattern of their articulation is negotiable and negotiated constantly. Although the three may be popularly perceived as irreducibly joined or aligned, such alignment remains a situational and not a permanently fixed condition: "*Man* and *masculine* might just as easily signify a female body as a male one, and *woman* and *feminine* a male body as easily as a female one" (Butler 1990:6; italics in the original).

Among Japanese feminists, and scholars influenced by feminist theory, sex and gender and sexuality have been distinguished in principle since around 1970 (Yuri 1985). Linguistic distinctions in Japanese between sex and gender are created through suffixes. Generally speaking, *sei* is used to denote sex, and *seisei* "sex-ness" (literally, "the sex of sex")—as in *josei* for "female" and *dansei* for "male." Since the *dan* in *dansei* can refer both to male sex and "male" gender, the suffix *sei*, with its allusions to fundamental parts (for example, genitalia), is necessary in order to specifically denote sex. Gender is denoted by the suffix *rashii*, with its allusion to appearance or likeness (*Kōjien* 1978:1214, 2300; Fukutomi 1985; Yasukawa 1989).[21] A feminine body is *onnarashii;* a masculine body, *otokorashii.*[22] The emphasis here is on the proximity of a body to a gender stereotype. When a speaker wishes to draw attention to a body's resemblance to a particular female or male, the term often used is *joseiteki* (like a/that female) or *danseiteki* (like a/that male). The difference between *onnarashii* and *joseiteki*, or *otokorashii* and *danseiteki*, is significant, although each set of terms is often used interchangeably in popular parlance. Further complicating matters is the use of the terms *onna* and *otoko* to refer to both sex and gender, distinguished only by the context.

STATION BREAK

This is the appropriate juncture to address a related issue concerning sex and gender terminology that challenges ostensibly well-meaning but relativistic and reductive notions of cultural encounter and exchange. Persons who are unfamiliar with the intellectual climate and popular culture of twentieth-century Japan might doubt that terms such as "homosexual," "heterosexual," "lesbian," "butch-femme," and so forth can be appropriately applied to Japanese sexual practices, assuming that there must be more "culturally specific" terms. If by culturally specific is meant "Japanese," then yes, of course there are such terms and I list them below. But just as important, there are historically specific terms as well, and "homosexual" and so forth are among them.[23]

Since the turn of the century and even earlier, Japanese pundits have been adept at selectively adapting, for domestic (and often hegemonic) purposes, institutions and terminologies that were devised and first popularized outside of Japan. With respect to sexological terms, Euro-American loanwords and Japanese neologisms rapidly made their way into professional and lay parlance alike. They can be found in a wide range of printed sources, including translations of foreign texts; moreover, there are many dictionaries devoted to introducing and defining such words. Loanwords and Japanese social scientific neologisms that became household words in the early 1900s included *fuan* (fan); *rabu retā* (love letter); *rezubian* (lesbian); *dōseiai*, for "homosexuality" (also referred to as *homosekushuaru*); and *iseiai*, for "heterosexuality" (also *heterosekushuaru*). Other loanwords referring to sexual practices that were introduced at this time included sapphism (*saffuo*), tribadism (*tsuribadeizumu*), and uranism (*uranizumu*) (e.g., Hayashi 1926; Kuwatani 1911; Ōzumi 1931).

Obviously, social and sexual practices labeled and categorized in the "feudal" Edo period were followed and perceived differently in the early twentieth century when the country was embarked on a course of modernization, industrialization, and selective Westernization (see Gluck 1985; Roden 1990; Robertson 1992c; Westney 1987). In fact, a new interpretation of sexual relations between females prompted the introduction of the term *dōseiai* at the turn of this century to distinguish such activities from those of males, although before long the neologism became a standard word for homosexuality in general regardless of the sex of the individuals involved (Furukawa 1994:115; see also chapter 2). Among the "indigenous" terms past and present for lesbians are *tachi* (an abbreviation of *tachiyaku*, or "leading man," similar in meaning to "butch"), *neko* ("cat," similar in meaning to "femme"), *onēsama* (older sister), *imōto* (younger sister), *join* (female licentiousness), *joshoku* (female eroticism), *gōin* (joint licentiousness), *tomogui* (eat each other), *shirojiro* ("pure white," with etymological implications of falseness and feigned ignorance), and *kaiawase* (matching shells) (Sugahara 1971:4–5). In the 1910s, words for lesbians were distinguished by girls' school: *ome* (male-female couple) was used at prefectural schools,[24] *odeya* (lover) at private schools, *onetsu* (fever) at Ochanomizu, *ohakarai* (your own discretion) at Gakushūin, and *oshinyū* (best friend) at Atsumi (Kuwatani 1911:35). Japanese lesbian feminists today translate "butch" and "femme" as *tachi* and *neko*, and they often use the loanwords *butchi* and *fuemu* (Mizukawa 1987:23). Another current Japanese term for "butch" is *onabe*, or "shallow pot," which is a play on *okama*, or "deep pot," a slang word for a feminine or "passive" gay male.

For Japanese social scientists and critics, the imported terms *homosexual* and *heterosexual* helped explain historical phenomena in a new way and make sense of new categories of phenomena, such as "female" psychology, neurasthenia, and fandom. Like all other methods of classification and analysis, these terms and their definitions both opened up some new insights and closed off others. Although they are not exhaustive, the sources in my bibliography attest to the compelling interest in Japan in sexual psychology (see Frühstück 1996a, 1996b). The works of Freud, Krafft-Ebing, Carpenter, Ellis, Hirschfeld, Weininger, and others were imported directly to Japan; they were translated, often by Japanese scholars who had studied abroad, and employed immediately in the identification of social problems and their analysis and resolution, exercises in which the state became increasingly invested (see Frühstück 1996b; Furukawa 1994). I was interested to find a number of these sexological treatises in the archives of the Takarazuka Revue.

Thus my use of terms, including *homosexual* and *heterosexual*, patently is culturally and historically specific, and I am attentive to the particular ways in which they were interpreted and employed in Japan. I am also perhaps more critical than many of their Japanese users past and present of the binarist readings they could impose on the sexual practices of Japanese (and others), which are not easily containable by dichotomous categories.

PREVIEWING THE BOOK

The question of how modern Japanese reflexively create a sense of themselves as female or male, or both, as well as how some of them attribute maleness and femaleness to others, is one of the underlying themes of this book. It is also central to the discourse of national cultural identity in Japan. The Takarazuka Revue lends itself to an exploration of this discourse: it is simultaneously a popular and mass cultural formation, a contested icon of modernity, and a site of struggle over the relationship of sex, gender, and sexuality. In chapter 1, I juxtapose current theoretical approaches to popular and mass culture with the terms and definitions developed and used by Japanese scholars and critics. One of the questions I explore is how these theories and definitions actually constituted the cultural debates in modern Japan in which Takarazuka figured significantly. But I am also committed to looking at how persons who are not and were not professional historians, social psychologists, or literary critics have negotiated the interwoven politics of sexuality and modernity. I draw an analogy between the "excessive semiosis" of popular culture and the practice of cross-dressing in an attempt to clarify the ways in which ambiguity and ambivalence have been used strategically both to contain difference and to parody the artifice of containment—as in gender. Similarly, I also address the politics of representation, which determines how "the people" are variously claimed as agents of, an audience for, and products of popular cultural forms and practices. In the process, I have taken pains to distinguish what people actually like from what critics and theorists of popular culture claim people like.

In chapter 2, I focus on androgyny, embodied differently by Edo-period Kabuki *onnagata* and modern Takarazuka *otokoyaku*, whose gender(ed) performances constitute a type of strategic ambivalence: that is, they create bodies capable of being read or understood in more than one way. This subject was inspired by the many early articles, which I excerpt, linking the establishment of the Takarazuka Revue to the problematic emergence in Japan of "androgynous" females and the diagnosis in women of the newly coined affliction, "abnormal sexual desire" (*hentai seiyoku*). I analyze at length the two basic ways in which androgyny has been rendered in Japanese either to stress sexuality or to bracket it. The fetishized, Janus-faced *shōjo* (girl) is introduced here, as she symbolizes the problematic ambivalence of modernity, the Revue theater, and female and male sexuality alike. Here, as elsewhere, while acknowledging areas of historical conjunction and cultural exchange, I take care to avoid succumbing to the tendency of forcing Japanese cultural practices into Western analytical categories and to distinguish those practices from the dominant sexual and gender ideology operating in Japan.

The general pattern of Takarazuka-state relations during the wartime years (1931–45) in particular is the subject of chapter 3. Here, I examine the role of the montage-like Revue theater in dramatizing and aestheticizing Japanese imperial ideology, including the practice of assimilation. I review intersections of gender, sexuality, ethnicity, and nationalism on and off the Revue stage, together with the specific Japanese orientalism informing both the imperialist project and the formation of an ambivalent national cultural identity. In this connection, I draw analogies between cross-dressing and what I call "cross-ethnicking," both of which are at once strategies of containment and transgression. As a technology of imperialism, the Takarazuka Revue helped bridge the gap between perceptions of colonized others and actual colonial encounters; it was one way of linking imperialist fantasies and colonial realities. Consequently, I examine closely several conflicting interests—those of the state, military, corporations, fans, revue management, and social critics—that converged in and were transformed by the Takarazuka Revue. The wartime period provides an important context not only for historicizing the characteristics by which the Revue is known today but also for demonstrating the implications and ramifications of Takarazuka in Japanese society at large, past and present. Put differently, the Revue's own cultural history and social reception complicates our understanding of Japanese society itself.

In chapter 4, the first of two chapters on fans, I trace the transformations in and discourses of fandom in modern Japan. Audiences and especially female fans of all-female revue theaters figured prominently in social critiques of modernity, and fandom was interpreted as a pathology of modernity. Male fans were not exempt from scrutiny, and I investigate their presence and stake in Takarazuka historically and at present in both chapters 4 and 5. Profiles of fans, fan etiquette, translations from fan magazines, and my own observations of Takarazuka fan clubs are among the subjects treated in chapter 4. In chapter 5, I explore the text-making activities of fans in the form of fan magazines and fan letters and the imaginary but contingent worlds they conjure up. I am also interested here in the supposedly unorthodox script in which fan letters are written, a script labeled "abnormal *shōjo* script" by detractors. Finally, I discuss the homoerotic aesthetic linking the Takarazuka actors and the New Half phenomenon in Japan, here speculating about androgyny as a body politics that serves to interrogate the naturalized dualities of male and female, masculine and feminine, and Japanese and others (Asian and Euro-American alike). I argue that the ambivalence of the modern Japanese nation, an eclectic composite of Asian and Euro-American elements, is transposed as androgyny in the ongoing discourse of national cultural identity. An epilogue draws together the threads of the basic argument informing the book, focusing on the androgynous ambivalence of Japanese modernity.

I should make clear at the outset what this book is not: it is neither a history of the Takarazuka Revue, nor a biography of its founder, nor a history of (homo)sexuality in Japan. It is, as I have outlined, an exploration of the overlapping discourses of gender, sexuality, popular culture, and national identity as they erupted into the world framed by Takarazuka. Any interpretation of the Revue's popularity today must take into account its historical beginnings and unprecedented impact on "common sense" or the status quo. Therefore, a substantial part of my book focuses on prewar and wartime developments in the Revue and Japanese society at large. Disciplined and strategic eclecticism mark my use of theories, which I do not separate out from ethnographic description but rather use to shape and guide my narrative. As will be evident, the material under discussion does not, nor should it be made to, fit into a particular theoretical box. Rather, I have used various theories at different junctures to help orchestrate the cacophonous welter of data in ways that resonate with the historical and contextual circumstances of the phenomena producing them.

I have spent over a decade studying the Takarazuka Revue and its fan clubs from different historical and practical angles. However, the chronicle of my extensive experiences in the field is limited to those instances when their mention illustrates an important feature of the Revue. There is far too little on Japan in the Anglophone literature, and much less on the revue theater, sexuality, and gender in that country; I have no desire to dilute this investigation with an autobiographical account. Reflexivity for me lies in my sensitivity and attention to the competing historical forces and discourses shaping specific Japanese practices. I aim to complicate our image and understanding of Japan and not to problematize my own long and complex relationship to that country and culture. That is another book— a memoir perhaps, to be written much later.

By the same token, the comparatively small Anglophone literature on Japanese mass and popular cultures calls for a premium to be put on the inclusion of more Japanese "stuff"; this is not the time and place to simply recycle old material in new theoretical vocabularies. After all, theory can only be developed and modified, as it must if it is to remain theoretical, by engaging with an ever-expanding body of tangible information (Vance 1985:18). Finally, although I am familiar with much of the scholarly literature on the relationship of theater, cross-dressing, and gender ideology, and cite some relevant sources, I have kept analogies between Takarazuka and its global counterparts to a minimum. This has been done partly for reasons of space, but also because I am in a better position to provide otherwise inaccessible information to scholars that augments the larger—mostly Eurocentric—literature. Obviously the gist of anthropological interpretation and translation relies on analogies and affinities between, across, and among cultural areas and practices. But those analogies and affinities should work together to catalyze new perspectives, insights, and understandings about a subject: they should not simply explain or rationalize B in terms of A, in which case no new information is yielded. Taking a clue from the Takarazuka Revue itself, which I conceptualize and position as a thematic nexus or node, I employ a montage-like approach: I juxtapose and layer into my narrative the relevant material necessary to make new associations and connections as a way of contributing to a new cultural history of Japan constituted by popular practices.

Ambivalence and Popular Culture

From Class S to Feverish Yearning for *Otokoyaku* . . .
[Takarazuka] Is the Cause of Torrid and Prolonged Lesbian
Pleasure.[1]

"Takarazuka bijin hensen-shi"
(4) 1930, headlines

Takarazuka is, if anything, completely lacking in sexuality.
J. Singer 1996:165

EXCESS AND POPULAR CULTURE

A brief English synopsis of "Asian Love" (*Eijin'an rabu* [sic]), a three-part scene in the glittery revue *Jump Orient!* (*Janpu oriento!*), reads: "It is the present day in Hong Kong. Two groups of young people fight late at night. A young man is deeply in love with a beautiful girl. A gangster is in love with the same girl. The fight between the friends of the two love-struck guys results in a victory for the gangster [sic]" (*Janpu oriento!* 1994:70). Although sketchy, this synopsis encapsulates the stock features of shows staged by Takarazuka today: an exotic foreign setting, a triangulated love affair, a tragic ending.

In the first scene, "Hong Kong Storm," Roy Fong, a gangster, dances with his girlfriend, Wan Ran, and sings about eating forbidden fruits and behaving like a drunken wolf. In the second scene, "Hong Kong Love," Kenny Kao, a Chinese mainlander, and his group dance and sing about chasing after elusive dreams and unrequited love. Kenny's girlfriend, Veronica, cozies up to him. Roy then appears on the scene and, dazzled by Veronica's beauty, tries to seduce her. She calls to Kenny for help, and he overwhelms Roy, who scatters with his gang. The final scene, "Hong Kong at Night," has Kenny singing a love song to Veronica as the two admire the pearlescent glow of the harbor lights. As they embrace, Roy returns with his gang and picks a fight with Kenny's group (figure 5). The jealous Wan Ran pulls out a pistol and takes aim at Veronica. But Kenny is shot instead when he throws him-

Figure 5.   *Jump Orient!* Roy (left) and Kenny (center) fight as Veronica (right) looks on worriedly. From *Janpu oriento!* (1994:11).

self over Veronica protectively. Kenny's friends, overcome with sorrow, collapse in tears. Blackout.

Takarazuka is, if anything, characterized by excess: the exotic settings, flamboyant costumes, and convoluted scenarios of the Revue conjure up a parallel world of gripping melodrama, wild fantasy, ambiguous ethnicity, daring adventure, thwarted passion, and tortured romance. Whereas Kabuki could be similarly described, it is the Revue's excessiveness that has invited many theater critics, Japanese and non-Japanese alike, to deride it as "nylon Kabuki," superficial, florid, gaudy, dreary, banal, and cheap (Arnott 1969:248–49). It is described as "airy soufflé," "Kitsch Heaven" (Mackrell 1994:sec. 2, 20), or "the adolescent girls' chewing gum—nonsexual, romantic and harmless" (Bowers 1989:H10). At first glance, *Jump Orient!* seems to fit these descriptions (though as we shall see in chapter 3, its themes are far more complex). What, then, is the place of Takarazuka in the history of Japanese popular culture? How has it been treated by the scholarship on popular cultural practices?

The two contrasting epigraphs that preface this chapter make a point that I recapitulate in subsequent chapters. Contrary to the second epigraph and in keeping with the first, the one excessive feature that remains unacknowledged or bracketed in virtually all the books and articles on the Revue (Japanese and Anglophone alike) is sexuality. From its first public performance in 1914, the Revue has been the focus of a fractious public debate in the Japanese mass media concerning the relationship of sex, gender, and sexuality. As I detail in connection with fans and fandom, Takarazuka actors have long stoked the libidinous desires of the women and men under the spell of their spectacular performances. And it was the excessive and unfeminine charisma of the Modern Girl that in part prompted Kobayashi Ichizō to establish an all-female revue in the first place.

Excessiveness has been claimed as a defining characteristic of popular culture, itself a concept central to the discourse of sexuality and nationalism in Japan and elsewhere. In John Fiske's account, the excessiveness of popular culture can be understood as "overflowing semiosis"—as "meaning out of control . . . meaning that escapes ideological control and is free to be used to resist or evade it" (1989:114). From the outset, Takarazuka fans and detractors alike recognized and appropriated the Revue's excessiveness for very different social and political agendas, and in ways that—contrary to Fiske's definition—both parodied convention and reinforced the status quo. But before we can consider further the contradictions, ambiguities, and ambivalence embodied in the Revue, especially with respect to the intertwined discourses of sexuality and nationalism, we need a working definition of "popular culture," its ideological and material forms and their operations.

The conceptual tools that Japanese scholars developed to frame and analyze popular culture are worth considering both in their own right and in relation to the Anglophone literature on the subject. How did these terms, definitions, and theories actually constitute the cultural debates in modern Japan in which Takarazuka and other all-female revues figured significantly? The question informs my book as a whole; here I would like to outline just one set of answers. We shall see that the Japanese terms carry a similarly complicated but different range of meanings than that conveyed in English by "popular culture." A cursory comparison suggests that like the French *culture populaire*, itself a tangle of usages and meanings (Rigby 1991), Japanese notions of popular culture are laced with nostalgic references to "folk" and "traditional" ways of life in addition to less sanguine associations with nationalism, mass consumption, and citizens' movements.

IDEOLOGIES OF POPULAR CULTURE

For Fiske, popular culture exceeds and escapes "the norms of ideological control" and in that way becomes a site of parody, resistance, evasion, and alternatives of and to convention and the status quo (1989:114). He perceives of popular culture as a domain of social relations characterized by struggle, opposition, and reaction to the forces of domination, be they capitalist, consumerist, sexist, ethnocentric, or racist. Popular culture therefore is "potentially, and often actually, progressive, for it finds in the vigor and vitality of the people evidence both of the possibility of social change and of the motivation to drive it" (21). However, Fiske insists, it is not radical, for rather than undermine or revolt against the forces of dominance, popular culture makes it necessary for those forces to work hard and insistently on maintaining their hegemonic values. In Fiske's optimistic scheme, "popular" thus refers to "the people," understood as a subordinated but coherent "homogeneous will" whose "expressions are by definition politically virtuous" (Frow 1995:62); by extension, popular culture is a process of struggle by "the people" over the meanings of social experience (Fiske 1989:28). A pessimistic scheme, articulated by Theodor Adorno and Max Horkheimer (1972), instead equates popular culture with the commodity form of capitalism and attributes to it passivity, ennui, and antisocial isolation.

A position intriguingly similar to Fiske's was assumed by Yanagita Kunio (1875–1962), a nativist ethnographer especially active in the early twentieth century whose work has been rediscovered as part of the folk culture revival accompanying the willfully nostalgic climate that has infused postwar Japan since the 1970s (see Ivy 1995; Robertson 1994 [1991]). Yanagita was perhaps the most celebrated of several social-critics-*cum*-ethnologists troubled by what they saw as the "nonsynchronicity" of city and country and their respective modes of production, an incompatibility precipitated by urbanization and massive industrialization in the decades before World War II (Harootunian 1990:100). The unprecedented physical transformation, and even ruination, of the rural landscape was especially disturbing and provided the major stimulus for their social theorizing. Yanagita, for example, coined the term *jōmin* in reference to "ordinary and abiding people" who resided in the countryside of a "timeless Japan that was 'always, already there'" as a source and locus of authentic cultural identity (106, 100).

Only as idealized reifications did rural peoples and practices figure in the romantic exaltations of village life that formed one side of the ideological coin of national cultural identity. The other side was etched with a condescending attitude: farmers lacked "a sense of nation, motivation for progress, adequate powers of observation, and an ability to socialize that was sufficient to civilized times" (Gluck 1985:183). Whereas for sympathizers such as Yanagita, the people qua *jōmin* were repositories of ancestral customs, and, by extension, were paragons of Japaneseness, for detractors, "the people" were boorish and backward relics of an uncivilized, unenlightened time (182–86). H. D. Harootunian suggests that Yanagita's imaginary, purely discursive invention of an otherwise absent Japan precluded the people from mobilizing to subvert the prevailing ideology of the militarizing state; instead, his "Japan" became an integral part of that ideology (1990:105–7). Of course, Yanagita's concern here is not actual people living in rural areas, who maintained a complicated relationship to the state, but his own inability to use social science (ethnology) to contest the state, which appropriated the folkloristic conception of a fixed, homogenous identity "attesting to sameness among all Japanese" and extended it to support a doctrine of "cultural exceptionalism and racial uniqueness" (107). "War," claimed one ideologue active in promoting organized recreation in interwar and wartime Japan, "may be destructive, but it provides an opportunity to forge a national culture (*kokumin bunka*)" (Iizuka 1941:44). The state-sanctioned Citizens' Theater Movement (*kokumin engeki undō*) inaugurated by nationalists in the mid-1930s, for example, was premised on the centrality of theater in everyday life and thus its usefulness as a vehicle through which the "spiritual essence" of the Japanese people could be nurtured (Fuwa 1941:2; Iizuka 1941:45; Ōyama 1941). In the context of war and imperialism, then, the enforced interiorization of a homogeneous will ultimately contributed to the formation of a national cultural identity—a New Japan that was overdetermined or excessive in its "Japaneseness."

Fiske, unlike either Yanagita or the proponents of the Citizens' Theater Movement, endows popular culture with a political essence:

> There can be no popular dominant culture, for popular culture is formed always in reaction to, and never as a part of, the forces of domination. This does not mean that members of dominant social groups cannot participate in popular culture—they can and do. But

to do so they must reform their allegiances away from those that give them their social power. . . . "The popular," then, is determined by the forces of domination to the extent that it is always formed in reaction to them; but the dominant cannot control totally the meanings that the people may construct, the social allegiances they may form.

(Fiske 1989:43, 45)

Yanagita and his nationalist colleagues had more in common with their French counterparts (see Rigby 1991); contrary to Fiske's views, they aestheticized and spiritualized the political potential of popular (*jōmin*) culture. For them, popular culture *was* the national, dominant culture. As reiterated in the late 1980s by Japanese sociologist and media critic Hidetoshi Kato, popular culture is "*the* culture that is shared by every single individual"; it is "the social cement that closes the gaps between upper class and lower middle class, between highly educated and high school graduates, and sometimes even between male and female" (1989a:315). Kato concludes that "Japanese popular culture is unique, and its research methodology requires that special consideration be given to this singularity" (316). In other words, because Japanese popular culture is indistinguishable from hegemonic culture and is shared across lines of region, class, and sex, it is not determined in relation to historical exigencies; it just is. Yet Yanagita and Kato's and Fiske's formulations are similar in that they effectively "sanitize" the popular by expelling from it "all ambivalence, all complexity, all perverse pleasure"; it is clear that for them, the category is "purely prescriptive (that is to say, a fantasy)" (Frow 1995:61–62).

Kato, who coedited the *Handbook of Japanese Popular Culture*, presents Japanese popular culture as a gloss for a singular, homogeneous impulse that "feeds into and through the cultural forms adapted to its expression" (Frow 1995:82–83). His definition depends on a notion of culture as a self-contained, self-evident, undifferentiated whole that perdures unchanged over time and space, across history and geography. Obviously, on a very general level, there is something distinctive— collective but not unitary—about the contexts within which Japanese peoples give meanings to their actions and experiences, and make sense of their lives. While there is no "true" definition of the term "culture," it is usefully understood as a space-time manifold in which potentially self-aware human beings "construct and represent themselves and others, and hence their societies and histories" (Comaroff and Comaroff 1992:27; see also Mohanty 1989:19–20). This is by no means a smooth, simple process. Only a willfully nostalgic pundit can ignore sociohistorical relations of inequality premised on sex, gender, sexuality, age, religion, ethnicity, race, region, education, and so forth that occasion differences in people's lived experience. However, that these relations have potentially divisive effects does not automatically preclude the possibility of an overarching national popular culture. In Japan, such a culture has been constructed and represented in this century regardless of, in spite of, and because of such differences—an observation quite at variance with Kato's insistence that popular culture presumes and reflects an absence of internal differences.

The ethnographic work of two less acknowledged contemporaries of Yanagita Kunio, in fact, is striking for its focus on differences within the Japanese culture of modernity—as opposed to modernity's effect on "Japanese culture"—and for its interrogation of the "productivist and essentialist ideology" of early-twentieth-century Japan (see Silverberg 1992). As detailed by Miriam Silverberg in her exemplary article on the Japanese ethnography of modernity, Gonda Yasunosuke (1887–1951) and Kon Wajirō (1888–1973) "alert us to the construction of a historically grounded and historically conscious culture constituted by practices of daily life. They insert class and gender into our understanding of the state of Japanese mass culture through their documentations of how the place of production was also a place of consumption. . . . [They] recognized that within contemporary consumer culture a struggle for meaning, symbols, and images was . . . taking place" (1992:32, 35).

Kon conducted his investigations of urban life and everyday practices under the rubric of "Modernology" (*kōgengaku*), and Gonda focused on "living social facts" (*ikita shakai jijitsu*). Unlike Kon, however, Gonda collaborated with the state; by the mid-1930s, he had dispensed with a class-based notion of "the people" (*minshū*) to focus on the "general masses" and specifically "the citizens" (*kokumin*), in keeping with his new interest in the formation of a national popular culture.[2] (This shift and wartime developments in general are conveniently ignored by Kato in his "reconsideration" of the history of Japanese popular culture [1989a].) Silverberg oversimplifies in suggesting that "Gonda did not subscribe to an essentialist ideology of 'Japaneseness'" (1992:36–49).While not joining Yanagita in advocating the revitalization of a nativist-inspired, uniquely authentic Japanese culture, he did call for the construction a new Japanese popular culture from select Western and Japanese institutions, as did Kobayashi of the Takarazuka Revue. Thus we see at least two competing ideologies of Japaneseness operative in the early twentieth century. As will become evident in subsequent chapters, the state was more interested in opportunities to mobilize the population than in maintaining any ideological consistency as they did so. The process of such mobilization incorporated both ideologies of Japaneseness in crafting a New Japan and a new culture of and for East Asian co-prosperity. In attending to competing popular discourses within Japan past and present, including those that promote an essentialized Japaneseness, I am taking issue with the prevalent stereotype of cultural homogeneity promoted by and about the Japanese.

JAPANESE TERMINOLOGY

What are the closest equivalents of "popular culture" in the Japanese language? In the late nineteenth century, the discovery of "social problems" (*shakai mondai*) as a distinct category of causes and effects, coupled with an "outburst of nation-mindedness" (Gluck 1985:27, 23), provided the impetus for efforts to consolidate cultural unity and fabricate a national identity based on symbols selectively drawn from Japanese history and non-Japanese institutions alike (Gluck 1985; Westney 1987). These symbols were disseminated rapidly through universal compulsory education and mushrooming mass media in the service of the state (Kasza 1988:3–27).[3] Distinctions were drawn between two contrasting categories of people based on their class and regional affiliations or lack thereof, signified by *taishū* and *minshū*. Prefixed to *bunka*, or "culture," both terms are translated into English as "popular/mass culture," although their connotations are quite different.

Taishū was first used centuries ago in a Buddhist context; pronounced *daishū*, it referred to acolytes and all sentient beings (*Kōjien* 1978:1336; Noguchi 1980:24). From roughly the turn of this century, it has been compounded with *bunka* to denote something akin to both popular culture and mass culture. Although the dictionary referent of *taishū* is also the so-called working class (*Kōjien* 1978:1336), the term is widely used today in reference to the "middle mass": that is, to the proverbial 80 to 90 percent of Japanese who supposedly identify with the label "middle class." *Minshū*, literally "the people en masse," connotes a populist politics and alludes to human agency in the construction and reproduction of social life. Whereas *taishū* emphasizes the sheer size of the great mass of people, *minshū* evokes the instrumentality of "the people" or "the folk" as a collective body.

Yanagita's *jōmin* and the nationalist *kokumin* are two more terms that were invested with the scope of *taishū* and a claim to represent the "really real" Japanese people. Kato, committed to the stereotype of a superior, unique, and homogeneous Japan, interprets *taishū* culture, with its totalizing compass, as "egalitarian" in emphasizing the leveling capacity of popular formations. Whether popular culture is viewed as egalitarian or hegemonic, or both, depends on which configuration of which of its components is under critical consideration at which historical juncture and by whom.

The Edo period, during which the Tokugawa Shogunate limited international trade contacts to a small, artificial island off the coast of Nagasaki, is widely regarded as the historical moment when, as sociologist Kurihara Akira claims, from an urban-based mercantilist economy emerged a popular culture that scholars generally refer to as *tsūzoku bunka*: literally, a culture permeating the laity or the mundane world (1980:59). Another common term for this emergent social formation is *shōmin bunka*: literally, the culture of peoples without a pedigree (e.g., Ichikawa K. 1972).[4] Kabuki, *ukiyoe*, woodblock-printed books whose topics ranged from racy fiction to farm manuals, teahouses, "temple schools" (*terakoya*), pilgrimage-based tourism, and so on were among the institutions and practices characterizing Edo-period popular culture. In contrast to Kato, Kurihara argues that popular culture (*taishū bunka*) today is not simply an extension of Edo-period artifacts, institutions, and practices, but a whole new "formation" (*keiseibutsu*) occasioned by the high-growth industrialization and associated technological inventions of the postwar period (1980:59).[5]

Kawazoe Noboru, a postwar social critic, summarizes the differences between the terms *taishū* and *minshū* as they are used today:

First, because *minshū* culture existed in opposition to aristocratic (*kizoku*) culture, it was from the outset a classlike conception. *Taishū* culture transcends class. Second, as folk songs (*minyō*) and folk dances (*minzoku buyō*) attest, *minshū* culture tends to be regionally focused while *taishū* culture is beyond any class or regional affiliation. *Taishū* culture is growing among those individuals who have become distanced from class and region, who have become locked into the circumstances of the expanding [classless, regionless] masses.

(Kawazoe 1980:7)

Reading between the lines, we see that Kawazoe represents *taishū* culture as a transcendent category—occasioned by certain forces, such as industrialization and modernization—that is virtually synonymous with the nation in its superclass, superregional orientation and its affective reach. By extension, we can understand *taishū bunka* as referring to a national popular culture: national in the sense that it encompasses and affects all peoples within the borders of Japan, and popular because it is familiar to or experientially available to all Japanese, albeit not necessarily in equitable ways.

This last point is the key to my understanding and use of "popular culture" in the Japanese context. It is also central to my attempt to sort out the concept's general theoretical parameters. I have elected to translate *taishū bunka*, the most widely used of the terms reviewed above, as both "popular culture" *and* "mass culture," which I am treating more or less synonymously. I will use "popular culture" as the generic term and "mass culture"—or "popular/mass culture"—when the hegemonic and homogenizing characteristics of popular media and practices are at issue. Although, as other theorists have remarked, it is difficult to maintain a rigid separation of these two terms, the tendency is to use "popular" as something, such as television, favored by the people and "mass" as something produced for the people (Shiach 1989:175). Whereas "popular culture" thus retains a sense of the people's agency, individually and as a group, "mass culture" emphasizes people—"the masses"—as the object of technological developments and social actions.[6] It is crucial to consider the Takarazuka Revue within the semantic frameworks of both terms simultaneously, for the complicated relationships of the theater's administrators, actors, audiences and fans, and critics assumed different arrangements at different historical junctures. These shifting configurations confound any easy formal categorization of Takarazuka as *taishū* or *minshū*, mass or popular.

UBIQUITY VERSUS POPULARITY

I locate popular culture in an encompassing cultural matrix, in this case Japanese culture, in which sociohistorical forces and relations are generated and reproduced, stimulated by encounters with ideas, things, and peoples both within and outside the matrix as a whole or any area in particular—in this case, the Takarazuka Revue. The figure-ground relationship between popular culture and culture emerges and develops continuously as a complex series of responses to communications technologies, increased literacy, a market economy (nominally) premised on choice and competition, and other factors; these factors, moreover, appear in different combinations at different historical moments.

As I see it, popular culture comprises social formations that mark and sustain, for an indeterminate period, some distinction among the ubiquitous elements of everyday life.[7] But the *ubiquitous* must be clearly distinguished from the *popular*: that which is everywhere *and* has been framed and mobilized as particularly salient. This framing activity usually is simultaneous with a thing's dissemination through a mass medium accessible and intelligible to the broadest possible population. Sometimes, however, media worthiness does not help to make something popular but rather acknowledges that very popularity, its distinctiveness among all other mundane things. The necessary, prior condition of ubiquity from which what is popular emerges differentiates "the popular" from the related process of *popularization*, whereby information broadcast about a rare, singular, or esoteric thing lends it topical conspicuousness. And, by the same token, something that once was but is no longer popular can be (re)popularized in this way. Or, as in the case of Kabuki history, something popular can over time or at a particular juncture bifurcate into (at least) two different trajectories, one codified as traditional, classical, and/or orthodox and the other as contemporary, vulgar, and/or unorthodox.

If the ubiquitous refers to dynamic but taken-for-granted or unframed components of everyday life, then the popular is a special category of the ubiquitous, consisting of certain artifacts and practices that are distinguished and mobilized from among all things under the sun. The recent valorization of "popular culture" as a legitimate subject for academic study might also be understood as a process whereby a selection of mundane items are framed and temporarily made discursively visible or canonical. As John Frow observes, "reggae, hip-hop, and scratch video are given a status which is denied to Val Doonican, Kenny Rogers, and family sitcoms" (1995:82). However, a long-standing premium on "discovery," in conjunction with the fickle politics of the academy, guarantees that in due time Kenny Rogers will win his proverbial fifteen minutes as a subject worthy of scholarly attention. Not without irony, this same premium informed the inauguration in 1993 of *Beer Frame: The Journal of Inconspicuous Consumption*. The mission of the journal's creator and editor, Paul Lukas, is to draw attention to the remarkable design values of "gizmos" and packaging that are either taken for granted or unattended to in the critical discourse of popular culture (see Lukas 1997).[8]

The question of why one ubiquitous thing and not another achieves popularity is related to the who or what are the agents of the process of selection and mobilization—of framing. The spectrum of agents ranges from the power bloc, the bourgeoisie, and the elite to the working class, the subordinated and disempowered, and "the people"; from those on top to those below; from the haves to the have-nots, the have-mores to the have-lesses. No single agent or agency has sole responsibility, although one may wish to claim that privilege. How one perceives the power of "the dominant class," "the power bloc," "the bourgeoisie," and even "the people" in this respect is largely determined by one's theoretical and ideological orientation and priorities. Popular culture is the result not of a homogeneous will—although it can be deployed in an *attempt* to create one (as in the case of a national popular culture)—but of many wills; therefore it is a knotty, composite category whose many components are differently mobilized by a variety of people and groups with different—sometimes overlapping, sometimes antithetical—agendas. Popular culture can provide visibility, autonomy, and power, and it can even be deployed as an instrument of domination. It is a place of encounter and contestation, and a process to be struggled over (cf. Kipnis 1986:32–33).

The process of selection and appropriation is also shaped by assumptions about culture, history, society, gender, race, and so forth and their particular configuration at particular times. Thus, ideological positions on, for example, the identity of "the people" are "mobilized in different combinations at different periods" and yield "different sorts of claims about popular culture" (Shiach 1989:6). There is no one continuous and coherent approach to the formation, deployment, and analysis of popular culture, although some of the same appropriations, arguments, and tropes have been recycled, albeit for different purposes, as I noted earlier regarding the state's use of Yanagita's ethnological theories about ordinary Japanese. This "consistency in difference," Morag Shiach suggests, "lies in the extent to which analyses of popular culture are always connected to, and motivated by, problems and perceived limitations within the dominant culture, rather [than] emerging from an engagement with the material forms of popular culture themselves" (6). I basically agree, although Shiach's emphasis on theoretical models of popular culture and their critique keeps her from paying equally astute attention to agents other than professional historians, social psychologists, and literary critics.

My study of the Japanese all-female revue theater and its retinue (such as fans, public cross-dressers, same-sex sexual partners, etc.) reveals that nonprofessionals were equally concerned, even preoccupied, with the relationship between popular culture and the dominant culture, or the status quo, precisely *because of* their creative engagement with the material forms of popular culture and their associated behaviors. I therefore treat the Takarazuka Revue not as a closed, self-contained, and transcendent entity but "as the product of specific historical practices on the part of identifiable social groups in given conditions" (Wolff 1981:49). As Janet Wolff points out, such products bear the imprint of the ideas, values, and conditions of existence of those groups and their representatives at particular historical moments in the form of social performances—including revues and that of their audiences.

Usefully characterized as a node of clamorous debates and contested ideas about the relationship of sexuality, racism, and nationalism, the all-female revue theater has informed my thinking about agency and popular cultural formations, both in general and particularly with respect to Japan. I layer into my narrative of the Takarazuka Revue contested as well as agreed positions and priorities about popular cultural formations and practices already in play. I investigate how and under what conditions "popular" formations and practices are mobilized for a period from the ubiquitous, and how some of them even become dominant.

SEXUALITY AND AMBIVALENCE

I began this consideration of popular culture by remarking that excessiveness is a hallmark of both the Takarazuka Revue and popular culture in general. In the struggle among peoples and groups with different priorities to frame the popular, whatever emerges as especially prevalent is necessarily overdetermined, as indicated by its formal excessiveness.

Cross-dressing—to take an especially pertinent example—is a practice that exemplifies the excessiveness of both the Takarazuka Revue and popular culture. Let us consider the case of a male who chooses to assume publicly a feminine appearance. He must overdetermine his desired look by displaying excess markers of femininity—the more stereotyped the better—so that he can "pass" as a female without raising any doubts among passersby. His excessiveness is carefully contained within a conventional model of femininity, which is itself overdetermined; if it were not, his cross-dressed appearance would be read as comical or even scandalous (cf. J. Roberts 1988 [1986]:26–27).[9]

I generally agree with Marjorie Garber that cross-dressing challenges "easy notions of binarity, putting into question the categories of 'female' and 'male,' whether they are considered essential or constructed, biological or cultural" (1992:10). However, it seems to me that cross-dressing within the bounds of convention—in short, passing—can also reinforce the dualism of oppositionally constructed images of females and males. For cross-dressing to truly frustrate binary thinking, the element of serious parody (as opposed to comedy) must also be mobilized, whereby the appearance of conformity becomes a challenge to conformity: in performing credibly as a woman, a male implicitly reveals gender itself as a type of artifice and performance and not a natural, uniform, original fact of female or male bodies. Although this revelation has come only recently to Euro-American theorists (despite the phenomenon being new to neither Europe nor America), the notion of gender as a performance has a centuries-old history in Japan, as demonstrated most eloquently by the Nō and Kabuki theaters; the concept itself is evident in the eighth-century mytho-histories (Nakamura 1983). In Kabuki, an actor becomes a type or style of woman or man, as opposed to imitating an actual (feminine) female or (masculine) male. The gender ideal is carefully crafted from a repertoire of markers or forms (*kata*)—gestural, sartorial, bodily, cosmetic, linguistic—that are coded masculine or feminine. Historically, Japanese females have been encouraged to follow the ideal standard of femininity constructed and performed by the Kabuki *onnagata*, or player of women's roles.

In the United States, a somewhat similar process of gender crafting is described in a guide to cross-dressing by Joanne Roberts, a male
cross-dresser and "transgender counselor":

> Let us talk a bit about "passing." . . . I am going to assume that you
> are among those crossdressers [sic] who have a strong desire to
> appear in public as a woman, i.e., you want to "pass" as a female.
> Much of being able to pass is related to your physical image. Women
> come in as wide a variety as men, so that if you have applied your
> makeup well and wear appropriate clothes, you will most likely pass
> for female. However, there is an emotional/psychological side as
> well. Once you have achieved an acceptable (to the rest of the world)
> outer image, you must build an inner one. You must believe that
> you will pass. If you do not believe, then you will be sending subtle
> signals to those who get a little too close that something is not quite
> right. Confidence comes gradually and by placing yourself in con-
> trolled situations you will achieve your goal of passing.
>
> (J. Roberts 1988 [1986]:26)

The idea that sexual anatomy and gender are not naturally identified is common to both Roberts and the Kabuki actor. Actually,
Roberts's account is closer to the experience of nonprofessional cross-
dressers in Japan, who may not have a sanctioned rationale for their
behavior but who do have access to "controlled situations" and, by
extension, an opportunity eventually to pass confidently in public, if
that is what they want to do. For example, the Elizabeth Club (discussed in chapter 5), one of hundreds of cross-dressing clubs for Japanese males, boasts a well-stocked wardrobe, a staff of beauticians, and
the presence of like-minded peers to ensure that members make the
transition to feminine personas successfully.

What the Kabuki theater, Roberts's guide to cross-dressing, and the
Elizabeth Club all signify is the performativity of gender and its dis-
sociation from sex, in the sense of genitals. Of course, the situation
becomes more complex if we take passing to apply beyond the realm
of theater or the practice of cross-dressing. Since gender is an effect
of culturally coded markers of behavior and style that are only presumed to be the natural attributes of one sex rather than the other,
then passing as feminine pertains to males and females equally, as
does passing as masculine. To put this differently, a cross-dressed male
is to a feminine female *not* as copy is to original, but rather as copy is
to copy. And, ultimately, the original is revealed to be "nothing other

than a parody of the *idea* of the natural and the original" (Butler 1990:31). In this connection, as I discuss in the next chapter, "original gender" is a matter of a stock character, such as the Good Wife, Wise Mother, or the trademark style of a particular actor: composite forms or pastiches, which can only ever be approximated. The relation of original to copy is also at the root of Japanese national cultural identity and the colonial policy of assimilation discussed in chapter 3.

To a certain extent, then, everyone is passing—she or he is selectively (over)acting and (over)dressing in order to be perceived unequivocally as female or male. Cross-dressing (as a gender and gendered performance), like popular culture, involves framing: select components (artifacts, practices) are assembled and configured in desired ways. The composite character of gender and popular formations alike is what, in my view, makes them fundamentally ambivalent and ambiguous; they are capable of fluctuating between or being assigned to more than one referent or category and thus are capable of being read or understood in more than one way. Such excessive semiosis reflects an epistemology of both/and rather than either/or. Throughout this book, I examine how ambiguity and ambivalence can be used strategically as grounds for containment (resolution, control) *and* as a basis for parody that draws attention to the artifices that uphold the status quo. Parody itself is ambivalent and ambiguous: it can be intended and read as merely comical and playful, *and* as demystifying and subversive (cf. Kleinhans 1994:194–97).

While negotiating everyday life *as a* man or *as a* woman is an unproblematic process for most people, becoming conscious of the arbitrariness of convention quickly leads one to doubt the very notion of an original or real femininity or masculinity. For those whose identity depends on the essential and a priori nature of these categories, this consciousness can be terrifying. But knowledge of the sociohistorical constructedness of gender need not preclude acting within those constructed parameters. Whether illuminating or subverting, passing—and by extension parody—depends on a context in which and an audience by whom its transformational potential can be fully recognized and mobilized. In Japan, the Kabuki and Takarazuka theaters have long been two such receptive contexts, and popular culture in general constitutes a major site of change. The presence of a receptive context alone does not an epistemological revolution make, however. Such is the indeterminate politics of ambivalence and ambiguity.

THE OFFICIAL STORY

Since my argument on strategic ambivalence relies almost exclusively on the very large Japanese literature on Takarazuka, a comment is in order here on the comparatively scanty non-Japanese, mostly Anglophone, literature on the Revue. Virtually all of these writings recapitulate Takarazuka's "official story," which is reproduced with great regularity in the Japanese literature as well, most of which continues to be published under the auspices of the Revue. One of the two exceptions—at least in some respects—is Ingrid Sischy's article on Takarazuka in the *New Yorker*, which broaches the subject of sexuality through the voice of one anonymous female fan who admitted that her "attraction [to Takarazuka] was sexual" (1992:98). The fan insisted on anonymity because she worked "in a straight world" and had "to be careful about [her] homosexuality."[10] The other exception is an article on the "Japanese Girls' Opera" (i.e., Takarazuka Revue) by Mamoru Mochizuki, who remarks that "the star-fan relationship is based on a latent homosexual interest" (1959:172). He further notes, altogether dismissively, that the "homosexual tendencies" of fans are "temporary[:] . . . something like the measles, a childhood disorder, which will soon pass away" (170).

Mochizuki, a Japanese sociologist who also publishes in English, had an opportunity to observe the theater firsthand and was probably familiar with mass media exposés of the Revue's sexual milieu (though not a single source is cited by him); he thus incorporates the subject of sexuality into his essay. However, he opts to radically delimit and to belittle the so-called homosexual tendency as a "childhood disorder." Sischy, on the other hand, despite her reliance on translators, administrators, and the Revue's public relations literature, seems to have an inkling of Takarazuka's significant subtext. Yet, apart from transcribing the one fan's account of her sexual attraction to Takarazuka, the perceptive Sischy ends up recapitulating the Revue's official story of its historical and social significance.

The film *Dream Girls* (1994), which attempts to document the parallel production of shows and their stars, encourages viewers to read a lesbian/gay consciousness at work, however implicitly, into footage of Academy students and actors rehearsing juxtaposed with the steamier scenes from an actual revue *as if* Takarazuka were, in fact, a lesbian feminist theater. That the film is advertised as a "lesbian film," and has been shown widely at lesbian and gay film festivals, has facilitated this overly simple reading, which is erroneous. The apparent motive of the directors[11]—to narrate the sexual politics of the theater—was severely constrained by the Takarazuka administrators, who fiercely guard the "wholesomeness" of the Revue. Consequently, the film instead encourages through innuendo—for those "in the know"—a lesbian reading of the various activities shown. As one reviewer remarked, "Although the film's attitude toward the school [i.e., the Takarazuka Music Academy] is respectful, the movie maintains a deadpan satiric undertone" (Holden 1994:B3). I am somewhat perturbed by the facile manner in which *Dream Girls* inserts itself—or has been inserted—into a presentist and universalizing (homo)sexual politics. To be credible and comparative, research on the discourse of sexuality must be attentive both to historical specificity and to the competing and contested views and practices that inform the text and subtexts of that discourse. Nevertheless, *Dream Girls* provides viewers with a glimpse inside Fortress Takarazuka; with more research and ethnographic depth, it could have been a film as complex as the Revue itself.

It is hard not to retell the Revue's official story. The alternative involves, as I have discovered, spending thousands of hours riffling through thousands of pages of yellowed newspapers and magazines, or unwinding dozens of rolls of microfilm at libraries and archives; meeting with and earning the trust of Revue fans over a period of years; and, of course, attending Takarazuka shows. But without this level of research, the tenacious and historical connections linking Takarazuka, popular culture, imperialism, and same-sex sexual practices will remain obscure—hinted at, but not detailed in a grounded and nuanced way.[12]

My own first glimpse into the charged history of the Revue's sexual politics was also my first encounter with the company's almost impenetrable defense of Takarazuka's public image. It was June 1987, and I had been given permission to peruse and order photocopies from the otherwise noncirculating scrapbooks maintained by the Revue's archival staff. They were housed in the Ikeda Bunko, a public library near Takarazuka supported by the Hankyū Tōhō Group, which has the largest collection of Takarazuka Revue literature in the country. Filled with newspaper clippings of practically every article that had ever appeared on some aspect of Takarazuka since its founding, the scrapbooks facilitated immeasurably the archival component of my research project. Focusing on the 1920s and 1930s, I came across article after article highlighting the connection between Takarazuka and lesbian practices. Although the staff photocopied them for me, once I filled out the long request form, it became obvious to me the next day that my choice of subject—actually one among many—had touched a nerve. I was told that today was the last day I could use the scrapbooks. "Why? I only started looking at them yesterday!" I protested. "Because they are scheduled to be microfilmed." "All of them at once?" I asked in astonishment—there were at least twenty thick volumes. "Yes."

The following year I returned to do more research at the library and asked to see the microfilms of the scrapbooks; I had since collected numerous articles on various aspects of Takarazuka by paging laboriously through bound newspapers and scrolling through reels of microfilmed texts at the Diet Library, but I wanted to see if there were any important articles that I might have missed. "What microfilms?" was the answer I got. Whatever their actual condition, the scrapbooks were no longer available for my use. Then one of the senior male librarians drew me aside and told me in a hushed, urgent voice that my research was "inconvenient" (*chotto komaru*). Clearly my interest in the sexual politics of the Revue was viewed by the administration as provocative.

Gradually, over the ensuing years, the librarians—who considered themselves Takarazuka employees—grudgingly came to accept me as a scholar, although they, and the Revue's administration, remained less than thrilled about my subject, the sexual component of which they had blown out of proportion. Administrators who at first had been so warm and accommodating became cool and dismissive: I was not perceived by them as one of the "friendly" foreigners whose work extended the Revue's public relations agenda. At one point during my eight-month field trip to Japan in 1990, I received a telephone call from a woman, a Takarazuka fan, who warned me that the Revue administrators were not pleased with my research and that if I were Japanese, I would not be allowed to continue: "They're mean. They have their ways. They could twist your arm the way developers do when they want to force people to sell their land."[13] That was not a comforting thought, but the only action the administrators undertook was to keep me at arm's length.

It was not until the fall of 1995, when I returned to Japan for two months, that I learned just how many documents had been withheld from me at the Ikeda Bunkō. Most of the defensive older staff had retired earlier that year, and young, college-age clerks had taken their places at the main desk. A self-service photocopy machine had just been installed, eliminating the need to request copies from the censorious staff. Sensing a concomitant change in policy, out of curiosity I asked to see script anthologies of revues staged in 1944 and 1945—volumes I was told had been destroyed during the war—and was delighted when a new clerk brought me all of the supposedly nonexistent volumes, which I was then able to photocopy freely. Previously the staff had tried to keep from me not only information about the actors' sexual practices but also material related to the Revue's wartime role in empire building and its production of nationalistic, promilitary plays.[14]

This digression on my experiences during fieldwork is relevant here for two basic reasons. First, it imparts a sense of the fiercely protective stance of the Revue and its loyal employees, whose mission is to promote the theater's official story and to squelch all others; and second, it underscores the necessity of diligent and thorough archival and library research, in addition to "live" fieldwork. Most fans and critics have neither the resources nor inclination to reconstruct Takarazuka's knotty history, and so the Revue is able to reproduce without challenge its official story in the numerous publications under its purview. Japanese critics and authors interested in the all-female theater are well aware of the limits set on their research. In a recent newspaper article, sociologist Ukai Masaki marvels at how Japanese books on Takarazuka invariably promote a sparkling image of the Revue—"they're all public relations books. . . . [You] just don't see books with titles like *Takarazuka's Backstage Corruption, Grotesque Takarazuka,* or *Takarazuka Babylon*" (1995). He suggests, with a touch of sarcasm, that a book that dealt with homosexuality (*dōseiai*) among actors and fans, bullying at the Music Academy, and other backstage "scandals"—"information that would destroy fans' dreams"—would likely make Takarazuka an institution more closely resembling today's Japan and would attract more people's interest.[15]

Similarly, it seems that for a wide variety of reasons, ranging from inadequate language skills to an unfamiliarity with the broader historical significance of all-female revues, the few non-Japanese re-

searchers writing on Takarazuka have simply continued to disseminate the "straight" version of the company's history and contemporary circumstances. For example, in his 1988 dissertation, Zeke Berlin
points to the dearth of English and European sources on the Revue
as the stimulus for his own research, which dwells on the contemporary Revue. However, relying on translators and on books published
under the Revue's auspices, Berlin recapitulates Takarazuka's official
story. Nevertheless, his work does offer readers a brief if standard history of the Revue and a profile of the theater, its actors, and its fans
in the late 1970s and early 1980s. Earlier, Dennis Atkinson wrote a
short introductory paper on Takarazuka in the same vein (Atkinson
1984).[16]

For the reasons suggested above, and as will become clear in what
follows, the Takarazuka Revue is an ideal site for an exploration of
the contested discourse of sexuality, among other subjects, in modern Japan. That such a connection has either been overlooked or dismissed is one manifestation of the relative lack of serious attention
that scholars of Japan pay to ideas about gender and sexuality beyond
the completely normative. Some shortsightedly eschew the subject
itself as unscholarly and/or motivated by a radical (i.e., feminist or
lesbian/gay) agenda; others apparently are afraid of being stigma-
tized and ostracized for undertaking research on the subject of sex and
gender—and especially on the subject of homosexual practices. Apparently the threat encoded in the insidious expression "It takes one
to know one" overpowers the fear of incomplete or even bad scholarship. It still is too often the case that indifference, ignorance, and
prejudice prevent researchers from considering the historical and cultural significance of gender attribution and sexual practices; in the case
of Japan, these have actually been part of a very *public* discourse.[17]
Imagine scholars fifty or one hundred years from now writing about
marriage in the late-twentieth-century United States without men-
tioning the enormous amount of attention, popular and legal alike,
paid to the issue of same-sex marriage. Similarly, one cannot understand or convey fully the cultural politics of, say, *bushidō* (way of the
samurai) without an earnest attempt to situate and analyze the place
of male-to-male sexual relations in the construction of both power and
samurai masculinity during the Edo period, examining also how they
affected the dominant construction of femininity.[18]

Consider a few concrete examples. In the course of researching the relationship between sexuality and suicide in modern Japan, I discovered that the several Anglophone works dealing analytically with "Japanese suicide" avoided any mention of "same-sex love double suicide" (*dōseiai shinjū*), even though this category has figured prominently in the Japanese social scientific literature on suicide since the turn of this century (see Robertson forthcoming and chapter 4 below).[19] By the same token, whereas the long history in Japan of same-sex sexual relations between males (specifically Buddhist priests, samurai, and Kabuki actors) is well represented, albeit largely descriptively rather than analytically, in English and Japanese publications past and present, sexual relations between females have remained largely unrecognized, unacknowledged, invisible, and inaccessible in the postwar scholarly literature in and on Japan until very recently.[20] Yet unlike the muzzled scholarship of today, various types of lesbian practice, including double suicide, were widely and openly highlighted, discussed, sensationalized, and analyzed in the scholarly and popular media of the early twentieth century. The complexities of sexual practices and the instability of their categories, together with a perceived and internalized stigma applied to lesbian subjects, jointly have induced Japan scholars to disregard *even what had captivated the Japanese public and scholarly community at a given historical moment.* Ironically, the space of sociosexual (in)difference is evident not in the popular cultural discourse shaping a specific period but in the academic scholarship on Japan. The persistence of the dominant sex-gender ideology, which views females as objects of male desire and not the subjects of their own desire, effectively inhibits both naming that desire and identifying modes of female *and* male sexualities in Japan. Attending to the early debates on sexuality, and conveying a sense of the contested rhetorical climate in which they took place, is a necessary beginning for a more responsible anthropology of sexuality, gender ideology, and popular culture.

2

Staging Androgyny

Today is my farewell party.
To love?
N-O.
Inside am I a man? A woman?
I strike a pose as one
and the other grows bored.
Well,
when the next page is turned
another me.

Mine izu main (Mine is mine) 1986:[46]

DISRUPTING STEREOTYPES

The epigraph is from an album of photographs featuring Mine Saori, a top *otokoyaku* who retired in 1987. Mine's poem about (her) androgyny is superimposed on a photograph of her: she is sporting a black satin tunic, black leather pants, lacy black socks, and black high heels, reclining on a sofalike object draped in black cloth. One foot is on the ground, the other raised to rest on the arm of the sofa. She has a bemused but serious look on her face, and her eyes are cast down and sideways. Mine's poem and picture allude to the constructed and performative aspects of gender and its distinction from sex that have been much invoked of late. Such an analysis is not merely a theoretical premise or literary exercise; these aspects are unquestionably evident in the Takarazuka Revue and Kabuki, two sites of my investigation into the politics of androgyny in Japan.[1]

Androgyny, as I employ the term here, refers not to a physiological condition (that is, an intersexed body) but to a "surface politics of the body" (Butler 1990:136). It involves the scrambling of gender markers—clothes, cosmetics, gestures, speech patterns, and so on—in a way that both challenges the stability of a sex-gender system premised on a male (masculine)/female (feminine) dichotomy and also retains the components of that dichotomy, now juxtaposed or combined. For an androgynous appearance or performance to turn heads on a street or to draw stares—and applause—in a theater, it must do both. Because so many critical analyses of Kabuki and virtually none of the Takarazuka Revue have been published, and also because I am interested in a female-embodied androgyny, my focus here is on the Revue—its actors, audience, and critics—and particularly on its early history. After summarizing the spectrum of English-language and Japanese terms for and usages of androgyny, I shall move on to the main project of this chapter: to explore some of the ways in which androgyny has been differently deployed to support and subvert dominant representations of females and males in Japan.

Since the early twentieth century, androgyny has been used in both dominant and marginalized discourses of sex, gender, and sexuality to camouflage "unconventional" female sexual practices by creating the illusion of an asexual—in effect, a disembodied—identity. Androgyny has identified Takarazuka actors who perform both "female" and "male" gender roles without being constrained by either. How is a dominant gender ideology constructed, reproduced, resisted, and even subverted, sometimes all at once, by women and men whose private and professional lives confound tidy, universalistic schemata, whether those derive from literature or theory? Real people tend to be messy, inconsistent, hypocritical, and mostly opaque when the relationship of sex, gender, and sexuality in their own lives is at issue. Moreover, the stereotype of *the Japanese* as a homogeneous people has had the corollary effect of whitewashing a colorful variety of gender identities and sexual practices. More often than not, the lived experiences of female and male members of Japanese society have not been sufficiently problematized; rather, they have been collapsed into dominant, naturalized gender ideals. The male workaholic and female housewife are two stock images that come readily to mind. In the larger scheme of things, this chapter—and book—seeks to dismantle some of the more tenacious stereotypes of Japanese women and men, in the process provoking new insights into the complicated relationship of sex, gender, and sexuality in Japan and elsewhere.

WORDS AND USAGES

The English loanword *andorojenii* (androgyny) has appeared frequently in the Japanese mass media since the mid-1980s in reference to clothing fashions—particularly the men's clothing adapted by and for women and the skirts worn by all-male pop music groups, such as the Checkers (Asano 1989; Nishiyama 1984; *Otoko ni mo sukāto jidai?* 1985; Yagi 1989). Since *andorojenii* is a transliteration, the term is often simultaneously defined in Japanese as *ryōsei* (both sexes/genders) and *chūsei* (between sexes/genders), the differential use of which I will elaborate later.[2] In English, following ancient Greek usage, "androgyny" literally means "man-woman," although what the word signifies and represents is far from literal. Carolyn Heilbrun, for example, presents androgyny—which she defines as the realization of man in woman and woman in man—as an ideal, nonpolarized way of being that is necessary for the survival of human society (1982 [1964]:xx). Adrienne Rich, on the other hand, argues that the very structure of the word androgyny "replicates the sexual dichotomy and the priority of *andros* (male) over *gyne* (female)" (1976:76–77).[3]

Japanese scholars have taken similar theoretical and political positions. Asano Michiko, for example, adopts Carl Jung's quasi-biological theory of androgyny in exploring the idea of androgyny as it has been expressed historically in Japanese popular religious texts (1989).[4] She bemoans the loss of "traditional" androgyny (as "the harmony of 'male' and 'female' qualities") over the course of Japan's modernization but observes a revival of androgyny (as "cross-dressing") in the present time (201–2). Similarly, Akiyama Satoko employs Jung's theory of the "inherent androgyny" of all people to debunk the notion of "sexual perversion" (*seitōsaku*), insisting that the sexual choices available to females and males are as varied as the combinations of feminine and masculine tendencies they embody (1990; see also Ifukube 1932). And Kurahashi Yukiko suggests the corporeality of Jung's *animus*, or "male archetypical essence," in her neologism for "a female who wants to be a man": *penisuto* ("penist") (quoted in Hyūga 1971:26). Yagi Kimiko, on the other hand, like Rich, dismisses androgyny as an idea (and ideal) that suppresses women's sexual difference in the name of equality (1989).

Medical—anatomical and psychological—descriptions and interpretations of androgyny were especially plentiful in early-twentieth-century Japan. The works of Euro-American sexologists—Sigmund Freud, Carl Jung, Richard von Krafft-Ebing, Havelock Ellis, Edward Carpenter, Magnus Hirschfeld, Iwan Bloch, Leopold Lowenfeld, Wilhelm Gustav Liepmann, Otto Weininger—were exported directly to

Japan, where they were studied, translated, adapted, and augmented by Japanese sexologists (Fujikawa 1919a, 1919b, 1923; Hanafusa 1930; Hayashi 1926; Ifukube 1932; Izawa 1931; Ōzumi 1931; Yasuda 1935; see also Hirschfeld 1935; Roden 1990). Physiological androgyny—that is, an intersexed body—was of special interest at that time to scholars of forensic medicine, who addressed the phenomenon in terms of conscription, patrilineality (specifically family name and inheritance), political service, and civil rights, all of which were contingent on the establishment of a person's body as male (e.g., Takada 1926 [1917]:285–91).

Two of the most frequently encountered Japanese terms referring to androgyny are *ryōsei* and *chūsei*, which were coined in the early twentieth century; they first appeared in journal and newspaper articles on homosexuality and "abnormal sexual desire" (Kabeshima, Hida, and Yonekawa 1984:185). *Ryōsei* was and is most generally used to label either someone with both female and male genitalia or someone with both feminine and masculine characteristics. Consequently, *ryōsei* has been used to refer intersexed bodies as well as to persons who behave as if they were at once masculine and feminine (Hyūga 1971; Komine and Minami 1985:57, 296–301). The latter combine and embody the stereotyped characteristics attributed to females and males, which are commonly seen as polarized and mutually exclusive (see Akiyama 1990; Asano 1989; Ifukube 1932; Komine and Minami 1985:57).

Chūsei, on the other hand, has been used to mean "neutral" or "in between," and thus neither female nor male, neither woman nor man. Whereas *ryōsei* emphasizes the juxtaposition or combination of sex or gender differences, *chūsei* emphasizes the erasure or nullification of differences. A person whose body is intersexed usually is raised or passes as one or the other sex/gender (see Sawada 1921; Komine and Minami 1985:296–301). A "neutral" body, in contrast, is one whose surface appearance (costume, hairstyle, intonations, speech patterns, gestures, movements, deportment, and so on) confounds the conventional alignment of sex with gender and scrambles received gender markers. The normalizing principle at work here posits that, say, masculinity is a "natural" attribute of male bodies. However, masculinity is not a product of nature—that is, some sort of agentless creation—but a sociohistorical representation of male bodies, a representation that is subject to manipulation and change. Gender, in other words, names an ultimately unstable "amalgam of signifiers" (Pacteau 1986:80). Despite the workings of this normalizing principle, it remains the case that in Japan historically, as attested in part by Kabuki and Takarazuka, neither femininity nor masculinity has been deemed the exclusive province of either female or male bodies.

CROSS-DRESSING HISTORICALLY

For centuries in Japan, cross-dressed performances have characterized ritual practices such as shrine festivals and the Nō theater, have lent spice to many novels, and have even figured in the eighth-century mytho-histories. However, I will limit my review of the history of gender ambivalence to the Edo period, when sexual and gender transformations became a subject of popular and legal fascination.[5]

The earliest Kabuki stage included females who performed men's roles while male actors often took women's roles. Female actors were first banished from the stage in 1629. Apparently, the Confucian Shogunate was disturbed by the general disorder, including unlicensed prostitution, associated with women's Kabuki. Patrons quarreled with one another for access to their favorite dancers. Replacing the females with boys did not solve the problem, for the male patrons were equally attracted to the boys. Eventually, the prohibition of females and later of boys prompted the sanctioned emergence of the *onnagata*, adult males who specialized in performing femininity.

Early accounts of female Kabuki actors were as polarized as the actors' gender was ambiguous. The seventeenth-century Confucian scholar Hayashi Razan (1583–1657) was not complimentary in his description of these shows: "The [males] wear women's clothing; the [females] wear men's clothing, cut their hair and wear it in a man's topknot, have swords at their sides and carry purses. They sing base songs and dance vulgar dances; their lewd voices are clamorous, like the buzzing of flies and the crying of cicadas" (quoted in Shively 1970 [1955]:232). In contrast, another early-seventeenth-century work provided a glowing description of a female Kabuki actor's stage entrance: "The figure . . . did not appear to be that of a woman but of a true-hearted man: it was indeed the image of Narihira, who long ago was called the spirit of *yin* and *yang*. . . . Anyone who would not fall in love with such a beautiful figure is more [frightening] than a ghost" (quoted in Shively 1970 [1955]:233).

Narihira, a ninth-century courtier known for his bisexuality, was eulogized in Edo-period fiction as "the god of *yin* and *yang*" (Schalow 1990:10). His name formed the basis of a term used in the Edo period to denote androgyny: *futanarihira*, literally "double-bodied" or "body double" (Imao 1982:145–46; Maeda 1973:750, 867, 884; Takada G. 1926 [1917]:287). The *futa* (double) preceding *narihira* would seem to imply an "overdetermined" Narihira, in the sense of a person—in most cases a male—who performs both in a feminine and masculine manner.

What is interesting in the passages just cited is the authors' fixation on the female actor's ability to appropriate the markers of masculinity. Yet these and similar accounts seem to presume a priori a male's ability to perform femininity—and thus theater historians have taken for granted the availability of males to play women's roles when females were banished from the public stage.[6] Indeed, whereas males could perform openly as women on the Kabuki stage, and also live as women offstage as well, females who appropriated masculinity as a social guise were criminalized. This double standard is poignantly illustrated by the case of a woman named Take who, in the 1830s, openly defied the sex-gender hierarchy. Her case is recorded in the women's section of *Oshioki reiruishū*, a collection of crimes and their punishments published between 1771 and 1852.[7]

As a girl, Take had played with boys and later found men's work and activities more exciting than women's work. Cutting off her hair, she created a new persona for herself as a young man named Takejirō. This act so provoked the indignation of the male innkeeper who employed her that he raped her, ostensibly to make Take/Takejirō aware of her female sex. She became pregnant and ran away from the inn, but not before stealing an obi and a straw raincoat to hide her pregnancy and to protect her masculine appearance. When the child was born, she suffocated it. Thievery and infanticide notwithstanding, when Take/Takejirō was captured she was charged with having committed the newly coined crime of "corrupting public morals" (*jinrin o midashimasu mono*) by dissociating sex from gender. Her second arrest came in 1837 when it was discovered that she was both passing as a man and impersonating a deputy magistrate, a flagrant violation of both the sex-gender hierarchy and the social status hierarchy. Ironically, she was rearrested after attracting the attention of a real magistrate who saw her capture a thief committing a robbery.

Take/Takejirō was fined, imprisoned, and eventually exiled for her appropriation of a masculine gendered appearance.

Take/Takejirō's actions indicated that she was aware of the arbitrary nature of gender attribution and of the sexual and gendered division of labor. Her punishment illustrated the tenacity of the Tokugawa Shogunate's emphasis on the fusion of female sex with femininity, although the authorities were considerably more lax toward cross-dressing males. In the case of Kabuki, the Shogunate was less concerned with cross-dressing than with class-crossing sexual relations between males. Nevertheless, Shogunate officials condoned female-embodied masculinity in at least one context. The term *bōzu*, or "shaved head," for example, referred to male and female priests who had taken the tonsure, as well as to female employees in the various castles who were assigned masculine gender. Dressed in formal men's attire (the *haori* and *hakama*), these women were responsible for mediating between the innermost, "female"-gendered and outermost, "male"-gendered sections of the castles (Takayanagi 1965:17). The difference between the *bōzu* and Take/Takejirō is that whereas the *bōzu* were assigned a masculine gender, Take/Takejirō chose hers; accordingly, she was punished severely. Also, the *bōzu* were likely selected from among older, postmenopausal females whose sex and gender were consequently regarded as ambiguous. That is, they were no longer classified as "feminine" females or "really real" females.

CONCEPTUALIZING ANDROGYNY

There seems to have been no formally developed concept of androgyny prior to Yoshizawa Ayame's development of a theory and method for Kabuki *onnagata* in the early Edo period. Ayame himself (historical figures are often referred to by their given name) was a Kabuki *onnagata*, and his theory was a twist on the Buddhist concept of *henshin*, or bodily transformation or metamorphosis. *Hen* is the term for "change," in both a transitive and intransitive sense. *Shin* (also pronounced *mi*) is the term for "body" in the most comprehensive sense: that is, a physical, mental, social, historical, and spiritual entity (Gunji 1988:4–9; Hattori Y. 1975:31–35; Ichikawa H. 1985:38–47; Imao 1982:29). The term *henshin* originally referred to the process whereby deities assumed a human form in order to better promulgate Buddhist teachings among the masses of sentient beings.

Related to *henshin* is the process of *henjo nanshi* (also *tennyo jōnan*), whereby a female body becomes transformed, or metamorphoses, into a male body. Since female bodies are regarded in Buddhist doctrine not only as polluted but also as representative of a lower form of existence, enlightenment is not possible for them unless they manage to metamorphose into male bodies. The net effect is not the creation of an androgyne but rather a female's total transformation into "the opposite" sex: in short, rebirth as a male over the course of several generations. It is clear that the orthodox Buddhist concept of *henshin* refers to physical bodies (including genitalia) and not only to embodied markers of gender.[8] However, the term *henjo nanshi* was also used popularly during the Edo period in reference to intersexed bodies. For example, a peasant woman was deemed suffering from the "*henjo nanshi* syndrome" (*henjo nanshi sho*) when, at the age of twenty-seven, she developed male genitalia (Tomioka 1938:104).

Henshin is also central to the Kabuki theater and refers specifically to the received process by which an *onnagata* becomes Woman, as opposed to impersonating a given woman. Ayame's theory resembles the Buddhist concept of *henshin* with the exception that gender (and not sex) is involved in an *onnagata*'s transformation from a man into Woman. He perceived the woman's role player not as "a male acting in a role in which he becomes a 'woman,'" but rather as "a male who is a 'woman' acting a role" (Imao 1982:149).[9] In other words, the actor's transformation precedes his assumption of the woman's role.

The original Woman is a male invention: an amalgam of signifiers of ideal femininity embodied by the Kabuki specialist. Ayame insisted that an *onnagata* "embody femininity in his daily life."[10] Simply impersonating a given female was neither adequate nor appropriate. To clinch his point, Ayame insisted that the construction of Woman could not be left up to the idiosyncratic notions of a particular actor. Instead, he introduced categories of the ideal Woman, each with predetermined characteristics. The role of a "chaste woman" (*teijo*), for example, was to be based on *Greater Learning for Females* (*Onna daigaku*, 1672), an influential primer on "female" gender written by a leading (male) Confucian scholar (Imao 1982:147–53). Given the Kabuki theater's mixed reception by the Tokugawa Shogunate, and the low, outsider status of actors during the Edo period, basing the construction and performance of femininity on *Greater Learning for Females* quite likely added a modicum of legitimacy to the urban theater.[11]

Ayame eschewed what he called the prevailing androgynous figure of the *onnagata*, describing it as *futanarihira*, or "double-bodied,"
as noted earlier. In his view, an androgynous *onnagata* blurred the
boundaries between sex and gender, female and male, femininity and
masculinity (Imao 1982:145–47). Ayame's apparent objective in for-
mulating a theory and method for the player of women's roles was
to make distinct both those boundaries and the bounded, all the while
recognizing that sex and gender were not naturally aligned in any one
body. An *onnagata*, then, according to Ayame, was not an androgyne
but the embodiment of patriarchally inscribed, state-regulated "female" gender. The actor was unequivocally Woman, a model for females offstage to emulate and a sex object for males offstage to proposition. Apparently, during Ayame's time, there was even "tacit
approval" for the *onnagata* "to bathe at the public baths reserved for
women" (T. Watanabe and Iwata 1989 [1987]:86).

From Ayame's point of view, the process of *henshin*, or transformation, precluded a blending of the two genders. However, sexologist
Watanabe Tsuneo asserts that because an *onnagata* was a male body
enacting a type of femininity and thus displacing the conventional
alignment of sex, gender, and sexuality, the Kabuki actor was indeed
an androgyne (74–135). For Ayame, "female" gender superseded and
even negated a male body, and thus the *onnagata*, having become
Woman, bathed with females at public bathhouses; in Watanabe's view,
the "female" gender and male body of the Kabuki actor formed a dialectic. According to Watanabe, the androgyny of the *onnagata* was
achieved by style (coiffure and clothing) in addition to same-sex sexual practices—specifically, by the "passive" feminine role.

With the Meiji Restoration of 1868, the modernizing state discour-
aged gender ambivalence and sexual confusion, which were associated with social disorder (cf. T. Watanabe and Iwata 1989 [1987]:127).
Sex and gender were to be strictly delineated: males were to keep their
hair short and dress in Western-style clothing; females were to wear
their long hair swept up in a traditional chignon and clothe themselves
in kimonos. On the surface, it seems that the state got its way: a one-
day survey of 1,180 people in Ginza (Tokyo's premier boulevard), conducted by the "modernologist" Kon Wajirō in 1925, revealed that 67
percent of males wore Western-style outfits, while all but 1 percent of
females appeared in Japanese dress (cited in Silverberg 1992:38).
Nevertheless, the 1 percent (and probably more) of females who did

wear "modern" clothes rankled critics, who connected Westernization with the masculinization of *the* Japanese Woman and the neglect
of Japanese customs (cf. Tachibana 1890; see also citations in Roden
1990; Silverberg 1991). As Donald Roden reports, "the expression and
representation of gender ambivalence captured the imagination of the
literate urban populace" in the 1910s and 1920s, sparking a heated
debate in the media between conservatives and liberals (1990:43).

Roden points to the Takarazuka player of men's roles and the *nimaime* (literally, "second"), or "effeminate male star" of the screen, as
"two of the most striking symbolic representations of androgyny in
Taishō mass culture" (47). However, it would be misleading to think
of the male *nimaime* as the structural homologue of the Takarazuka
man, even though she was called *nimaime* by all-female revue fans and
revue administrators alike (e.g., "Nimaime zadankai" 1936; Ueda
1974:211–37). I suggest that the male *nimaime* was the film media
equivalent of the Kabuki dandy (as opposed to the *onnagata*), usually
a pale-faced, merchant-class playboy with street smarts in lieu of
swordsmanship. To refer to him as "effeminate" both recapitulates and
confuses the conservative argument against a broader definition and
image of masculinity that seemed to be at issue at that time. Rather,
it is more accurate and insightful to refer to the *nimaime* role as characterized by a "charm born from indecisiveness," a charm that complements its gender ambiguity (Ueda 1974:113).

One could also argue that males were able to perform as indecisive
and love-struck men in the movies precisely because the patriarchal
ideology of the modern state, like its Edo-period counterpart, so per-
vasively suffused the structures and institutions of everyday life; sexual hierarchy within the household, for example, was an "organic component" of the state (Nolte 1987:67). The male *nimaime*, in short, did
not alter the dominant ideology of sex and gender. Whereas Roden implies that debates about gender and sexual ambivalence were directed
at men and women equally, my extensive perusal of hundreds of contemporary newspaper, magazine, and journal articles leads me to different conclusions: girls and women almost exclusively were singled
out as the sources of sexual deviance and social disorder and as the
targets of acrimonious debates about the relationship of sex, gender,
and sexuality.[12] Just as the Takarazuka man inspired far more commentary about androgyny and sexual deviance than did the sensitive

male screen star, so too the Modern Girl (*moga*) completely overshadowed the Modern Boy (*mobo*), her almost token male counterpart, in the critical social commentary of the early twentieth century (see Silverberg 1991). If the sexes were converging, as some pundits argued (e.g., Nogami 1920), it was because the masculinization of females was compromising the masculinity of males, who appeared more feminine in contrast; that is, the markers distinguishing male from female, masculine from feminine, were losing their polarity.[13] Today, the self-conscious visibility of assertive females, in spite of the corporate glass ceiling and other forms of institutionalized sexism, has prompted pundits to once again argue that the sexes are converging. Ōhira Ken, a psychiatrist at St. Luke's International Hospital in Tokyo, has claimed that "male high school students today have entirely lost the idea of 'masculinity'" (quoted in "Sexual Revolution in the Making" 1996). In the zero-sum game of sex-gender polarity reflected in these sorts of proclamations, which seem to be reinvented by each generation of social critic, any transformation in the dominant ideology of gender is perceived as pathological and socially disruptive.

The one exception to the overwhelming focus on the "woman problem" (*fujin mondai*) was an intense debate about the place of *onnagata* in modern Japan. One prominent forum in which the debate was waged was a special issue of the theater journal, *Engei Gahō* (*Theater Graphic*), published in 1914. The constituent articles were fairly evenly divided between those who were in favor of retaining the *onnagata* institution, and those who felt that it was unnatural and perverse. Supporting arguments stressed how

> in Japan, males are superior to females in every way—from the shape of the face, eyes, nose, and mouth to body type and size. Females can be beautiful too, but they usually have some flaw: for example, a lovely face but a short body. Since these flaws do not allow an actress to complement a male lead, it is only obvious that males should continue to perform as women onstage.
>
> (Naitō 1914:102)

> Real *onnagata* do not perform as men, but now that there are actresses, *onnagata* are also performing men's roles. Previously, a male actor became a woman; now he trains to become an *onnagata*. . . . Adding females to Kabuki is like mixing oil and water. . . . Actresses

have the smell of girls' school students about them. People who watch Teigeki [Imperial Theater] Kabuki, in which both sexes perform, will forget the authentic Kabuki tradition.

(Osanai 1914:83, 86–87)

These and other supporters of the Kabuki *onnagata* proceeded from the assumption, also voiced in the Edo period, that female anatomy precluded womanliness and femininity. The ironic logic of anatomical reductionism virtually ensured that females could participate only in the *deconstruction* of femininity as it was defined by dominant males and, by the same token, provided a rationale for the existence of *otokoyaku*, or female men. As Adrian Kiernander notes in a related context, "The similarities and differences between the terms 'female' and 'feminine' . . . can be seen as a kind of conceptual oxymoron" (1992:187).

Detractors such as Hasegawa Tokiame seconded the point of view voiced by leading feminists, such as Yosano Akiko, Tamura Toshiko, Hiratsuka Raichō, and Iwano Kiyoko, that "now was the time for independent-minded actresses." In Hasegawa's words, "Although the *onnagata* has the weight of history and tradition on his side, all I see is a middle-aged male wearing face powder trying to play the part of a young woman. It is in bad taste and wholly unconvincing. He doesn't even try to hide his Adam's apple!" (1914:97–98).

The same debates continued through the militarizing 1930s. One side argued that "as an art form, *onnagata* imparted a flavor that actresses could not hope to produce" (Hanayagi 1939; see also Hasegawa Y. 1931:82–88); the other side stressed the "unhealthy" (i.e., homosexual) lifestyle of the *onnagata*, insisting that women's roles should be played by females ("Onnagata kikin" 1939:3; see also Watanabe Y. 1965). Tradition and flavor triumphed over feminist arguments and charges of sexual perversion. And, as we shall see in the next chapter, the valorization of "tradition" as part of the spiritual mobilization of the people during the wartime period included the promotion of Kabuki as a classical art form of Japanese theater, a status that ensured its central place in the cultural archive of the Japanese Empire as a living symbol of Japanese cultural superiority.

The Takarazuka Revue, founded at a time when the *onnagata* debate was heating up, created an ambivalent public space for the performance of masculinity by females. *Henshin* was not a process officially prescribed for Takarazuka *otokoyaku*. Kobayashi, the Revue's founder, was no Ayame, and he was keen on limiting an *otokoyaku*'s appropriation of "male" gender to the Takarazuka stage. Along with many early-twentieth-century social critics, he believed that a masculine female outside the context of the Revue was something deviant. Although her body served as the main vehicle for the representation and enactment of the ideal man, an *otokoyaku* was not to become unequivocally Man herself, much less a model for males offstage to emulate. Whereas the *kata* in *onnagata* means "model" or "archetype," the *yaku* in *otokoyaku* connotes the serviceability and dutifulness of a role player: "The Takarazuka *otokoyaku* affects a masculine guise, while the [Kabuki] *onnagata* . . . is completely transformed into a woman. As the term *otokoyaku* attests, the female who plays a man is but performing a duty" (Nōzaka Akiyuki, quoted in Tanabe and Sasaki 1983:130). Thus, Revue directors refer to the actor's achievement of manliness not in terms of transformation or metamorphosis (*henshin*), but in terms of "putting something on the body" (*mi ni tsukeru*)—in this case, markers of masculinity.

METHODS OF ANDROGYNY

Any discussion of the construction of gender on the Takarazuka stage must consider the Stanislavski System of acting employed by the Revue since at least the mid-1920s and probably earlier. Konstantin Stanislavski (1863–1938) developed a system of training and rehearsal at the Moscow Arts Theater for actors that, generally speaking, bases a performance on inner emotional experience rather than relying on technical expertise per se, although technical expertise (*kata*) was also central to Takarazuka stage roles. The system's premise is that the "quality of an actor's performance depends not only upon the creation of the inner life of a role but also upon the physical embodiment of it. . . . An actor must . . . answer the question, 'What would I do *if* I were in . . . [X's] position?' This 'magic *if*,' . . . transforms the character's aim into the actor's" (Moore 1988 [1960]:52, 25).

Using the "magic if" techniques for the inner construction of male-authored characters means that the Takarazuka actors inevitably reproduce hierarchical gender typologies. The femininity performed by the players of women's roles serves as a foil, highlighting by contrast the masculinity of the players of men's roles. Despite a history of protest from Takarasiennes and their fans, the (male) directors continue to use *musumeyaku* to define the gendered contours of the Revue's men.

Takarazuka directors, notably Kishida Tatsuya and Shirai Tetsuzō, probably encountered the Stanislavski System firsthand during their travels throughout Europe in the latter half of the 1920s, although they were already familiar with it through the efforts of the playwright Osanai Kaoru, who met Stanislavski in Europe in 1913 and applied his methods in Japan (Rimer 1974:34). Many of the initial Takarazuka staffers had also studied with foreign playwrights and directors residing in Japan, such as Giovanni Rossi, who introduced them to various European acting methods. By the mid-1930s, knowledge of the system was widespread in Japanese modern theater circles and Stanislavskian principles were incorporated into treatises on acting and acting manuals (Hiroo 1936; Hachida 1940 [1937]). Stanislavski's writings (in Russian and English) were shelved in the Revue's library, where they could be perused and adapted by the theatrical staff.

The tension pervading gender issues cannot be accounted for in terms of simple oppositions—an all-male management versus female actors, for example, in the case of the Takarazuka Revue. Directors and actors are only two of the many agents in this ongoing, highly charged and sexually divided discourse; fans and critics are among the others. These interlocutors engage each other on several overlapping levels or thresholds of significance, including the textual, performative, allegorical, and political. Moreover, as Stanislavski recognized, it is important to see drama itself as dialogical, for it includes "inner dialogues": "the character's 'I' is also a 'you' with whom he [or she] is in dialogue" (Moore 1988 [1960]:71). The theoretical and existential implications of a female actor in dialogue with her "male" character—or her "female" character, for that matter—are significant.

One of the key modes in which competing discourses of gender are manifested in the theater and in general is in the dissonance and disjunction between text and subtext. Let me digress for a moment on the relationship between the two. Deidre Pribram's explication of a text offers a useful clarification of the term as I employ it here in the sense of dominant discourse or master narrative.

> The function of a text is to position the spectator to receive certain
> flavoured—and restricted—meanings which the text "manages" for

the viewing subject in keeping with dominant ideology. In this model the spectator is not an active part of the production of textual meaning but the passive side of a unidirectional relationship in which the text disperses meanings while the spectator . . . receives them. The spectator can only interpret (be interpreted by) a text in terms preformulated by gender difference. There is no possibility of a mutually informing relationship between spectator and text, and therefore no accumulative building of textual meaning. . . . The intention of the text and the reception of textual meaning are defined as one and the same.

(Pribram 1988b:4)

A text then, as a technology of gender, is invested with "power to control the field of social meaning and thus produce, promote, and 'implant' representations of gender" (de Lauretis 1987:18). But, as Teresa de Lauretis argues, "the terms of a different construction of gender also exist, in the margins of hegemonic discourses" and texts (18). I use the term "subtext" to refer to marginalized, alternative discourses—which are marginalized and alternative only in relation to a dominant ideology and its attendant practices.

It has been said of the Stanislavski System that the priority given to training actors "led to the deconstruction of performance texts" (Schechner 1988:210). In the context of the Takarazuka Revue, one might restate the claim: the emphasis on training actors in their secondary genders has at the same time undermined Kobayashi's patriarchal text and underscored a lesbian subtext.

FEMALE SEXUALITIES
AND THE "WOMAN PROBLEM"

Any interpretation of the popularity of the Revue today must take into account its historical beginnings and its unprecedented impact on the status quo. Such an account requires a review of the discourses of gender and sexuality that informed the social climate in which the Takarazuka Revue was established and received, which follows. When pertinent, and especially in the last section of this chapter, I discuss gender and androgyny as performed and constructed in the Revue from the 1960s onward.

It was in the context of state formation and nationalism that Good Wife, Wise Mother (*ryōsai kenbo*) was codified as the model of "female" gender in the Meiji Civil Code. The discourse of sexualities is closely linked to nationalism and state formation (see Corrigan and Sayer 1985; Mosse 1985; Parker, Russo, Sommer, and Yaeger 1992; Watson 1990). At the same time, the printed word has been key in conceiving of the nation and promoting nationalism (Anderson 1983). Many of the dozens of articles on femininity, marriage, sex, gender, sexuality, androgyny, and the revue genre published in the early twentieth century were written from a nativist and nationalist angle. Some of the authors even elaborated on the link between all of these issues (e.g., Sugita 1935; Takada T. 1934), and one Japanese sexologist claimed in a newspaper interview that cross-dressing among girls and women was fostered by the revue theater and foreign films (Hori Kentarō, quoted in "Dansō hi ari" 1935). Kobayashi himself recognized the potential of theater in orchestrating the construction and regulation of gender and in literally staging the enactment of gender roles in society.

Newspaper, magazine, and journal articles on these themes published between 1900 and 1945 make it clear that female sexualities, and particularly certain homosexual practices, provoked the most perplexity among social commentators and made the biggest headlines. The "woman problem" (*fujin mondai*)—the term for issues related to females' civil rights that were made problematic by feminists—appeared to be fueled by problem women.[14] Before and even after the Meiji period, published writers and critics—the vast majority of whom were male—relegated sexual desire in females to courtesans and prostitutes (see Robertson 1991a). "Ordinary" women were defined by the gender roles of daughter, wife, and daughter-in-law. Motherhood and mothering emerged as additional components of state-regulated sex and gender in the Meiji period (Koyama 1982, 1986; Mitsuda 1985; Nolte and Hastings 1991). Nearly all of the women's journals founded in the first two decades of the twentieth century were devoted to promoting among their hundreds of thousands of readers the socialization of women as Good Wives, Wise Mothers (Watashitachi no rekishi o tsuzuru kai 1987). One exception was *Seitō* (*Bluestocking*), a feminist journal founded by Hiratsuka Raichō in 1911 and put under surveillance by the government shortly afterward for publishing articles critical of the patriarchal household and family system (Hara 1987:16, 22). The so-called Taishō Democracy was hardly democratic with respect to women. Not only was the

Seitōsha (Bluestocking Society) banned, but under the auspices of the Peace Police Law of 1900, women were forbidden to congregate in public and were prevented from participating in political activity in general. In the spring of 1938, the military government banned from women's journals any articles related to sex and sexuality that did not trumpet the state's paternalistic values and pronatal policies (Hara 1987:16–21). Not surprisingly, in August 1939 Osaka outlawed Takarazuka *otokoyaku*—"the acme of offensiveness"—from public performances in that prefecture; it was the only prefectural government to do so ("Dansō wa shūaku no kiwami" 1939; "Dansō no reijin shōmetsu" 1939).

Kobayashi, who from July 1940 to April 1941 served as minister of commerce and industry, colluded with government censors to produce musicals that exalted the image of the Good Wife, Wise Mother, an image further reified at that time as *Nippon fujin*, or Japanese Woman. Typical of the revues staged during this period of militarization and state censorship was *Legends of Virtuous Japanese Women* (*Nippon meifu den*, 1941), a nationalistic extravaganza dedicated to heroines, mothers of heroes, and "women of chastity" (Matsumoto 1941a). Takarasiennes were also recruited into patriotic women's associations and charged with entertaining not only troops in the field but also farmworkers and the war wounded. Kobayashi introduced a "national defense color" (*kokubōshoku*, i.e., khaki) uniform for daily wear (figure 6) to ensure that the Revue kept in step with the militarization of the society as a whole ("Jishuku wa seitō dake" 1940; "Takarazuka kageki ni seifuku chakuyō" 1939; "Zuka gāru ga jishuku" 1940; "Zuka musume danzen jishuku" 1940). Kobayashi also moved to reorganize the Revue, including the widely publicized temporary addition of a male pit chorus whose mere presence would apparently help to deflect allegations of deviant behavior among Takarasiennes and their fans ("Kindan no Takarazuka e" 1940; "Takarazuka kageki no dansei kashu" 1940).[15] The adverse publicity, which I elaborate on below, had also motivated Kobayashi in 1940 to remove the problematic term *shōjo* in the Revue's final name change for two ostensible reasons: to acknowledge the more "adult" content of the revue and to prepare for the inclusion of the male chorus ("Shōjo no niji massatsu" 1940; "Takarazuka shōjokageki wa doko e yuku?" 1940).

In Japan, the key indicators for females of social adulthood are marriage and motherhood. *Shōjo* is the term coined in the Meiji period for

Figure 6. Takarazuka uniforms: Wartime and current. *Top*, Takarasiennes posing in their "national defense color" uniforms introduced in 1939, which served as the prototype for today's military-like uniforms worn by Academy students, *bottom*. As evident from their haircuts, the students are assigned their secondary genders at the end of their first semester at the Academy. From Hagiwara (1954:21) and Ueda (1986 [1976]: cover).

unmarried girls and women and means, literally, a "not-quite-female" female. Its usages and modifications reveal much about the vicissitudes of the discourse of gender and sexuality since the Meiji period. In recent years "gal" (*gyaru*) has been employed as the term for an older, more "female," *shōjo;* and in 1990 the expression "older-man gal" (*ojin gyaru*) was coined by a leading (female) cartoonist to refer to "gals" who enjoy drinking, gambling, and singing (*karaoke*-style) after work, presumably just like their fathers and older males.[16] The "older-man gal," today's Modern Girl, can be construed as an expression of androgyny inasmuch as the phrase refers to a female who has appropriated "masculine" pastimes (Horiuchi 1990:24). "Gal" might also be read as a revival and abbreviation of *garçon* (*gyaru-sonnu*), one of the common terms in the 1930s for a masculine female. *Shōjo* now tends to be used in reference to teenage girls, and *gyaru* to unmarried women in their early twenties. *Shōjo* denotes females between puberty and marriage, as well as that period of time itself in a female's life (*shōjoki*) (Kawahara 1921:112; Tamura 1913:165–68). *Shōjo* also implies heterosexual inexperience and homosexual experience, a point to which I shall return. *Gyaru,* on the other hand, has quite different associations, conjuring up the figure of an assertive, self-centered woman who is in no hurry to marry and who maintains a stable of boyfriends to serve her different needs.

The modernizing state emphasized universal—if segregated and sexist—education, together with the notion that a brief stint in the burgeoning urban industrial and commercial workforce was a desirable thing for females. This policy had the effect of increasing the number of years between puberty and marriage (see Murakami 1983). Kobayashi was among the many influential persons who published articles in women's journals reminding their female readers that working outside the home for wages should not be construed as a career in itself, but rather as preparation for marriage (Shida and Yuda 1987:115).

Included in the *shōjo* category of female were the New Working Woman (*shinshokugyō fujin*) and her jaunty counterpart, the Modern Girl, herself the antithesis of the Good Wife, Wise Mother. The flapperlike *moga* fancied themselves actors whose stage was the Ginza, at that time Tokyo's premier boulevard (see Bollinger 1994; Silverberg 1991). Along with the New Working Women, they were Takarazuka fans. Many of the urban-based New Working Women aspired to the revue theater; by the same token, Takarazuka players of men's roles were often referred to in the press as Modern Girls, especially after 1932, when the *otokoyaku* began sporting short haircuts (Maruo 1932; "Yōsō danpatsu no shiiku na sugata" 1932).

Generally speaking, not only sexism but ageism was the rule in the workplace. Male employers preferred women up to twenty-four years of age, and there were few employment opportunities for women over the age of thirty. In fact, not many women could afford the financial strain of remaining single; those who did manage to support themselves included doctors, teachers, midwives, nurses, and, to a certain extent, actors (Shida and Yuda 1987:114). Some women, in the first half of the twentieth century at least, passed as men in order to secure employment as rickshaw drivers, construction supervisors and laborers, fishers, department store managers, grocers, and so on (Tomioka 1938:103).[17] Passing was associated unequivocally with sexual deviancy in the case of urban middle- and upper-class girls and women who, it was argued, wore masculine attire not to secure a livelihood but as an outward expression of their "moral depravity." As privileged and educated—in short, bourgeois—girls and women, they were supposed to fulfill the state-sanctioned Good Wife, Wise Mother gender role. Consequently, those who resisted were vilified in journal and newspaper articles on "masculinized" (*danseika*) females, and roundly critiqued in texts and treatises on "female" psychology (Sakabe 1924; Sugita 1929, 1935; Ushijima 1943; Yasuda 1935).

Ironically, given Kobayashi's views on work and marriage, tenure in the Takarazuka Revue further lengthened the *shōjo* period, and many of the actors continued to perform into their thirties before retiring well beyond the average age of marriage.[18] Perhaps in response to criticism, the Revue management crafted an informal "retirement policy" (*teinensei*) in 1936, the first of several up to the present time, whereby Takarasiennes whose tenure in the Revue exceeded twenty years would be encouraged to retire (Kudō 1963; *Shin Nippō* 1936). For the most part, however, it continues to be the case that provided an actor does not marry or leave to pursue other avenues of show business, she can spend her life as a Takarasienne—if not always onstage, then as an instructor or in a supervisory capacity.

Apart from conceiving of an all-female revue as a commercially viable complement to the all-male Kabuki theater, Kobayashi perceived the Takarazuka theater to be an appropriate site for the resocialization of (bourgeois) girls and women whose unconventional aspirations had led them to the Revue stage in the first place (Kobayashi 1961b:408). In his essays and articles, he makes clear his antagonism toward the Modern Girl and masculinized females. To a certain extent, Kobayashi agreed with reactionaries for whom such females were examples of *eroguro nansensu*, or "erotic-grotesque nonsense," a trendy expression in the 1930s for hitherto unthinkable juxtapositions—such as females dressed as men singing love songs to their feminine partners on a public stage advertised as "wholesome family entertainment." But whereas the critics regarded the *otokoyaku* and her fans as living examples of grotesque eroticism, Kobayashi cast the player of men's roles as a paragon of idealized masculinity and by extension, an emblem of patriarchy—a formulation that was compelling so long as her stage expertise did not carry over into her private life.

Kobayashi, like Stanislavski, used the theater as a pulpit and maintained that the Takarazuka Revue served a didactic purpose. He theorized that by performing as men, females learned to understand and appreciate males and the masculine psyche. Consequently, when they eventually retired from the stage and married, which Kobayashi urged them to do, they would be better able to perform as Good Wives, Wise Mothers, knowing exactly what their husbands expected of them (Kobayashi 1961b:467 and 1948; Ueda 1974:139). In other words, the actors were trained to perform gender roles that would facilitate their postretirement reentry into a more conventional lifestyle. Significantly, Kobayashi referred to the actors as "students" (*seitō*). The term not only justified his paying them less than fully professional actors but reflected his belief that a wedding ceremony marked the start of a woman's real career, whereupon she became a full-fledged actor, with the conjugal household her stage, and her husband and children her audience. Their stage duty as members of the Takarazuka Revue was deemed analogous to their eventual duty as Good Wives, Wise Mothers in a patriarchal household.[19]

Kobayashi anticipated the attacks of and defended the Academy and Revue against social critics and sexologists who singled out girls' schools and their (unmarried) female instructors and students as the primary sites and agents of homosexuality among females (see Furuya Tsunatake 1932; Sugita 1929, 1935; Tamura 1913; Ushijima 1943).[20] In 1910 one of the first articles on this subject was published in a leading women's newspaper, the *Fujo Shinbun* (*Women's Newspaper*). Two types of homosexual relationships between females were distin-guished: *dōseiai* (same-sex love) and *ome no kankei* (male-female rela-tions). It is clear from the article that what the editorial staff meant by "same *sex*" was actually "same *gender*" and that *ome* referred to a butch-femme-like couple: that is, same sex, different genders.[21]

Dōseiai was coined at the turn of this century to refer specifically to a passionate, but supposedly platonic, friendship between females, although sexologists found it difficult to distinguish friendship from homosexuality among girls and women: where did one end and the other begin (Yasuda 1935:151)? Such friendships were regarded as typ-ical among girls and women from all walks of life, but especially among girls' school students and graduates, female educators, female civil servants, and thespians (Fukushima 1984 [1935]:561; see also Tamura 1913; Yasuda 1935). The *ai* alludes to the term's original def-inition, although *dōseiai* soon came to be used as the standard word for homosexuality in general without any distinction by sex. *Ai*, of-ten translated as "agape," is contrasted with *koi*, or "eros." Because female homosexuality was understood as spiritual and male homo-sexuality as physical, *dōseiai* was preferred by some sexologists to un-derscore the spiritual aspect of same-sex love between women (Fu-rukawa 1994:115–16).[22]

Passionate friendships and same-sex relations among females were also referred to as "S" or "Class S" (*kurasu esu*), with the S standing for "sister," "*shōjo*," "sex," or all three combined. Additional mean-ings of S (*esu*) included the German "*Schöne*," or "beautiful woman," a popular loanword at the time, and "escape" (*esukeipu*), a popular word among students in the 1920s that meant to skip class (Hattori K. and Uehara 1925:83–84; Kabeshima, Hida, and Yonekawa 1984:41). Class S continues to conjure up the image of two schoolgirls, often a junior-senior pair, each with a crush on the other (Miyasako 1986:61). *Ome* relationships, on the other hand, were described as

> a strange phenomenon difficult to diagnose on the basis of modern psychology and physiology.[23] . . . One of the couple has malelike (*danseiteki*) characteristics and dominates the [femalelike] other. . . . Unlike the [*dōseiai* couple], friends whose spiritual bond took a passionate turn, the latter have developed a strange, carnal relation-ship (*niku no sesshoku*) . . . stemming from their carnal depravity (*nikuteki daraku*). . . . The malelike female is technically proficient

at manipulating women . . . Doctors have yet to put their hoes to this uncultivated land (*mikaikonchi*).

(Fukushima 1984 [1935]:562)

This article, and others like it (e.g., Tamura 1913; Yasuda 1935), makes it clear that even an overheated *dōseiai* (that is, homogender) relationship was not pathological in the way that an *ome* (that is, heterogender) relationship was, the latter being not only explicitly sexual but also a heretical refraction of the heterosexual norm formalized in the Meiji Civil Code. The most objective writers, not surprisingly, referred to an *ome* couple as "husband and wife" (*fufu*), a marital metaphor that safely contained (and in effect neutralized) the sexual difference represented and practiced by the two women.

The *Fujo Shinbun* article introduced recent "medical" findings in surmising that females were more prone than males to homosexuality. It was postulated that women's "natural" passivity (*muteikōshugi*) made them susceptible to neurasthenia (*shinkeishitsu*), which, in turn, occasioned a pessimism expressed in the form of homosexuality.[24] However, *ome*, or "butch-femme" relationships, seemed to stymie the sexologists and worry the social critics of the day since unmarried women (that is, *shōjo*) in particular were stereotypically regarded as blissfully unaware of sexual desire, and since women in general were certainly not supposed to play an active role in sex. "Moral depravity" fostered by modernization (or Westernization) seemed to be the only viable "explanation" for *ome* relationships among urban women, at least until the appearance of the Takarazuka man prompted critics to come up with new ideas to account for the increasingly visible masculinized female.

Overall, it seems that much more print space was devoted to defending the typicality and relative "normality" of *dōseiai* (homogender) relationships among *shōjo* and to insisting on their—ideally, at least—platonic character. Apart from eye-catching headlines and titles, relatively little attention was paid to the actual *ome* relationship itself, although the "origins" of the "deviant and anomalous" (*hentaiteki*) masculine partner generated several speculations. The author of a 1930 newspaper article on the Takarazuka Revue, for example, went so far as to assert that the emergence of *ome*-type relationships was the "direct result of females playing men's roles" and to suggest that the Revue was the medium through which Class S couples were transformed into "butch-femme" couples, an evolutionary thesis absent from the *Fujo Shinbun* article published twenty years earlier ("Takarazuka bijin hensenshi" [4] 1930).[25] The headline sums up the gist of the author's argument: "From Class S to Feverish Yearning for *Otokoyaku*."[26]

ANDROGYNY AS ERASURE

The "psychiatric style of reasoning" imported from Europe and the United States late in the second half of the nineteenth century—and alluded to in the 1910 *Fujo Shinbun* article and others—provided a whole new set of concepts that made it possible to separate questions of sexual and gender identity from facts about anatomy (Davidson 1987:22; see also Hanafusa 1930; Izawa 1931; Kure 1920; Yasuda 1935). Female sexualities, now problematic, were linked to experiences, to environment, and to "impulses, tastes, aptitudes, satisfactions, and psychic traits" (Davidson 1987:22). For example, in the *Fujo Shinbun* article, "abusive stepmothers, exploitative employers, constant hardship, others' callousness, false accusations, and unrequited love" were blamed for causing girls and women to adopt homosexual practices. The so-called masculinized female in particular was regarded by some sexologists and social critics as a prime example of the newly defined disorder, "abnormal or deviant psychology" (*hentai seiri* or *hentai shinri*). After establishing cross-dressing (*hensō*) itself as "abnormal" (*fuseijō*), one sexologist went on to distinguish between "natural" or congenital cross-dressing and "unnatural" or acquired cross-dressing among females and males.[27] According to this writer, the former involved an intersexed person attempting to pass as either a woman or a man, while the latter involved a person motivated by curiosity, criminal intentions, or the desire to secure a livelihood. Masculinized females associated with the theater, the author claimed, cross-dressed out of curiosity (Tomioka 1938:98–103).

Beginning in the 1920s, so far as I can assess from print sources, Takarazuka *otokoyaku*, as well as the girls and women who were attracted to them (and sent them "love letters"), were referred to by unsympathetic critics as "deviant" and "anomalous" (Kawahara 1921:13; Sugita 1935; "Takarazuka bijin hensenshi" [4] and [5] 1930). Their desire was interpreted as being misaligned with their female bodies. The sympathetic use of the term *chūsei* ("neutral," or in between woman and man) to describe the Takarazuka man and masculinized females in general conveniently circumvented the issue of erotic desire and parried allegations of "abnormal" sexuality. *Chūsei* was used defensively to deflect negative attention away from both the sexual difference represented by the Takarazuka player of men's roles and the social ramifications of that difference. Describing someone as *chūsei* suggested that she had a childlike naïveté about anything beyond a passionate friendship between *shōjo* sisters. A group interview with ten Takarasiennes on their thoughts about a Hungarian movie actress known in Japan for her "*otokoyaku*-like" appearance illustrates the deflective, defensive use of *chūsei*. Active in the 1930s, she is described in the article as not only neutral (*chūseiteki*) but also childish (*kodomoppoi*), mischievous (*itazurakko*), and "not coquettish, but rather romantic in a childish sense" (*kodomoppoi romanchikusa*). The reporter notes that she is *chūsei*, "in the sense of childlike" (*chairudo to iu imi*), the implication being that despite her provocative wink, she was asexual (*Yomiuri Shinbun* 1935).

Some of the more "progressive" writers and critics sympathetic to the Revue, such as the novelist Yoshiya Nobuko (1904–73), a lesbian,[28] preferred the safe ambiguity of *chūsei*, with its allusions—like Yoshiya's fiction itself—to a "dreamworld" (*yume no sekai*) free from the constraints of fixed, dichotomous, and hierarchical gender roles. Takarazuka itself was conceived of as a dreamworld—"a place where dreams are made and sold," according to the Revue's advertisements —and the early theater complex was named, appropriately, Paradise. Kobayashi collaborated with Yoshiya and shared her romantic vision, but he colored it heterosexual: his dreamworld was one in which gallant men were sustained by adoring women (figure 7).[29]

Detractors, on the other hand, referred to the players of men's roles and other Modern Girls as abnormal, masculinized females, who sported short hair (*danpatsu*) and wore pants (Maruki Sunado 1929; Sugita 1929:80 and 1935). Such females were also called *garçons*[30] since they had "forgotten what it means to be feminine"—one of the accusations leveled at Yoshiya Nobuko herself ("'Watashi' wa 'boku' e" 1932). Among the detractors singled out for criticism by Kobayashi was the feminist writer and editor Hiratsuka Raichō, who was more concerned about cross-dressing onstage than its practice offstage. Her criticism of the *otokoyaku* was directed toward the gender ideology

Figure 7.   Yoshiya Nobuko and Kobayashi Ichizō. The setting is
Yoshiya's home in Kamakura, a seaside resort south of Tokyo. From
Maruo (1981:2).

promoted by the Revue; she apparently did not recognize the potentially subversive implications of the all-female Revue's subtexts. Raichō argued that there was no reason to have "girls who know nothing about males expressing earnestly emotions such as passion and
love." Kobayashi claimed that she dismissed Takarazuka as "mere fiction; a superficial performing art form," declaring that "we women
view [the *otokoyaku*] as a disfigured and deformed person" (Kobayashi
1961a:395; source of original citation unknown).

From the mid-1930s onward the expression *dansō no reijin*, literally "a beautiful person [i.e., a female] in masculine attire," was used
sympathetically in reference to both Takarazuka *otokoyaku* and masculinized females. This expression, a euphemism for *chūsei*, was apparently coined in 1932 by the novelist Muramatsu Shōfu. His serialized short story "Dansō no reijin" was inspired by Kawashima
Yoshiko (1906–48), who had donned a military uniform and passed
as a man during the early stages of Japanese imperialism in China and
Manchuria.[31]

In an editorial titled "What is the *'dansō no reijin'*?" Kobayashi ex-
presses his concern that the current spate of scandal-mongering press
reports on all-female revues was bound to create public misunder-

standings about Takarazuka, the "'main household' (*honke*) of the *shōjo* revue": "The *dansō no reijin*, . . . a symbol of abnormal love, . . . is becoming a social problem. . . . [G]ood [i.e., middle- and upper-class] households especially are affected. . . . Nothing must compromise [Takarazuka's] reputation or worry the parents of [Takarazuka Music Academy] students" (1935a:10–12). He quotes part of his letter to Ashihara Kuniko, a leading *otokoyaku*, asking her to make sure that new students understood that they were not to use masculine words or to behave in a manly fashion in their daily lives. For Kobayashi, the most problematic "male" words were *aniki* (elder brother), *boku* (a self-referent denoting "male" gender), and *kimi* (a masculine form of "you") (Kobayashi 1935a). Ashihara's fans called her *aniki*, which distressed Kobayashi greatly and for which he had chastised her two years earlier (Ashihara K. 1979:157). Her reply—which, in keeping with precedent, may actually have been written by him—was included in the editorial.[32] In it, the senior *otokoyaku* reassured Kobayashi that she and "the others are all just 'ordinary girls' . . . who practice the tea ceremony and flower arrangement when not performing onstage." "Masculine words," she added, "are not used by any of the students or actors even though their use is popular among girls' school students and [Takarazuka] fans" (Ashihara, quoted in Kobayashi 1935a:11–12).

But even sympathetic contemporary accounts of the Revue contradicted this "ordinary girl" image of the Takarasiennes: mention is made by one critic of a player of men's roles who is "malelike in her everyday life" (Hirai 1933:168). It appears, rather, that Kobayashi's editorial was a timely and opportunistic measure undertaken to minimize any negative repercussions from the highly publicized lesbian affairs at that time (detailed in chapters 4 and 5) and also to reinforce his patriarchal agenda for the Takarasiennes.

POSTWAR ANDROGYNY

Knowledge of past precedents and of the early, varied reception of the Takarazuka Revue is necessary to fully recognize the significance of contemporary experiments with androgyny. The Revue continues both to uphold the dominant ideal of heterosexuality and to inform a lesbian subcultural style. In this connection, the sexual tension that has marked Takarazuka from the start still frustrates the paternalistic management. With respect to state formation (i.e., the production and reproduction of the status quo), the Revue continues to attract the attention of the mass media, although the charges of "moral depravity" and "abnormal sexual desire" are now rarely leveled, as openly at least, at the Takarasiennes and their fans. But this waning of overt criticism is due less to an acceptance of lesbianism than to the Revue's tighter management of public relations and newspaper coverage.

The Rose of Versailles (*Berusaiyu no bara*) is regarded by the Revue and fans alike as the most memorable and successful postwar revue to date. It was based on a best-selling, multivolume *shōjo* comic book of the same name first published between 1972 and 1974 by Ikeda Riyoko, one of Japan's most successful female comic book artists. First staged over the period 1974–76 and revived in the years 1989–91, the hugely popular revue illustrates the resilience of the androgynous image of Takarazuka.[33] *The Rose of Versailles* dwells on the adventures of Oscar, a female raised as a boy in order to ensure the patrilineal continuity of a family of generals. The late cartoonist Tezuka Osamu's popular postwar comic, *Princess Knight*, doubtless inspired Ikeda's Oscar just as Takarazuka inspired Tezuka. In that earlier comic, Princess Knight, or Sapphire, is raised as a son, having been born to a royal couple in need of a male heir. Sapphire switches costume-*cum*-gender several times in the story before emerging as a woman at the end (Schodt 1983:96–96).

The Oscar character, who represents the slippage between sex and gender (figure 8), is referred to in the literature as a "classic" *dansō no reijin* (Tsuji 1976:97, 107–8; Yabushita 1990:108). Significantly, Oscar has been acted by *otokoyaku* exclusively, whose own acting careers in the Revue have followed a similar trajectory. Clothing is the means to, and even the substance of, the character's commutable gender, as the expression *dansō no reijin* suggests; accordingly, Oscar switches at one point from masculine to feminine attire. This play's alternative subtext is that gender as performance undercuts the ideological fixity of received gender differences (see Kuhn 1985:53; see also Komashaku 1989; Tsuji 1976:107–30).

The Rose of Versailles is one of the Revue's most reflexive productions in that the relationship between Oscar and her/his father is analogous to that between the player of men's roles and the Revue's patriarchal administration. When reading the following dialogue between Oscar and the General, bear in mind that Kobayashi had insisted that the Takarasiennes call him "Father."

Figure 8.   Oscar. Haruna Yuri as Oscar and Hatsukaze Jun as Marie Antoinette in the Moon Troupe's 1974 performance of *The Rose of Versailles*. From Hashimoto (1994:108).

OSCAR: Father, please answer me!
GENERAL: Oscar?!
OSCAR: If . . . if I had been raised as an ordinary female, would I have been forced to marry at the age of fifteen like my sisters? I could be playing the [clavichord], singing arias, dressing up every night in fine clothes and laughing away the time in high society. . . .
GENERAL: Oscar!!
OSCAR: Please answer me! I could be wearing velvet beauty marks and rose perfume; I would fill my arabesque compact with cosmetics; I could bear children—and raise them.
GENERAL: Oscar!!
OSCAR: Answer me, please!
GENERAL: (Pensively.) Yes, it's as you say—had you been raised as an ordinary female.
OSCAR: Father, thank you.
GENERAL: (Taken aback.)
OSCAR: Thank you for giving me a chance to live the kind of life I have, in as broad a world as I have, even though I am a fe-

male. Even while struggling to deal with the stupidity of
pathetic people . . .
GENERAL: Oscar.
OSCAR: I am no longer remorseful. I . . . I'll live as the child of Mars,
god of war. I'll devote this body of mine to the sword; I'll
devote it to the cannon. My livelihood is the military and
I'll serve as the child of Mars, god of war.

(Ikeda Riyoko, quoted in Tsuji 1976:165–66)

Oscar (and by the same token, the Takarazuka *otokoyaku*) is able to
transcend the fixed, narrow life course of "ordinary females" because
of Father's pragmatic decision to name her "son." Recognizing that
"male" gender affords access to a wider world, Oscar is effusively
grateful for the opportunity to be the household's *otokoyaku*. Oscar's
military uniform not only accentuates the difference between masculinity and femininity—the former identified with swords and can-
nons, the latter with flowers and children—but also magnifies the tension between "male" gender and the female body it camouflages. The
overall effect at once exaggerates and masks the slippage between sex
and gender. Both the General and the audience know that Oscar, like
the Takarasienne, is a masculinized female. That gender is a property
of attribution and convention, and not anatomy, is made doubly obvious by the synonomy between Oscar and the *otokoyaku* performing
Oscar. At the same time, both role players demonstrate the irony that
access to a supposedly more "liberating" gender identity is granted
by privileged father figures.

Annette Kuhn observes that if "clothing can be costume, capable
of being modified at the wearer's will, it follows that the gender identity conventionally signified by dress may be just as easily change-
able" (1985:53). What is most problematic with this theoretical statement insofar as Oscar and the Takarazuka *otokoyaku* are concerned is
the matter of the "wearer's will." "Will" does not figure in one's initial gender assignment (based on genitalia); nor is either Oscar's or a
Takarasienne's secondary gender assignment necessarily confluent in
every respect with her will.

The Rose of Versailles also illustrates how "the West" is positioned as
a site of transvestism in Japanese popular culture, although the implications are differently construed depending on the spectator. For ex-

ample, the Revue has deployed cross-dressing not only to represent ideal men and women, masculinity and femininity, but also to use non-Japanese (especially Western) characters as foils against which a homogeneous Japaneseness can be gauged and understood—the we-are-not-that maneuver. Thus, in American musicals, such as *West Side Story* (*Uesutosaido monogatari*, 1968–69), generic American gender markers are constructed and performed in opposition to dominant assumptions about Japanese gender ideals. Not surprisingly, therefore, some conservatives within the Takarazuka management were opposed to the production of *West Side Story* on the grounds that "vulgar street gangs should not appear on a [Japanese] stage renowned for its beauty and elegance" and that the "innocent" Japanese women should not portray coarse American characters (Berlin 1988:283; Hashimoto 1984:83). Whereas the ethnic and class tensions that informed the original *West Side Story* were absent, tensions between Japan and the United States were evident in the criticism directed at this and other Broadway musicals restaged by Takarazuka during the "miracle sixties," when postwar Japan began to rise as a economic giant.

A discussion about the Takarazuka production of *West Side Story* appearing in an official fan magazine is revealing: the director noted the difficulty of being Japanese and performing as Americans ("Enshutsuka ni kiku" 1968:67); the various ethnic identities of the American characters in the Broadway production were not at issue. One theater critic, in fact, criticized the Revue for the actors' inability to convey convincingly Puerto Rican "affectations" (*kusami*) ("Yukigumi kōen o mite" 1968:69). Equally problematic, of course, is the critic's reduction of ethnic difference to a matter of affect. I do not wish to imply here that Arthur Rollins's *West Side Story* was less ethnically essentializing; my point is that the specific ethnic differences informing the story were more or less homogenized in Takarazuka's "melting pot" version. This production points to a type of "cross-ethnicking" (discussed at length in the next chapter) that involves the enactment of reified national character stereotypes, in this case a singular *American* ethnicity. Takarazuka's *West Side Story* focused not on the convoluted and tragic ethnic politics coloring the love affair between Tony, an Italian American man, and Maria, a Puerto Rican woman, but on the "purity" of the couple's impossible love—a theme that is vintage Takarazuka ("Sutā to sutaffu" 1968:62).

ANDROGYNY REVUE

In the fall of 1985, the Takarazuka Revue staged a show called *Androgyny* (*Andorojenii*) that the (male) playwright/director felt captured the "bewitching charm" of the androgyne. The show called for players of men's roles to appear alternately as "neutral boys" (*nyutoraru boi*), resplendent in gaudy, glittery jumpsuits and equally colorful wigs, and as well-known (non-Japanese) masculinized females, such as George Sand. It was referred to in fan magazines as "unprecedented," a show "ahead of its time" (Mure 1985:38).

Although the 1985 revue may have been the first and only show titled *Androgyny*, the theme and phenomenon themselves have constituted an essential part not only of the Takarazuka Revue's repertoire but also of its public image, as we have seen. Already in the late 1960s *otokoyaku* were encouraged to impart an "androgynous charm" by blending markers of "female" and "male" gender. They did so mainly by teasing their often peroxided hair to create puffy pompadours and by using pastel makeup to soften the darker, sharper, deeply chiseled features of the "classic" *otokoyaku* (figure 9). These 1960s players of men's roles foreshadowed the interstitial Oscar character: Kō Nishiki described herself as "an *otokoyaku* who was close to being feminine," although she also threatened to resign if forced to appear as a woman onstage (Okazaki 1971:49; Yoshizawa J. 1966:52); Anna Jun claimed to have been a "womanish" (*onnappoi*) man (Anna 1979:197); Dai Takiko declared that even though she was a "leading man," she took care not to forfeit her femininity (Yamada 1968:70).

By allowing "the woman" to permeate "the man," these *otokoyaku* in effect drew attention to the facticity of their female bodies and, *from the standpoint of convention*, to the primacy of their femininity, thus ensuring that their secondary, "male" gender was kept in check by their primary, "female" gender. The directors did not want the players of men's roles to be too successful in their appropriation and performance of masculinity. Similarly—and here the Edo-period case of Take/Takejirō comes to mind—as a way of clarifying the limits of actors' "honorary" masculinity, the directors also staged shows in which *otokoyaku* were to appear as women, much to the consternation of the players of men's roles and their fans. Allowing "the woman" to permeate "the man" is one thing; being assigned to women's roles is quite another. Many *otokoyaku* protested the directors' gender-switching an-

Figure 9. *Otokoyaku*: Classic and androgynous. *Left*, Kasugano Yachiyo as a "classic" *otokoyaku*; *right*, Anna Jun as a 1960s "androgynous" *otokoyaku*. From *Takarazuka Fuan* (1954) and *Takarazuka Gurafu* (1968).

tics, and they claimed to have experienced a sense of conflict or resistance (*teikō*), along with a loss of confidence (Misato 1974:68; Okazaki 1971:49; "Sensei to kataru" 1977:38; Yamada 1968:70–71; Yoshizawa J. 1966, 1967). Gō Chigusa, an *otokoyaku* who retired in 1972, remarked that on the rare occasion she was assigned to perform as a woman, her fans complained bitterly of their resultant dis-ease, that eerie feeling (*kimochi warui*) when the familiar suddenly is defamiliarized (Yoshizawa J. 1967:71). The androgynous charm of the *otokoyaku* was compromised by the compulsory femininity of "the woman."

Some fans, however, drew attention to the difference between the female in the man and the woman in the female. *Otokoyaku* Daichi Mao, who retired in 1985 and is now a very successful stage actress, is the subject of the following "fan letter" published in a pathbreaking lesbian anthology. Daichi was often called the Japanese James Dean during her tenure in the Takarazuka Revue (figure 10).

> To Daichi Mao-*sama*: You were an absolutely new flower. There has been no other star in Takarazuka history who has displayed your gorgeous androgynous elegance. Before you, there were many orthodox *otokoyaku* . . . but you gave rise to a new type of player of men's roles . . . with your round face, slim body, and sinuous movements. . . . When we fans first heard you sing [about love],

Figure 10.   The Japanese James Dean. Moon Troupe *otokoyaku* Daichi
Mao. From Ueda (1986 [1976]:296).

we were swept away into a strange and fragrant world. Without question your charm was your very womanliness. Not the posturing come-on of mannish females, but an affirmation of the womanliness of female bodies. You symbolized a new era when females could begin to love themselves as themselves.

And so why have you become an ordinary woman?

There are millions of actresses. There's no reason for you to become yet another actress who titillates actual males. . . . Now all you do is take roles that have you pout at males and say things like, "Why don't you like me?" That kind of role is totally unrealistic; it's a pathetic joke. You've gone from being a jewel to being a mere pebble. I can never forgive your betrayal in playing women who exist for males. When we see you being embraced by a male, it's as though our dreams have been stolen.

You—Takarazuka's new flower, females' freedom and joy, our fin de siècle dream. Why did you become a woman? Just an ordinary woman!?

Yours, Hoshi Sumire.[34]

(Hoshi 1987)

The fan, who was thrilled by Daichi's precedent-shattering androgynous performances, is bitterly disappointed that the former Revue star capitulated to the sexism of show business and became a mere woman—a patriarchal invention that exists only to indulge and pleasure males. She adored Daichi as a female "doing" a man, but despises the petulant player of women's roles the female star has devolved into.

Otokoyaku have been characterized by sympathetic (and defensive) critics as sexy but sexless, the argument being that ambiguous gender is perceived as an asexual identity (e.g., Aoki T. 1934; Aochi 1954:231). An *otokoyaku* performing onstage as a man may be the object of desire, but she herself is purportedly without sexuality. Partly to sustain this perception of asexuality, all Takarasiennes must remain unmarried and ostensibly heterosexually inexperienced throughout their tenure in the Revue, a policy implemented by Kobayashi on founding the Revue. Yet the actors and the administration rationalize this policy in tellingly different ways. Implicitly acknowledging that a theatrical vocation virtually precludes distinctions between on- and offstage experiences, several players of men's roles have noted that "it would be ridiculous to be married *and* to perform as a man onstage," but their explanation contradicts the management's rationale: "Female fans probably will not be charmed by a married *otokoyaku*" ("Jidai ni kakaru hashi" 1962:41). Other players of men's roles claim—at least in official interviews—to sustain their stage roles in public out of respect for their fans: "The fans have this stereotype of what the [otokoyaku] should look like, and to wear a skirt [offstage] is just like shattering their dreams. . . . That's why whenever I get in a car, I never sit with my knees together. I just sit like a man" (Anju Mira, quoted in Rea 1994:S5).

From the beginning, the Revue management has sought to limit female fans' infatuation to the ideal man performed by an *otokoyaku*. My archival research and interviews suggest that, on the contrary, female fans of all ages, class, and educational backgrounds do not see a prototypical man onstage; rather they acknowledge and appreciate a female body performing in a capacity that transgresses the boundaries of received femininity and masculinity (Hoshi 1987; Maruo 1950:252–78; "Shōjo kageki o kataru" 1935; Tanabe and Sasaki 1983:135–36). The player of men's roles, in short, is appreciated as an exemplary female who can negotiate successfully both genders, and their attendant roles, without being constrained by either: like Daichi Mao during her Moon Troupe days, she successfully lives the contradiction.

And what about the *musumeyaku*? One aspect of the postwar revival of Takarazuka has been the efforts of *musumeyaku* to make femininity more than just a foil for masculine privilege. Takarasiennes and their female fans sometimes refer to the actor not as *musumeyaku* (literally, "daughter's role player"), but as *onnayaku* (woman's role player), thereby claiming a nomenclatural parity with the *otokoyaku*. This act of (re)naming is a reminder that the "sex-gender system . . . is both a sociocultural construct and a semiotic apparatus, a system of representation which assigns meaning (identity, value, prestige, . . . status in the social hierarchy, etc.) to individuals within the society" (de Lauretis 1987:5). The actors began to stress their female being over their daughter status, and, accordingly, demanded more prominent roles.

The all-male administration responded to these demands by creating highly visible, dynamic, and often overtly sensuous woman characters, such as Scarlett O'Hara in *Gone with the Wind* and Jacqueline Carstone in *Me and My Girl*. However, in a move that undercut *musumeyaku* intentions, the directors assigned these new roles to players of men's roles. As the director of *Gone with the Wind* explained, using a logic reminiscent of the arguments in favor of retaining the Kabuki *onnagata*, "the *otokoyaku* have an erotic appeal (*iroke*) that is missing in *musumeyaku*. The rationale for having an *otokoyaku* play Scarlett O'Hara is to revive her original femininity while at the same time retaining the sensuality of her 'male' gender, thereby doubling her charm (*nijū no miryoku*)" ("Dō, oiroke aru kashira" 1977). In this way, the construction and performance of femininity remain the privilege of both males and players of men's roles. *Musumeyaku*, in contrast, almost never have been reassigned to men's roles: the transposition of gender is not a reciprocal operation. As several players of women's roles have remarked, "Japanese society is a male's world, and Takarazuka is an *otokoyaku*'s world" ("Utsumi-sensei to onnayaku" 1967:54). Also significant is that the charismatic women characters performed by the players of men's roles are most often Euro-American. We saw that in the early twentieth century, the Paris-inspired revue and Western films were held accountable for the "masculinization" of Japanese females. But in this case, the directors felt that the requisite innocence and naïveté of the *musumeyaku* would be irreparably compromised by roles that called for (hetero)sexually active characters. Although all Takarasiennes by definition are unmarried and ostensibly (hetero)sexually inexperienced, *otokoyaku*, by virtue of their "male" gender, were perceived as less likely to be corrupted by assuming the roles of charismatic and lustful women—an ironic twist on the rationale for the emergence of the Kabuki *onnagata* in the 1600s.

Some actors, such as Minakaze Mai (retired 1988), who had enrolled in the Academy specifically to do "male" gender, were assigned instead to do "female" gender. Minakaze was assigned to perform women's roles because of her comparatively short stature. In order to resolve the conflict between her offstage desires and her onstage role—or, in Stanislavskian terms, in order to dialogue with her character's "I"—she "stopped wearing blue jeans" and "always exerted [herself] to the fullest to be a *musumeyaku*, even in [her] private life." Minakaze is not alone in believing initially that females encountered less resistance performing women's roles. She now agrees with several of her colleagues that locating "the woman within the female poses a perplexing problem" (*Nihonkai* 1987; *Hankyū* 1987). Similarly, after ten years of performing only men's roles, *otokoyaku* Matsu Akira (retired 1982), in contrast to Daichi Mao, was unable to perform a woman's role: "Even though I am a female, the thing called 'woman' just won't emerge at all" (quoted in Misato 1974:68). Whether in terms of "resistance" or "emergence," the Takarasiennes have drawn attention to the incompatibility between their femaleness and the dominant construction of "female" gender. The actors' training in their secondary genders has led in effect to the deconstruction of femininity, which, as a gender role, can be understood as a performative text.

Kobayashi's assertion that "Takarazuka involves the study of males" is only partially correct (1948). "Female" gender is also taught and studied; this, in fact, is the ultimate objective of the Takarazuka Music Academy and Revue. Students who are assigned a secondary gender contrary to their personal preference are in a position analogous to all Japanese females who are socialized into gender roles not of their own making. And like the players of women's roles in particular, girls and women are suspended between the depiction and definition of "female" gender and the achievement or approximation of such. Ironically, it is just this limbo that many young women have sought to avoid by enrolling in the Academy.

Nevertheless, the Revue offers Takarasiennes an alternative to, or at least a respite from, the gender role of Good Wife, Wise Mother. One actor declared that for her to become a player of men's roles was tantamount to "realizing [her] personal ideals" ("Tsurugi Miyuki katarogu" 1986:45). Another enrolled in the Takarazuka Music Academy specifically because "despite the fact that [she] was female, [she] could assume a masculine persona" ("Kakko yosa" 1969:39). And many *otokoyaku* regularly speak of themselves offstage as *boku*, a self-referent that signifies masculinity. As players of men's roles, the actors have access to, and provide fans with vicarious access to, a wide range of ranks and professions still limited to males, from military general to revue director. Many *otokoyaku* have noted that had they not joined Takarazuka, they would have pursued—as if employment opportunities were equal—such careers as import-export trader, airplane pilot, train engineer, and lumber yard manager, among others, occupations underrepresented by females.

Leading *otokoyaku* have been provided the opportunity to realize their forfeited careers in one fan magazine's "magic if" series, titled "What If You Had Not Joined Takarazuka?" Asami Rei and Haruna Yuri, for example, would have been a train engineer and airplane pilot, respectively. For the series, the two players of men's roles dressed in the appropriate uniforms and assumed their forgone careers for a day. Haruna toured but did not pilot a jet, and Asami was given lessons and actually drove a Hankyū train ("Untenshi ni charenji" 1976:50–51; "if . . . " 1977:60–61). Theoretically, they subverted the male-dominant occupational hierarchy; but in actuality, as well-known *otokoyaku*, their act was not perceived as redressing conventional "female" gender roles. So long as they remain members of the Takarazuka Revue, the *otokoyaku* are able to operate as hinge figures whose very bodies mediate the fantasies of the stage with the realities of everyday life. Like the theater itself, they represent excess—overflowing semiosis—and its containment. Once they retire, the players of men's roles are expected to return to their primary feminine selves.

In recent decades, Takarasiennes and their fans have often referred to the *otokoyaku* as a female who has metamorphosed (*henshin shita*), indicating a recontextualization of this hitherto androcentric term to fit their stage experience (e.g., "People: Ōura Mizuki" 1986:48). Their use of the term outside the Buddhist and Kabuki (*onnagata*) contexts may have been prompted by the tremendous, continuing popularity of the "morph dramas" (*henshin dorama*) that were first aired in the late 1960s. These television dramas, some of them animated, feature mostly "ordinary" boys and young men who have the ability to suddenly morph into another, more powerful form. The brainy Pa-man, for example, in another incarnation is Mitsuo, an average elementary school student. His inventors suggest that what audiences find intriguing is the possibility of "one person living in two worlds" ("Kodomo no suki na henshin dorama" 1968:11).

I would argue that the Takarazuka Revue was and is attractive to audiences for much the same reason. For over eighty years the excessively wrought Revue has provided viewers in Japan with glimpses and dreams of other, exotic worlds. And for female fans in particular, the tuxedo- and gown-draped actors enabled the vicarious experience of an alternative to the traditional kimono, as well as an alternative to the Good Wife, Wise Mother role—or at least a respite from it. Of great significance in this connection is that the public vocation of the Takarazuka actor reverses the conventional association of females with the household; in a particularly vivid way, the player of men's roles negotiates both the public and the private spheres, her androgynous image symbolizing their fusion.

It is in this light that the impressive popularity of Takarazuka among girls and women especially is partly explained, as is the fiery criticism aimed at the *otokoyaku* in earlier years. Voting rights and nominal equal employment opportunity laws (in effect since 1986) notwithstanding, sexist discrimination against girls and women—from the boys-first order of school roll calls to short-term "mommy track" jobs—is the prevailing state of affairs. "Women inside, men outside" remains the dominant gender ideology, which is further reinforced by "public opinion" polls commissioned by the Prime Minister's Office and others despite the facts: over 60 percent of all adult females work for wages outside their homes, 80 percent of whom are married and mothers (Atsumi 1988; Pollack 1994:17, 19; Radden 1991; "3.4% of Women Feel Equal at Work" 1994:2; "Women's Work Conditions" 1990:4).

ANDROGYNY AS AMBIVALENCE

"Performance at its most general and most basic level is a carrying out, a putting into action or into shape" (Maclean 1988:xi). Takarazuka performances "carry out" at least two competing actions that correlate with the text and the subtext of the Revue. Indeed, a theatrical performance always exceeds the elements—such as the "master" text—from which it is composed, extending into many spheres of action (xi–xii). In addition, the interaction of performers—who, in the widest sense, include actors as well as directors, fans, critics, "I," and "you"—may be cooperative or contentious. The influence of the Takarazuka Revue on the discourse of gender and sexuality has been evident at different historical junctures in several, often contradictory ways, as I have shown. For example, whereas Kobayashi argued that the players of men's roles participate not in the construction of alternative gender roles for females but in the glorification of males and masculinity, both government censors and female fans viewed the actors as doing just the opposite. The former interpreted the *otokoyaku* as deviant and offensive enough to ban from the stage in 1939, even as the wartime state employed Takarazuka in its efforts to mobilize the population through entertainment, as we shall see in the next chapter. Female fans, on the other hand, continue to view the player of men's roles in a number of affirmative ways, including as a style-setting lesbian and as an exemplary female who embodies contradiction and bridges gender and its spatial domains. Watching the *otokoyaku* onstage, (female) fans enjoy vicariously what they too might be able to do *if*—magically—they were someone else: not male, but players of men's roles. The key to liberation, as it were, involves not a change of sex but a new gender identity, and by extension, a transformation in gender ideology. Like Oscar in *The Rose of Versailles*, Takarasiennes, and particularly *otokoyaku*, provoke a recognition of gender as, in part, a costume drama in which clothing—in addition to gesture and voice—undercuts the ideological fixity and essentialism of conventional femininity and masculinity (Kuhn 1985:53). The technologies (*kata*) of gender utilized in the Takarazuka Revue not only have drawn from and informed but also in some cases have redressed the dominant representations of male and female.

Androgyny has been used in Japan since the turn of this century to name three basic, but overlapping, types of androgynous females: those whose bodies approximate the prevailing masculine stereotype; those who are charismatic, unconventional, and therefore not feminine females; and those who have been assigned to do "male" gender or who have appropriated it on their own initiative. The characterization of their appearance as "androgynous" is necessarily premised on a priori knowledge of the underlying female body—knowledge that can nullify or compromise the "male" gender of the surface. Obviously, a female who passes successfully as a man does not appear androgynous. "Passing" can work in either transitive or intransitive ways, or both. It can refer to what someone does to purposively efface their difference or otherness, and it can refer to what is achieved, consciously or unconsciously, when an observer does not recognize one's difference or otherness. Successful passing was a source of great anxiety on the part of conservative pundits committed to retaining a polarized sexual hierarchy, which they equated with social stability. Others preferred to reassure themselves with the conviction that masculine females were asexual. *Dansō no reijin*, for example, was an expression that focused attention away from the body and onto the masculine clothing of an unconventional female.

I have shown that the appeal to and experiments with androgyny in the Takarazuka Revue served the different interests of both the patriarchal management and female actors and fans alike by deflecting negative attention from the sexual difference posed by the players of men's roles. (We shall return to the subject of sexuality and crossdressing in chapter 5, which considers very recent expressions of androgyny.) By allowing "the woman" to permeate "the man," the Revue's experiments with androgyny in the late 1960s and early 1980s in effect reemphasized the facticity of the female body doing "male" gender. The directors viewed this as an indication that an *otokoyaku*'s secondary "male" gender was kept in check by her primary or "natural" femininity. But many female fans continued to see the *otokoyaku* as a female unconstrained by a sexual and gendered division of labor. Androgyny, as a theory of body politics, continues to interrogate the naturalized dualities of male and female, masculine and feminine. At the same time, androgyny, as an embodied practice, also has been used to exaggerate, essentialize, and mystify those same dualities.

3

Performing Empire

[T]he greatest drama . . . is . . . war itself. The greatest
theatre is the theatre of war.

Dana 1943:5

The colonial policy of Orientals in dealing with Orientals is
a unique feature in the study of the general subject.

Asami 1924:[1]

To view those who are in essence unequal as if they were
equal is in itself inequitable. To treat those who are unequal
unequally is to realize equality.

Yamato minzoku o chūkaku to suru sekai seisaku
no kentō (An investigation of global policy
with the Yamato race as nucleus) 1943,
quoted in Dower 1986:264, 357

MADE IN JAPAN

"Made in Japan" ("Meido in Nippon") was the signature song in a
Takarazuka revue (of the same name) about foreign trade staged in
1941 at the height of Japanese imperialist aggression in Asia. The
sixteen-scene production opened with a swinging "money dance" on
a set decorated with large-scale copies of the currencies of eight countries. With prosaic lyrics and tune, the title chorus followed, celebrating the expansion of Japanese trade into global markets and alluding to Japanese colonialism in such "underdeveloped" areas as
Micronesia, a Japanese mandate since 1919:

> To global ports. Onward! To global markets
> So thrilling, Made in Japan
> Onward! To the Seven Seas
> Onward! Japanese commerce
> So thrilling, Made in Japan
> Spirits soar: Maritime patriotism
> Our flag waves in ports around the world
> Announcing, this is our Japan

89

> And inviting Japanese trade
> Our Made in Japan
> The less advanced
> Will join with us
> To revive their trade
> Our fortune is lucky for those
> who lack foreign currency.
>
> (*Sekai no ichiba* 1941:70–71)

The show earned glowing newspaper reviews:

> Ingeniously punctuated with pathos, comedy, and embellished
> with well-worked out gags, [*Made in Japan*] . . . depicts the silk,
> porcelain ware, musical instruments, bicycles, and other representa-
> tive manufactured goods of the Island Empire—and that in a
> remarkably artistic way. . . .
> As an added feature of the revue, scores of born-in-Nippon girls
> play made-in-Nippon violins, accordions, and organs on the stage.
>
> (N. Matsumoto 1941a)

In a spirited display of imperialist bricolage, the revue also linked together what the reviewer described as a Tyrolean clock scene, a view
of "bicyclists on an Annamese street," a "pathetic romance" set in
Mexico, a "rather weird" Thai dance, a "graceful" Indian dance, and
a "lively" Argentine tango.

This revue, *Made in Japan*,[1] alerts us to the role of the revue theater
as a technology of Japanese imperialism. Perhaps because the affective, aesthetic, and cultural dimensions of Japanese imperialism have
been much more neglected than the bureaucratic, military, and polit-
ical-economic dimensions, the mainstream historiographical consensus is that "imperialism never became a very important part of the
[Japanese] national consciousness" and that "there were no Japanese
Kiplings, there was little popular mystique about Japanese overlord-
ship and relatively little national self-congratulation" (Jansen 1984:76).
In considering the relationship between theater and the imperialism
I focus precisely on the affective, cultural dimensions of that expan-
sionist project. And because the political dimensions of theater in general have been neglected relative to its aesthetic and popular cultural
character, I highlight the politics of the Takarazuka Revue in order to
foreground the aesthetic and cultural aspects of Japanese colonial
practices. My project has been facilitated by an abundance of archival

and dramaturgic evidence suggesting that the mainstream consensus is premature. Theater, for one, was deployed as a powerful instrument in forging a national culture and in shaping popular attitudes about colonial subjects and the indisputable superiority of Japanese culture.[2] Japanese ideologues and impresarios were no different than their counterparts in Germany, Italy, Russia, and the United States in manipulating the relationship between entertainment and social engineering.

Generally speaking, it was during the wartime period (1931–45) that presentist plays, or "plays dealing with the present (emergency) situation" (*jikyoku engeki*), were staged. The majority of wartime revues produced were about military policies and exigencies, such as the "southward advance" (e.g., *Saipan-Palau: Our South Seas* [*Saipan-parao: Waga nan'yō*], 1940), immigration to Manchuria (e.g., *When Spring Orchids Bloom* [*Shunran hiraku koro*], 1941), patriotic college students (e.g., *College Students of a Military Nation* [*Gunkoku daigakusei*], 1939), and valorous nurses (e.g., *Navy Hospital* [*Kaigun byōin*], 1940).

I shall return to the braided motifs of ethnic tensions and impossible love, noted in our brief examination of the postwar revue *Jump Orient!* in chapter 1, as integral components of the Japanese orientalism informing Revue productions past and present. The intersections of gender, sexuality, ethnicity, and nationalism interest me here, as does the almost hyperconscious formation of an ambivalent national popular culture and identity. Moreover, these intersections, and the historical, ideological, and practical products of their convergence, reveal much about the sexual politics of Japanese imperialism—a sexual politics embodied by colonial subjects and Takarazuka actors alike.

ASSIMILATION ONSTAGE AND OFF

Central to my overall thesis of strategic ambivalence as a defining feature both of the gender ideology informing the Revue and of modern Japanese national cultural identity is the homology between the process of an *onnagata* or *otokoyaku* becoming Woman and a man, respectively, and the process whereby a colonial subject "became" Japanese. As we shall see, androgyny is conceptually related to hybridity, by which I mean, in a general sense, "a making one of two distinct things" (Young 1995:26). In a more specific sense, hybridity characterizes the composite construction of Japanese national cultural identity, the "Japanization" of Asian peoples incorporated into the Greater East Asia Co-Prosperity Sphere (*daitōa kyōeiken*),[3] and the embodiment of "outsiders" (*gaijin*) by certain Japanese. Kobayashi's industrial and government ties and positions, the martial cast of the Revue and the Music Academy, and the montage-like structure of the revue form, made Takarazuka, despite its all-female cast and attendant controversies, a useful vehicle for disseminating and enacting a pan-Asian vision of co-prosperity.

This vision of co-prosperity was premised on a doctrine of assimilation (*dōka*; lit., "same-ization"), or Japanization (*Nipponka*), which, by the 1930s, was a central issue in Japanese colonial affairs. It was also referred to more starkly as "imperialization" (*kōminka*) (lit., "imperial subject-ization"; Peattie 1984a:41). Assimilation in its theory and practice during the wartime period is of further interest to understanding the Revue since it is linked conceptually to the theory and practice of androgyny discussed in the previous chapter. Infused with a Confucian morality, the rhetoric of assimilation equated Japanese expansion in the Pacific with a mission to civilize and "equalize"— "by treat[ing] those who are unequal equally"—the peoples of Asia.[4] The assertion that the Japanese Imperial Household was the source of the Japanese "race" and the emperor was the head of the nation further distinguished Pan-Asianist ideas on assimilation. Mark Peattie explains, "The origins of the Japanese race were held to be mystically linked to the Imperial house and thus to constitute an Imperial 'family,' a principle which could be extended outward to include new populations brought under Japanese dominion, so that these too could become 'imperial peoples' (*kōmin*)" (1984b:97). Of course, becoming "imperial peoples" was by no means a straightforward matter of "becoming Japanese." In general, the proposition that colonized peoples were capable of becoming Japanese was contingent on their outward Japanization. The basic idea at work here was the notion that content— in this case, attitude, behavior, cultural identity—followed form. Thus, "concerned primarily with the problem of control, the Japanese colonial bureaucrat was delighted with programs which induced Taiwanese, Koreans, Chinese, and Micronesians to speak Japanese, live in Japanese style houses, dress in modern Japanese (Western) clothing, and reinforce their physical identity with the ruling elite" (Peattie 1984b:100).

In the prevailing Japanese colonialist rhetoric, assimilation did not imply an end state, that is, the emergence of "new" Japanese, with the "same claims to liberties and economic opportunities as the citizens of metropolitan Japan" (Peattie 1984a:40; also 1984b:96–104). Rather, assimilation was both a heuristically useful and compelling theory and a fundamentally ambiguous and contradictory process. On the one hand, attempts were made to remold colonial peoples as "Japanese" in outward appearance. They were encouraged, in other words, to become copies of the "original" in a manner analogous to the differently conceptualized gender (and gendered) performances of the Kabuki *onnagata* and the Takarazuka *otokoyaku* described in the preceding chapter. Whereas the "real" *onnagata* metamorphoses into Woman, the *otokoyaku* puts markers of masculinity on her body. So, too, whereas colonial peoples were induced to acquire bodily and behavioral markers of Japaneseness, they were neither encouraged nor allowed to metamorphose into Japanese.

On the other hand, assimilation ultimately defined a process whereby, as a strategy of colonial domination and control, the Japanese nation assumed a protean character capable of absorbing, reappropriating, and reinscribing cultural difference according to the dominant ideology and image of Japaneseness.[5] The protean nation was not unlike a "real" *onnagata*, a male who contains and controls the female by becoming the Woman: only in this case, specific Asian peoples were contained and controlled by pan-Asianist Japanese. Japaneseness, as especially evident in the theater of colonialism, can be summarized as simultaneously a condition of hybridity and a hybrid formation. Significantly, several postcolonial theorists have suggested that the production of hybridization through colonialism "enables a form of subversion" (Bhaba 1985:154; also cited in Young 1995:23), which, as "a monstrous inversion, a miscreated perversion of its progenitors" (Young 1995:23), either interrogates or exhausts the differences between colonizer and colonized.[6]

This interpretation of the operations of hybridity closely approximates the theory of transculturation, which was applied in the introduction to the dynamics of cultural encounter. I shall propose a different interpretation with respect to colonial Japan. By strategically assuming a protean or hybrid character itself, the Japanese nation neutralized the anxiety about hybridity that can accompany colonialism (Young 1995:22–26; see also Stoler 1989), in effect subverting the possibility of subversion (that is, of "monstrous inversions").

Such were the cultural politics of Japanese assimilation policies. The sexual (or sex) politics of assimilation was shot through with anxieties about hybridity expressed in terms of "mixed blood children" (*konketsuji*), where a hybrid was perceived as a cross between two "races" and "races" were equated with species. As I elaborate on the aspects of eugenics and "race hygiene" informing Japanese colonial policy elsewhere (Robertson 1997a), a summary will suffice here. By marshaling arguments from Euro-American (including Nazi) books, journals, and articles devoted to these subjects, a great many ideologues helped create a rhetorical climate favoring ethnic separatist, antimiscegenational policies. These policies included the "comfort women" (*ianfu*) system of state-sponsored, coerced prostitution and the harsh treatment of Eurasians, whose "enemy blood" was perceived as making them especially devious and untrustworthy (Frühstück 1996b; Hayashida 1976; Hicks 1996; Saitō 1993; Suzuki Z. 1983; Takagi M. 1989, 1991, 1993; Tōgō 1945; Touwen-Bouwsma 1994; Yoshii 1940).

In a less abhorrent way, the ambiguous referent of assimilation was also evident in Takarazuka's wartime productions, as captured by a headline: "'Zuka Assimilates *Midsummer Night's Dream*." The author of the accompanying article on the Japanized version of Shakespeare's comedy remarks that "orthodox lovers of the Shakespearean play will undoubtedly be disappointed in seeing the 'Zuka comedy, as it is different from the original, but, so far as its entertainment value is concerned, this abridged Nippon version is worth seeing" (N. Matsumoto 1944). The settings, costumes and atmosphere are described as "entirely Nippon"; "Nippon names" were given to the various characters; "Nippon fairies" replaced the spirits of flowers, acorns, mushrooms, and dragonflies; and *joruri* music, the traditional musical narrative associated with Bunraku (the puppet theater) and Kabuki, clinched the "Nippon background." However, as the reviewer notes, the multicultural finale, featuring Takarazuka actors performing as Shirley Temple, Miura Tamaki,[7] and other international celebrities, was excessive even for the Revue—a case of "too many cooks spoil[ing] the broth."

In the example of *Midsummer Night's Dream*, "assimilation" corresponds to the two, somewhat tautological meanings noted above: Japaneseness is synthesized from an appropriation and adaptation of the foreign, while the foreign is Japanized. Assimilation (*dōka*) was also the term used by performance theorists, influenced by Stanislavski and William Archer,[8] to describe the twofold process by which an actor identified with her or his stage character (Matsui 1914:95). Acting, as a process of assimilation, involved the production of the external markers of a character through technical expertise (*kata*), as well as the dialogical creation of a character's inner life, in order to animate the role.

A similar twofold process characterized assimilation in the service of Japanese colonialist policy. The five basic means through which Japanization was pursued in the colonies incorporated both the physical and mental dimensions of *dōka*: the education of children and their acquisition of Japanese for everyday use; the exaltation of state Shintō and the veneration of the Japanese emperor and, by extension, the Japanese people in general; the organization of youth into public service groups and auxiliary military corps to defend the empire; observation tours to Japan, the showcase of Asian modernity and coprosperity (Peattie 1988:104); and the organization of theater groups and theatrical performances as a means of affective social engineering. Assimilation was pursued both abroad in the colonies and on Japanese turf: Asian peoples were pressed to become Japanese in outward appearance and behavior, and in Japan, foreign institutions and artifacts were rendered indigenous by their infusion with an ineffable "Japanese spirit."

Okada Keigo, a Revue director, explained the cultural logic of assimilation and hybridity in a 1940 newspaper interview:

> As long as the Nippon spirit is interwoven in [a] show, it seems to me, one need not bother very much about the subject matter and the form of expression. . . . [What's important] is to reproduce Japanese life, sentiment, and morale in our stage productions. Mere introduction of Japanese characters and Japanese costumes may be meaningless. . . . I am of the opinion that the Nippon spirit is big enough not to reject the [*sic*] Western music and Western costume—it has a bigger embracing capacity than that.
>
> (quoted in "What Will Become of Girls' Revue in Japan?" [*sic*] 1940)

Okada provides an important reminder of the limits of the colonial policy of assimilation and also of the limits of cross-dressing in the Revue theater. Colonial subjects and *otokoyaku* alike could only always approximate and never really become—nor should they ever become—either Japanese or Man, respectively. It is an ironic but crucial feature of the strategic ambivalence of assimilation that the prescribed technologies for achieving both Japaneseness and manliness drew attention to the artifice sustaining both identities. At the same time, those very technologies circumscribed and contained their potentially parodic and disruptive effects. Neither Japanized Asians nor masculine females could lay claim to the liberties and opportunities afforded real Japanese and real males; their assimilated identities were tantamount to a sanctioned form of passing. Passing in any other circumstance provoked anxiety and motivated defensive measures, such as antiespionage campaigns.

The relationship between the revue theater and the state was more a matter of mutual convenience and opportunism than of seamless consensus and total state control over forms of popular and mass entertainment. The state, which was not a singular formation, was more interested in mobilizing the population than in maintaining any ideological consistency in the process of reaching that end. As I elaborate below, the usefulness of Takarazuka in creating a vision of a global hierarchy headed by Japan, according to which all "nations and races" would assume their "proper place," owed much to two factors; first, to the symbolic ambivalence of the all-female theater, and second, to the structure of the revue form itself. Because revues consist of a montage-like display and concatenation of different, even contradictory, images, lands, settings, peoples, and scenarios, they offer a potent means of shaping and reshaping popular consciousness and national, cultural identity. Thus, just as Japanese colonial policy was both erasing and reinscribing the cultural difference embodied by colonial subjects, Takarazuka actors were recuperating that difference through wartime dramas, set in the colonies, that were designed to familiarize the public with the vast range of geographies and cultures contained within the Japanese Empire.

The oppositional construction of gender was refracted through the Takarasiennes, who embodied the eroticized tension between sexual and gender transgression and repression (cf. Theweleit 1989 [1978]:330). This tension, significant in the history of Japanese popular theater, was a main factor in the Tokugawa Shogunate's prohibition of "women's Kabuki" in 1629, along with proscriptions on cross-class sexual relations between male Kabuki actors and their patrons, as we have seen. It was also a significant component of the libidinal economy underlying Japanese nationalism and imperialism, realized metaphorically in the homologous relationship between androgyny and assimilation—or, to put it differently, between cross-dressing and cross-ethnicking. Gender is constructed on the basis of contrastive physical and behavioral stereotypes about females and males; similarly, the theatrical construction of ethnicity is based on reified images of "us" and "them." In addition to "doing" a wide range of men and women, the Takarazuka actors have also embodied and performed non-Japanese characters of diverse national and ethnic backgrounds. Just as *otokoyaku* signify idealized men, more debonair than actual males, so the various ethnic peoples performed by Revue actors signified colonial others reconstituted and pacified in wartime—and postwar—theatrical revisions of Japanese imperialist aggression.

The Revue's cross-ethnic performances were an extension of the official rhetoric of assimilation, which equated Japanese expansion with a mission to "civilize" through Japanization the peoples of Asia and the Pacific. The civilizing mission of the Revue's "ethnographic fantasies" was twofold. On the one hand, colonial subjects were represented on stage as objects and products of the dominant Japanese imagination of exoticized yet inferior otherness. On the other hand, according to a logic invested in the Kabuki *onnagata*, these representations were sometimes circulated as models of "cultural correctness" to be emulated by the colonized peoples objectified on the Takarazuka stage. In other words, just as the *onnagata* exemplified ideal femininity, so the Revue's actors portrayed the proper way—that is, the "Japanese" way—to look and sound Chinese and Indonesian. Radio broadcasts of wartime revues throughout the Japanese Empire and photographs of revues in colonial magazines (such as *Djawa Baroe* and *Fujin Asia*, among others), together with the Japanization efforts enumerated above, attempted to disseminate the "correct" images of Asians beyond Japan. The cross-dressed and cross-ethnicked actors were part of a larger, state-initiated process of locating and containing the gendered or ethnically marked other within, thereby assimilating it—but not without sometimes purging parts of it, as we shall see (cf. Bhabha 1983; Gilman 1985:14–35; Pease 1991; Pickering 1991; Renov 1991).[9]

JAPANESE ORIENTALISM

Orientalism is now a familiar component of anthropological discourse and needs no detailed introduction here. Recently scholars have effectively criticized the more monolithic and totalizing aspects of Edward Said's (1979 [1978]) initial formulation of Orientalism, arguing that the rubric glosses the messy knots of textual, imperial, social, historical, and cultural practices and discursive formations that constitute international relations (see Lowe 1991; see also Carrier 1992; Clifford 1988). Critical reappraisals of Orientalism presented in the guise of Western self-critique nevertheless retain an asymmetrical relationship between "East" and "West"; ironically, they further privilege Euro-American intellectual and theoretical trends as universal while at the same time obfuscating and trivializing the histories and legacies of non-Western imperialisms and associated "othering" practices. Indeed, a specifically Japanese orientalism characterized both colonial policy and revues built around the theme of Japanese cultural superiority and military supremacy.

Generally speaking the recognition of multiple Euro-American Orientalisms (see Lowe 1991) has not translated into genuine awareness of "the third world" as more than a singular formation defined in terms of its experience of colonialism and imperialism (Ahmad 1986:5). Japan, which arguably was not colonized by Euro-American powers but was itself a colonizer, complicates the critique of Orientalism and the oppositional construction of an internally coherent third world. Japan remains unmarked as a colonizer in Euro-American, but not Asian, eyes. (Of course, the metaphor of imperialism has been applied in recent decades by the American automotive industry to galvanize a nationalist response to the Japanese domination of the car market, an altogether disingenuous strategy given the transnational composition of "Japanese" and "American" cars.) Although "Japan" may have been appropriated by "the West's" orientalizing impulse, evident in literature ranging from Victorian travelogues to Roland Barthes's *Empire of Signs* (1982 [1970]), Japanese wartime ideologues were no less adept at creating various orientalist schema to rationalize and aestheticize their imperialist claims in Asia and the Pacific.

When referring to Japanese representational practices I therefore use *orientalism* in its lowercase form to distinguish it from Said's specific definition of *Orientalism* as a product of "the West's" presentation of the "Other" (the non-West) as "absolutely different" from the West. This makes the concept available as a useful theory of oppositional, essentialized constructions that work to intensify a dominant

cultural or national image by dramatizing the "distance and difference between what is closer to it and what is far away" (Said 1979
[1978]:55).[10] Unlike Joseph Carrier (1992), I find it unnecessarily complicated to divide O/orientalism into unmarked (what the West does)
and marked (the "ethno-orientalisms" of the non-West) categories. In
using the lowercase form, I also distinguish between the products of
Orientalism (i.e., the West and the Other) and the orientalizing process,
through which a dominant national cultural identity is constructed
and dramatized. Both the term and its overtones are salient in the context of Japanese imperialist expansion and colonial domination.

Orientalism in this generic sense has been deployed since the late
nineteenth century by influential Japanese historians and ideologues
in two apparently contradictory but actually mutually constitutive
ways. The first presents *the Japanese* as culturally and racially superior to other Asian peoples. The second claims an essential, mystify-
ing uniqueness that distinguishes *Japan* from nation-states perceived
as comparable in industrial and military power (i.e., the West; cf.
Tanaka 1993). Some scholars have even argued that Japanese orientalism was so totalizing that it obviated the need for the concomitant
deployment of an equally evolved Japanese occidentalism in order to
dramatize and allegorize cultural difference.[11] The widest line of difference was drawn thus not between Japan and the West but between
Japan and the rest of the world.

The Euro-American-influenced Revue was an ambiguous and unstable symbol of, and for, the New Japan, as the imperial nation-state
was called. On the one hand, the New Japan was an imagined community constructed from select artifacts of European and American
material cultures, a nation whose Western inflections would allow it
to withstand the encroachments of European and American powers
(Feuerwerker 1989). On the other hand, the New Japan was both the
legacy of, and repository for, the products of Asia's ancient cultural
histories, and it bore the burden of salvaging Asia for the Asians.

Figure 11 provides a striking illustration of Japanese wartime orientalizing, and this chapter presents others in the context of the revue theater. The cartoon, published in 1942, reveals many of the ways
the Japanese signified their superiority vis-à-vis other Asians. Here
the familiar purifying sun (labeled "Co-Prosperity Sphere") beams
down on Indonesia, driving out the Dutch, while the Japanese hand—
symbolizing a larger-than-life patriarch—clasps the native's. The

Figure 11.   "Person of the Southern Region." This cartoon appeared in *Osaka Puck* in December 1942 as part of a before-and-after sequence depicting Asia under Western domination and after Japanese liberation. From Dower (1986:200).

Japanese hand is far lighter in color than the dark-skinned native's, and a modern (Western) jacket cuff is evident, whereas the "southern person," obviously a manual laborer, is half-naked and implicitly half-civilized. His inferior but "proper place" as a race and culture is absolutely clear, as is his subordinate role in the division of labor within the Greater East Asia Co-Prosperity Sphere (Dower 1986:200). The Netherlands is represented disparagingly by a woman in archetypical Dutch attire, including wooden clogs, holding a lantern whose light is nearly extinguished by the advance of Japan into the former Dutch colony. Whereas the subjugated Indonesians are reduced to the image of a sarong-clad laborer, the Dutch, an enemy of equal status and power, are feminized: military regimes often reduce gender to a zero-sum game, where, as in this case, power is coded "masculine" and powerlessness "feminine."

The gender politics informing Japanese orientalism was not a simple inversion of the Eurocentric categorization of the East as feminine and the West as masculine. Rather, the deployment of gender was adapted to extenuating circumstances, as we shall see. When the martial spirit of the Japanese was at issue, the West and Euro-American cultural productions were cast as feminine and feminizing, and, by the same token, as unmanly and emasculating. Yet the nation was sometimes represented as feminine when the superior cultural sensibility of the Japanese was emphasized. As a discourse of comparative otherness, Japanese orientalism was activated through the wartime mass media and popular entertainment forums with the catalytic effect of enabling a broad spectrum of Japanese to think that they were familiar with, knowledgeable about, and superior to manifold cultures, European and Asian alike.

COLONIALISM AS THEATER,
THEATER AS COLONIALISM

As orientalism was the theory informing the representation of colonized Asian peoples, Japanization was the colonial practice. Although I have limited the scope of this chapter to the use of theater as a technology of Japanese imperialism, it is also useful to consider briefly the implicit theatricality of the colonialist project.

A newspaper photograph published in 1943 (figure 12) depicts a group of Japanese soldiers stationed in Burma performing the "East Asia Co-Prosperity Sphere South Seas Dance" (*Tōa kyōeiken nan'yō odori*). Brandishing spears and dressed in grass skirts and paper crowns, they appear as caricatures of South Sea islanders. One soldier-native pounds on a drum. The South Sea islands were incorporated into Japan's "southward advance" (*nanshin*), an early imperialist impulse that gained momentum in 1919, when, under the Versailles Peace Treaty, Japan gained the Micronesian islands formerly held by Germany (see Peattie 1988). Although the Japanese soldiers were in Burma as part of the imperial state's campaign to Japanize Asian and Pacific peoples, here they were parodying Pacific island rituals. However entertaining it might have been for the soldiers, the "South Seas Dance" also represented the protean way in which the dominant Japanese assimilated and reinvented cultural difference on their own terms. And by insisting on assimilation, or the outward invisibility of cultural difference, they were also able to rationalize a program of Japanization in the rhetoric of Pan-Asianism.

Figure 12.   "South Seas Dance." A newspaper photograph published
in 1943 of a group of Japanese soldiers in Burma performing, as the
sign indicates, the "East Asia Co-Prosperity Sphere South Seas Dance."
From Hosokawa Shūhei (1992:146).

This performance of cross-ethnicking complemented and overlapped with Takarazuka's colonialist revues and with the cross-dressing that constitutes a little-studied but nonetheless significant form
of Japanese "soldier show" entertainment. Inspired by memories of
all-female revues and Kabuki and stimulated by overseas tours made
by Takarazuka and its contemporaries, frontline soldiers staged
shows in which some of them performed as women. In one recorded
case, the cross-dressed soldier was the biggest attraction: "she" was
hugged, kissed, and had "her" dress lifted by the other men (Kamura
1984:121–22; also Maruki Sato 1930). The spectacle of males cross-
dressing as women was a regular feature of the mobile entertainment
troupes who performed for British and American soldiers during
World War II. As Allan Bérubé and Richard Fawkes have noted, the
players of women's roles often were more popular and sought after
than actual female actors and dancers (Bérubé 1990:67–97; Fawkes
1978:45, 53, 125, 163). Apart from Japanese accounts of similar mobile
troupes and recent scholarship on the traffic in "comfort women," little
research has been conducted on the organization of soldiers' recreation in the Japanese armed forces. Whereas state-sponsored wartime

prostitution paralleled mainstream sexual power relations, those same relations were exaggerated and parodied in the military's transvestite revues, in which women were erotically reappropriated in male-to-male sexual play.[12]

Markus Nornes makes a similar argument for *Dawn of Freedom* (*Ano hata o ute*, 1943), the first Japanese-Philippine coproduced propaganda film. The main focus of the film, he writes, "is the love between soldiers, funneling sexual energy into the war effort" (1991:260). Obviously homoerotic, *Dawn of Freedom* comes close to bringing male homosexuality and the desirability of "the other" to light: the scene in which the initially pro-American Filipino officer, Captain Gomez, says good-bye to his new Japanese soldier friend "is shot like a love scene with Greta Garbo. The two stare lovingly at each other and spout amazing lines":

JAPANESE SOLDIER (IN JAPANESE):   Now we must part company. You may not understand me now, but you must feel the mutual sympathies between us. That's all.

GOMEZ (IN ENGLISH):   I know you are going to Corregidor and saying goodbye to me now, but I'm sorry I cannot understand what you are saying.

JAPANESE SOLDIER: Capt. Gomez, please understand just this. Nippon and Philippines are not enemies.

GOMEZ: Nippon . . . Philippines.

JAPANESE SOLDIER: Nippon . . . Philippines. [They hold hands and stare dreamily into each other's eyes in a backlit (close-up).]

GOMEZ: Nippon . . . Philippines . . . Peace.

(Nornes 1991:260–61)

Military strategy afforded an easy transition from costume to camouflage: one of the more thespian tactics used by the Japanese in invading Malaya involved dressing their soldiers as Malays to confuse British troops (Hall 1981:859). This tactic was premised as much on the close relationship between camouflage and makeshift entertainment as on the Japanese belief that the British were unable to distinguish among Asian peoples.

A final example of the theatricality of colonialism comes from Indonesia. The stage was set in March 1942 for the induction of Indonesia into the Greater East Asia Co-Prosperity Sphere, as the Dutch regime was dismantled and local, regional, and governmental administrative apparatuses were reorganized and centralized under Japanese military command. One of the fundamental objectives of the Co-Prosperity Sphere policy in Indonesia was to eliminate as quickly as possible all signs of European and American influence. The Japanese pursued cultural hegemony in a variety of ways. They removed Dutch colonial monuments and constructed Japanese ones in their place, including Shintō shrines; replaced the Western calendar with the wartime Japanese one, including public holidays; renamed buildings, places, streets, squares, cities, and islands in Japanese and Indonesian; and mandated the compulsory study of Japanese, which was further enforced through the reform of the education system, press control and censorship, and the controlled use of radios, loudspeakers, films, photographs, music, and theatrical performances (Aziz 1955:174–77). In addition, Indonesian girls and women were encouraged to occasionally wear kimonos and to study Japanese dance and flower arrangement, formal practices that would reinforce their physical and cultural identity with, and obligations to, the superior Japanese. Artists were required to join a "cultural corporation" that regulated the production of orientalist works and "native" arts (Kurasawa 1991). My point here is not to inventory and measure the effectiveness of the cultural policies implemented throughout the Japanese Empire but simply to highlight the practice of assimilation as part of Japanization.[13] Indonesia, along with other areas under Japanese domination, was conceptualized as a newly constructed stage fitted with Japanese sets and backdrops on which native actors would speak their lines in Japanese and perform their lives as if they were Japanese. In a way, non-Japanese Asians were to become outwardly more traditionally "Japanese" than the (selectively) Westernized Japanese themselves.

In Japan, meanwhile, Indonesians, Chinese, Micronesians, Germans, and Italians and other colonized peoples and imperial allies were represented by Takarazuka actors enacting a spectacular vision of empire. The Japanese folktale "Peach Boy" ("Momotarō") was also adapted in Takarazuka as well as in local theaters throughout countries under Japanese domination. The story of Momotarō is one of the most popular of all Japanese folktales. He was born from a peach that an elderly couple plucked from a stream as it floated past. Under their tutelage, Momotarō grew to embody the quintessence of Japanese masculinity; later he was rewarded by the emperor for having subdued the demons of Onigashima. The wartime version of this story was about a miraculous Japanese boy who recruited a retinue of loyal followers from Indonesia, China, and the Philippines to help free Japan and Asia from American and European ogres (Dower 1986:253, 356). In addition to its imperialist theme, "Peach Boy" articulates in its subtext the ambiguity of Japan as an anticolonial colonizer.[14]

Although colonialism possesses a dramaturgy of its own, it cannot be reduced to theater. Theater, however, can and did expand the affective reach of colonialism (cf. Bratton et al. 1991). The Japanese cultural administrators appreciated theater as the preeminent mass medium, capable of providing a form of topical news show in which images and events, foreign places and peoples, were recaptured and recreated with "authenticity" (Holder 1991:135). Japanese cultural administrators were deeply influenced by their counterparts in the Allied and the Axis countries, and many articles on the American Federal Theater Project, as well as on Bolshevik, fascist, and Nazi uses of theater, were published in leading theater journals (Iizuka 1941:52; Nakagawa 1941; see also Dana 1943; de Grazia 1981; Stourac and McCreery 1986; White 1990; Zortman 1984).[15] Colonial administrators and state ideologues regarded theater to be far more effective a didactic medium than cinema (Endō 1943). They recognized theater not only as a means of organizing and rationalizing the leisure of soldiers and subjects but also as the art of "claiming the people" (cf. Dana 1943; de Grazia 1981; Schnapp 1993; Tsuchiya 1985).

Theater scholars have argued that the simultaneous interactions in theater between characters in a play, as well as between performers and spectators, produce a "performance consciousness": a collective capacity to engage imaginatively in the construction of potential worlds. The potential or possible worlds encountered in the performance are carried back by the audience into the wider—"real" —sociopolitical world in ways that may influence subsequent action (Kershaw 1992:25–29). The wartime state was especially interested in securing a link between a New World Order (*seikai shinchitsujo*) engineered by Japan and the potential world conjured by the theater (cf. Endō 1943). Revues such as *Children of the Sun* (*Taiyō no kodomotachi*, 1943), for example, were described as linking the "dreamy world" of children's stories to "wartime realities" in ingenious ways. *Children of the Sun* includes a scene in which "real" children visit the aged parents of Peach Boy (Momotarō), who tell them, "Our son is not the only Momotaro! Don't you know many Momotaros are now fighting in the North and in the South, waging a holy war for liberating the oppressed from the Anglo-American demons?" Sponsored by the Patriotic Industrial Association, the revue was trumpeted as "the right kind of entertainment which the people behind the guns most need for 'lubricating' their human mechanism" (N. Matsumoto 1943c).

INTERMISSION:
FROM *MON PARIS* TO MON JAPON

Well before Takarazuka and the theater world in general fell under state supervision, many of the Revue's performances were informed by a belief in the imperial prerogatives of the Japanese people. The 1927 revue *Mon Paris* (*Mon pari*) provoked a new discourse in Japan on the entertaining, didactic, and ideological possibilities of the revue form.[16] Written by Kishida Tatsuya, one of Takarazuka's leading playwrights, *Mon Paris* is generally recognized as Japan's premier revue. It was revived in 1947 and again in 1957, and its elements have been incorporated into countless programs since its debut.

Mon Paris consisted of a panoramic sequence of vignettes inspired by Kishida's travels through Asia and Europe the previous year. Most of the sixteen scenes were orientalist fantasies set in China, Ceylon (Sri Lanka), and Egypt—"exotic countries" through which the protagonist Kushida passed on his way to Paris (Shirai 1947:17; *Waga pari yo* 1927). The success of *Mon Paris*—the theme song sold over 100,000 copies—spurred the popularity of *parimono*, or revues with Parisian motifs, although Paris itself figured in only the last two scenes of Kishida's revue (Ōzasa 1986:113–14; Shima 1984:96).

The first *Mon Paris* anticipated the Co-Prosperity Sphere rhetoric of "interracial harmony"; this was particularly evident in the multicultural finale, in which all the countries visited by Kishida were represented by cross-ethnicking actors. The 1947 version of *Mon Paris* is less a revival than a whole new revue, in both senses of the word: a theatrical form and a looking back. Kushida remarks that "thanks to the Allies" the past (i.e., the Greater East Asia Co-Prosperity Sphere) is accessible as a zone of fun and adventure: "Everyone here can come on board and travel to Paris with us" (*Mon pari* 1948:11). But although Japan immediately after the war was portrayed as a radically changed society, socially and politically speaking, the countries through which Kushida and his party traveled en route to Paris had not changed; the orientalist stereotype of a static, "primitive" Asia employed in the original *Mon Paris* remained unchallenged. For example, China again was represented as teeming with "bandits"—by 1947 a code word for Communists—from whom Kushida rescues a feudal landlord's daughter. He was rewarded for his bravery with a banquet at which the grateful daughter sang "an ancient Chinese song" about a "beautiful flower: the red flower of my heart, to whom shall I give this flower?" (12).

Several days after visiting China, the travelers arrived in Sri Lanka and attended a religious ceremony performed at the Temple of the Tooth in the town of Kandy.[17] There, lotus-flower vendors danced gracefully before Buddhist sculptures that "came alive" momentarily to the sounds of swing music. The original *Mon Paris* included a subsequent scene in which Kushida cavorted with an "Indian mermaid" (Shirai 1947:17; *Waga pari yo* 1927:26).

On to Egypt, where the Japanese travelers toured the "pyramids, sphinx, and vestiges of Egypt's 5,000-year history" (*Mon pari* 1948: 14–15). The audience was then treated to an enactment of an "ancient Egyptian story" dreamed by Kushida. Among the "Orientals" featured in the dream sequence were a Cleopatra-like queen, her son the prince, manifold female attendants, grand chamberlains, and an evil sorceress from Libya, who appeared and disappeared in a cloud of smoke while snickering, *"ihehehe"* (figure 13). In short, Asia—the Orient—existed in a timeless vacuum: Egypt was a dreamland of magic and mystery, Sri Lanka was populated by pious natives who lived and breathed Buddhist ritual, and China was feudal and lawless.

Paris, in contrast, was portrayed as a marvel of modern, urban technology. Soaking up the ambiance of the lively, bustling, tree-lined boulevards, the characters profess, as they did in the 1927 version, that "Japan has much to learn from the West" (*Mon pari* 1948:15). Both Takarazuka and Japan are distanced from the rest of "sleeping Asia" and positioned within European modernity. Kushida and a friend decide to see a revue—and what else should they find playing in Paris but *Mon Paris!* Kushida declares, "[French revues] are nothing like Takarazuka, but let's go and see it anyway." Later, his friend remarks

Figure 13.   Egyptian royalty in *Mon Paris*. A scene from the Snow
Troupe's 1947 performance of *Mon Paris* featuring the court of the
Cleopatra-like queen. From Hashimoto (1994:67).

that "the French didn't overlook anything when they imported the
revue from Takarazuka" (15), and Kushida even refers to Takarazuka
as the "main household" (*honke*) of the revue theater (16). In another
assimilationist moment, Kushida notes that both Paris and France as
a whole resemble Takarazuka, which is described as "everyone's beautiful, enchanted country; a country of dreams smoldering since childhood" (16). The *Mon Paris* revision of theater history makes an ahistorical claim for the Japaneseness of the revue form and recalls the
expansive yet exclusive rhetoric of the paternalistic "family state system" that infused Co-Prosperity Sphere doctrine. This claim formed
the ideological basis for the Revue's inauguration of a Greater East
Asia Co-Prosperity Sphere series in 1941, discussed below.

The railroad in particular is an important framing device in *Mon
Paris* and other revues, particularly those staged during the wartime
period. It is employed as a metaphor of nation, empire, and progress.
In addition to a railroad's Taylorist qualities, geostrategists in Europe
and Japan were well aware of the "capacity of railroads for absorb-

ing small states into empires" (Robinson 1991:1). The South Manchuria Railway Company, for example, has been described as "having the appearance of a commercial company but really functioning
as an organization for the [Japanese] state to carry out colonial rule
and colonization" (Myers 1989:118–19). The Takarazuka Revue similarly was a commercial company that the state was keen on har-
nessing to help carry out the imperial project at home and abroad.

The two companies converged in another Kishida-authored revue,
From Manchuria to North China (*Manshū yori hokushi e*, 1938), that, like
Mon Paris, was described as a "stage version of a travelogue . . . intended to make the audience more conscious of the prevailing conditions in Manchuria and North China," where a full-scale war between the Chinese and Japanese had erupted in 1937.[18] Incorporated
into the revue was "a motion picture showing South Manchuria Railway's famed streamlined limited express speed across the wilderness
and fast developing regions of Manchuria" (N. Matsumoto 1938).

Train travel epitomizes the montage-like form of the revue in that
it too compresses space and time, geography and history: the loco-
motive signifies a teleological, modernizing force and allows travelers a view of its antithesis—namely, "natural" landscapes and "primitive" and "traditional" practices. The Takarazuka Revue, which
continues to operate under the aegis of the Hankyū railroad and department store conglomerate, celebrated and capitalized on the form,
function, and ideology of the railroad. Kobayashi initially developed
the theater and entertainment complex in part to increase passenger
service on his train line connecting Takarazuka with Osaka. Train
travel in Japan in general increased from 1927 onward, and domestic
tourism was promoted enthusiastically by the railroad ministry as a
form of organized recreation capable of linking the periphery to the
center (Takaoka H. 1993).[19]

Literally and figuratively, the railroad linked domestic strategies
of wartime mobilization with imperialist expansion and control. It also
signified the circumscription of the global by the local, and, within
Japan, the absorption of the local by the state, not to mention by commercial developers. On one level, *Mon Paris* was a traveling exhibition in which global sights/sites were brought to local audiences. On
another, it was an allegory about the Japanese people moving forward
in unison. Significantly, the "train dance" (*kisha odori*) was introduced
to audiences in the 1927 production of that revue (figure 14).[20] The

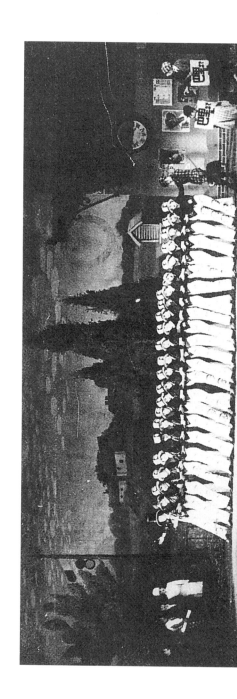

Figure 14. The "train dance" in *Mon Paris*. The "train" in the 1927 production of *Mon Paris* consists of a row of twenty-three actors, legs extended, linked hand on elbow so as to resemble the drivers connecting the wheels of a chugging steam engine (and wheels decorate the legs of their white trousers). Kushida, the protagonist, is clutching a carpet bag and umbrella in his left hand and grasping the right shoulder of the last "wheel" with his right as he leaves Marseilles for Paris. The train reappears in the last scene when Kushida reminds the audience that he has overseen their safe arrival in Paris and bids them good cheer (*Waga pari yo* 1927:30–31). From Hashimoto (1988:18).

image was one of Japanese people moving forward in mechanical unison, and the principle goal of the "train" was to keep itself moving and absorbing. No mere steam engine this: this train was the Japanese Empire.

SITING THEATER

Erika Fischer-Lichte's definition of theater as a cultural system that generates meaning in the moment of its performance sums up nicely the way in which theater was perceived by playwrights, theater critics, and state ideologues alike in wartime Japan. As she notes, an important ontological feature of theater is the dialectical relationship between, minimally, a spectator and an actor (and, implicitly, a character). Without an audience, there is no performance. Theater by definition is a public event; the production and reception of a theater performance are synchronous (Fischer-Lichte 1992 [1983]:1–10; McConachie and Friedman 1985a:7). Regardless of how many times a play is performed, each occasion constitutes a uniquely configured event since unlike cinema, subsequent shows are not—and cannot be—formally identical. As in the dynamics of everyday life, the transitoriness of theatrical performance in conjunction with the mutually constitutive relationship between actors and audiences renders the meanings generated both within and across performances inherently unstable. There is no guarantee that the meanings communicated by an actor in character, much less in a script, will be the meanings construed by members of an audience. The history of the Takarazuka Revue is characterized by a tension between the dominant text of a performance and the subtexts generated by it. As we shall see, theater reformers, including Kobayashi, and Japanese state ideologues grappled with the problem of how to measure and control the sociopolitical efficacy of wartime theatrical productions (Kobayashi 1961a: 207–21).

From this theoretical position, we are able to move beyond the simple notion that theater passively mirrors social reality and to recognize the role of the medium in legitimating and delegitimating certain forms of social interaction—forms that, in turn, may have their own impact on initiating, reinforcing, and ultimately altering theatrical events (McConachie 1985:17). I can never know firsthand the dialectical dynamics of the wartime revues I cite and analyze. Instead,

I must rely on scripts, photographs, critical reviews, memoirs, fan letters and literature, domestic and colonial government policies, newspapers and popular magazines, scholarly texts and journals, interviews, and other diverse historical and present-day sources to gain insights into the places, purposes, receptions, and efficacies of the revue theater in wartime Japan and in the colonies.

In Japan, the wartime revue theater generated subtexts that encouraged popular uncertainty and ambivalence toward militarization and imperialism. For example, a play about the valor of battlefront nurses (e.g., *Navy Hospital*) alludes to human casualties that, in turn, could raise doubts about the purpose of war. Admittedly, it is more difficult to account for instances of resistance occasioned by theaters not self-consciously agitprop, although such can be inferred by reading between the lines of official policies and regulations, as well as from the occasional documented case. Similarly, historian John Dower has documented how "sensational rumors" and "seditious graffiti" reveal the popular dissidence and declining morale that characterized social life in Japan during the 1940s (1993:101–54). As dominant ideologies themselves are potentially unstable and never totally effective, it was in the interest of ideologues to allow some of the subtexts to surface some of the time, a practice tantamount to an affective approach to social control. For example, state censors did not favor shows that presented the Allied countries in a less than critical light, although shows with foreign settings produced in the name of the Axis Alliance, Japan's southward advance, or East Asian development and so forth were lauded. Whenever a seemingly pro-American element was included in a revue, the indiscretion was quickly criticized even though the production was allowed to continue its run. Thus, in reviewing the fifteen-scene play *The Navy* (*Kaigun*, 1943), staged with the support of the Navy Ministry to celebrate Navy Day, a critic commented about the "musical side of the play": "One would find [*The Navy*] to be quite entertaining except for the inclusion of 'Aloha Oe.' One fails to understand the reason why the management has chosen this song of enemy character, especially at this time when the national drive is going on for eliminating the tunes of hostile states" (N. Matsumoto 1943b).

Given that "Aloha Oe" was among the sixty or so Hawaiian (i.e., enemy) songs banned by government censors (Hosokawa 1994:62), the inclusion of the tune in *The Navy* could be interpreted as a sign of the persistent resilience of popular cultural formations backed in part by the business sector. Similarly, in her book on the mass organization of leisure in fascist Italy, Victoria de Grazia argues that the vested economic interests of private enterprise often conflicted with the fascist regime's need for a politically responsive mass base (1981:243). Here, the conflict pitted the commercial success of Hawaiian music in Japan against the military's perception that the "effeminacy" of "exotic tunes" weakened the people's fighting spirit, even though a number of Hawaiian-style tunes eulogized Japanese imperial expansion. These included "Manchurian Snowstorm" ("Manshū fubuki," 1936) and "From a Cup of Coffee" ("Ippai no kōhii kara," 1939), which presented the act of drinking coffee as analogous to a tourist's possession of Java (the island being represented as a young woman) (Hosokawa 1994: 59–61). Moreover, despite the ban Hawaiian instrumentals were also used to score wartime newsreels and propaganda films, such as *Momotarō's Sea Eagle*, in which Peach Boy and his troops stage a surprise attack on Onigashima to the sounds of Hawaiian music, perhaps to draw closer analogies to Pearl Harbor (Komatsuzawa 1991:241).

The tension between text and subtext was also mediated through the architectural units of the theater, which enhanced the dialogical and dialectical character of performances. Wartime revues were especially illustrative of this synthesis, which was facilitated by the historical relationship in the Kabuki theater between stage and auditorium, a relationship adopted by the Takarazuka Revue—despite its Western veneer—to aid its audience-centered performances. Structurally, intimacy in the Revue is achieved above all through the use of a detached apron stage known as the "silver bridge" (*gingyō*), introduced as a permanent fixture in 1931. Its function follows from the primary impulse of Kabuki theater architecture: to move the actor toward the audience and to create a focal center of performance in the midst of the audience (Ernst 1956:65, 104).[21] Both the silver bridge, which encourages physical and direct eye contact, and, more recently, an illuminated mirror ball that splatters the audience with colored dots are used to make the audience an integral part of the staged activity.

During the 1930s and 1940s, the combination of presentist plays and interactive theater space incorporated the viewers into the staged scenarios, in theoretical terms interpellating them as agents of the New Japan. The Takarazuka Revue as a whole was positioned by Kobayashi as a bridge between Japanese society and an idealized vision of Asian co-prosperity.[22] Moreover, Takarazuka functioned as a "traveling bridge" when, in the late 1930s, mobile troupes of Takarasiennes were dispatched to factories, farm villages, hospitals, and even war fronts throughout China, Korea, and Manchuria to provide civilians and soldiers with "wholesome entertainment" and to weave together symbolically the disparate parts of the Japanese Empire (N. Matsumoto 1939; "Shasetsu" 1942; Takagi Shin'inchi 1942; Toita 1956 [1950]: 250–52; Uemoto 1941). Revue administrators even entertained, but never pursued, a plan to establish a Takarazuka-like theater in North China (N. Matsumoto 1939). As of 1932, there were 1,934 drama theaters of widely varying sizes in Japanese cities ("Monbusho goraku chōsa" 1932), and regional tours by commercial theater troupes were an important part of building a national community. The intensive activities of the mobile groups of actors in the late 1930s further popularized theater among diverse audiences in Japan and abroad (Toita 1956 [1950]:252) and helped disseminate a military and imperialist ethos in the guise of entertainment. Members of the Shōchiku Revue also toured the same war fronts and colonial outposts, as well as those in Southeast Asia and Micronesia (Shōchiku Kagekidan 1978:45–48).

Although mobile theater troupes have a centuries-old history in Japan, the specific use of such troupes during wartime was reinforced by the example set in fascist Italy, where the state deployed Thespian Prose Cars, basically portable stages, to bring sanctioned entertainment to the masses.[23] In 1941 the Japanese state pressured commercial theaters to organize the mobile troupes under the auspices of a national federation, the Japanese Federation of Mobile Theaters (Nippon idō engeki renmei). Three years later, citing an emergency economizing measure, the state closed nineteen commercial theaters, including Takarazuka—although the mobile units were retained—and levied a stiff tax on them (Toita 1956 [1950]:243–44). Six theaters were reopened the following month for a couple of hours daily during which patriotic plays, newsreels, and films were scheduled (Hagiwara 1954:150–51). Takarazuka revues were resumed in May 1945 at a movie theater, the main theater having been expropriated by the navy as an educational facility for air corps trainees. The Tokyo branch had been converted into a factory for the assembly of balloon explosives made from Japanese paper. Although the main theater was reopened after the war in April 1946, the Tokyo branch fell under the jurisdiction of the Allied Powers' General Headquarters headed by General

Douglas MacArthur. It was temporarily renamed the Ernie Pyle Theater—after the popular American war correspondent killed in action in 1945—and reverted back to Kobayashi's control only in April 1955 (Hashimoto 1993:78, 84; Toita 1956 [1950]:244). Throughout the Occupation period (1945–52), Tokyo Takarazuka performances were staged at other local theaters, and the Revue produced special shows for Occupation personnel at the Ernie Pyle (Hashimoto 1993:142).

REVUE THEATER AS MONTAGE

Japanese avant-garde social commentators called the 1930s the "revue age" (*rebyū no jidai*) (e.g., Takahashi 1930). It was an age of things "mass"—mass production, mass consumption, mass entertainment, mass mobilization, and, in the context of imperialism, mass assimilation. Even Takarazuka's founder was known as "Mr. Kobayashi of the masses," and he often boasted that the main theater in Takarazuka was the ultimate "mass theater" (*taishū engeki*) in Japan ("Ichizo Kobayashi" 1944:5). A conservative estimate of the total annual number of spectators at both the original Takarazuka and Tokyo Takarazuka theaters in the interwar period produces a figure in the several millions—a significant audience that, in the eyes of the state, could not remain unclaimed.

Kobayashi's profit-oriented, commercial interest in organizing and rationalizing leisure and entertainment overlapped with the state's interest in the same. Ever the entrepreneurial opportunist, Kobayashi promoted Takarazuka as the dramatic equivalent of the New Japan. Takarazuka, he proclaimed, represented a break with the past and captured the modern zeitgeist of the twentieth century. Kabuki, in contrast, was an "antique" (*koten*) theater whose "pathetic *shamisen* melodies did not resonate with the spirit of the times" (Kobayashi 1962:130; see also 1961a:343–44, 431–34, and 1961b:512–15). Nor was the *shamisen* suitable for military marches and the choral singing at school ceremonies. Kobayashi recommended instead the promotion of Western music (*seiyō ongaku*), emphasizing that it was already an assimilated musical idiom (1962:132–33).

Kobayashi's enthusiasm for the revue form and its manifold social, economic, and political possibilities was not shared by many of his contemporaries, who regarded the 350-year-old Kabuki theater as a cultural artifact in which they could admire the past and recognize themselves as a great nation. Although they recognized the class-crossing popularity and "awesome commercial appeal" of the Takarazuka Revue, and were impressed by both the disciplined actors and the rationality of Kobayashi's production methods, they dismissed the revue form itself as "devoid of content": "a fad . . . that, like people's lives today, is superficial, intuitional, divorced from tradition, and without systematicness" (Iizuka 1941:65, 66, 68, 69). Whereas Kobayashi gave Takarazuka a positive valence as signifying the differentiation of Japan—a unique hybrid culture—from Asia and the world, his detractors placed a negative valence on the revue form as signifying the Westernization and thus corruption of Japan. Other revue enthusiasts, however, were critical of efforts by entrepreneurs like Kobayashi to "exploit the new market for emergency-minded revues" even as they recognized wartime measures, such as mobile troupes, as ways of "bringing the revue to the people" (Okada 1938:10, 11).

The revue age was described by the avant-garde as "an age not of systematically argued essays, but of critical commentaries (*hyōron*) that capture [and generalize from] essential points. Today's aesthetic is represented not by the stable order of the classics, but by disorder and chaos. Consequently, the [mental] weapon (*buki*) of choice is not deductive logic (*en'eki*); it is induction (*kinō*)" (Sasaki Norio, in Sakata 1935:[i]).[24] The epistemological aesthetic of the revue age was also evident in the imperial state's slogan, "New World Order," which was shorthand for the liberation of Asia from Western imperialist powers and the consolidation of a new regional, and ultimately international, hierarchy headed by Japan. The New World Order signified a new chain of historical associations and newly historicized memories: a new system of cultural artifacts in the service of Imperial Japan. The revue theater was to serve the new order as an important proving ground where the composite image of the New Japan could be crafted, displayed, and naturalized.

The Japanese state found several characteristics of the revue form particularly useful. In keeping with its etymology, the "revue" theater represents a break from "the past"—that is, a break from a fixed, singular, canonical reading of events past and present. One commentator writing in the 1930s declared that the revue was the epitome of transformation: "The revue does not have a singular, fixed, immobile form; by definition, the revue is always moving and changing, always progressing and developing" (Ashihara E. 1936:7). Like

photomontage and cinema, the revue offered "completely new opportunities . . . for uncovering [and making] relationships, oppositions, transitions and intersections of social reality" (Joachim Büthe,
as translated in Ollman 1991:34). The performance efficacy of montage, or its potential to exert sociopolitical influence, whether in photography, cinema, or theater, is allegorical.[25] To work as allegory, montage necessarily requires the concatenation by the viewer or audience
of fragmented and juxtaposed images and scenarios. Because a single
reading cannot be guaranteed, montage generates a tension between
the dominant meaning and the subtextual, and potentially subversive,
readings of the same performance. Moreover, once an audience disperses and reenters the wider social realm, a twofold problem remains:
how to reinforce the official text of a play and how to measure accurately any influence that the performance may have had on their behavior (Kershaw 1992:2). In the case of wartime revues such as *Made
in Japan*, it was a common practice for a narrator, either an emcee or
a character in a play, to venture out onto the silver bridge at regular
intervals and synthesize the various dramatic elements for the viewers, thereby attempting to reduce the degree of slippage between the
performance, its reception, and its lasting effects.

The genealogy-building capacity of the revue theater was acknowledged in a two-part article on the production and goals of
wartime revues published in 1942 by a Takarazuka administrator in
Gendai Engeki (*Contemporary Drama*), an influential theater arts journal. The article defers to the state's interest in exploiting theater as a
cogent means of popularizing imperialism and Japanizing Asia.

> The Japanese revue theater is best described as a cultural engineering
> corps, and, as such, has a role in teaching and guiding East Asian
> peoples. The Japanese revue must work toward purging from Asian
> cultures the bad influence of Euro-American revues, which have
> all but eradicated local cultures with glorious histories spanning
> thousands of years. It is the responsibility of the Japanese to raise
> the standard of culture in East Asia; they [East Asians] are leaving
> that task to us. We must . . . pursue affirmative, spiritual ideals. The
> revue is a rich repository of cultural forms; [Asian] customs and
> manners must be incorporated into revues in order to capture the
> charm of ordinary people. The revue is a type of entertainment that
> can be deployed as war matériel (*gunjuhin*).
>
> (Komatsu 1942:67)

The administrator provided an example of a hypothetical revue, *East Asian Bouquet* (*Tōa no hanataba*), inspired by the Greater East Asian theater of war. *East Asian Bouquet* was to present various colonized Asian nationals and ethnic groups and their cultures to Japanese audiences. The scenes constituting the proposed revue were set in Japan, Manchuria, "New China," French Indo-China, Thailand, Luzon, Burma, Malaya, and Java (Bali), respectively; the tenth scene was a multiethnic finale (Komatsu 1942:65).[26] The people involved in its production—lyricists, choreographers, costume designers, and so on—were to travel to the featured sites in order to re-create "authentic" local settings for their Japanese audiences.

There is no record of *East Asian Bouquet* ever having been performed by either Takarazuka or Shōchiku. The closest equivalent to this revue was Takarazuka's *Children of East Asia* (*Tōa no kodomotachi*, 1943), a drama "dedicated to the juveniles of East Asian, especially the sons of Nippon who shoulder the future destiny of the East." The eighteen-scene revue was divided into three parts: Manchukuo, with an emphasis on the founding of the puppet state established in 1932; China, whose relationship with Japan was portrayed metaphorically as that between father and son; and the Southern Region, represented as a utopian garden whose feathered inhabitants happily chirped praises of Asian unity (N. Matsumoto 1943c).

East Asian Bouquet may have been a hypothetical revue, but it nonetheless accurately reflects the conception, dramaturgic organization, and production of wartime revues in general. The Revue's staff in fact often traveled to the countries and colonies represented on stage to gather firsthand culturally relevant material and ideas for their productions (Komatsu 1942:65; Miyatake 1942). Some wartime revues staged by Takarazuka were even written by army and navy playwrights who had access to classified military intelligence documenting daily life and social structures in areas occupied by Japan. Along with incorporating ethnographic data into their plays, the Takarazuka staff also wrote anthropological reports about the various cultural areas they visited, and these were published in script anthologies. In combining theater and ethnology as a "cultural weapon," they sought advice from various anthropological sources, including the very peoples who themselves were objectified on the revue stage. One theater critic, writing in 1943 about theatrical productions about and for export to the Southern Region, urged playwrights and directors to collaborate closely with anthropologists in order to create plausible representations of and for Asian and Pacific peoples (Endō 1943). But although Takarazuka playwrights and directors claimed to re-create culturally specific practices, they sometimes resorted to staging montage-like Pan-Asian spectacles, such as orchestrating Indonesian gamelan music and dances in plays set in Thailand (e.g., *Only One Ancestral Land* [*Tada hitotsu no sokoku*], 1943, as cited in N. Matsumoto 1943d).

Likewise, the revue *Saipan-Palau: Our South Seas*, composed by a Takarazuka playwright following his research trip to the Japanese-mandated islands, was described in a newspaper review as a "potpourri of the delicacies of South America, Mexico, Spain, and [North] America" (N. Matsumoto 1940). The reviewer was less disturbed by the cultural eclecticism of the spectacle than by the putative "mistake" the playwright made in musically representing native peoples who had neither dances nor tunes of their own. His assertion was, of course, erroneous and inconsistent with the well-documented ethnomusicological findings of Japanese colonialists and scholars active in the South Seas since the turn of this century, whose work was consulted by playwrights (Peattie 1988; Tsubouchi Hakase Kinen Engeki Hakubutsukan 1932:482). Moreover, a South Seas cultural exhibition, sponsored by the South Seas Bureau (Nan'yōchō)—basically the Japanese colonial government in the South Seas—was staged at the main theater complex in Takarazuka to augment what might be described as the ethnographic "infotainment" contained in the play (Hagiwara 1954:130). Such cultural exhibitions tended to be held in conjunction with revues set in areas of national interest to Imperial Japan, such as those created as part of the Greater East Asia Co-Prosperity Sphere series of plays.

Mongol (*Mongōru*, 1941), the first play in the series, was basically a love story in which was embedded Japanese colonial propaganda extolling Mongolia's natural resources and its entry into the Co-Prosperity Sphere. The country is referred to as the "land of dreams" (*yume no kuni*). Imperial dreams were the thread out of which many wartime revues were spun; Mongolia's dreamland status was achieved, two characters remind the audience, under Japanese guidance, whereby vast resources, such as coal and animal pelts, were being developed for export to North China and Japan (*Mongōru* 1941:60, 63–64). Japanese audiences were treated to actors dressed as Mongolians and to stage sets featuring the yurts inhabited by nomads. They could even learn a few key phrases in Mongolian that had been incorporated into the scripted dialogue in the *katakana* syllabary, such as *moroguchibaaina* (thank you) and *sainbaaina* (how are you).[27] Mongolian folk songs and dances were also performed throughout the eighteen-scene revue (*Mongōru* 1941).

Appearing with the *Mongol* script in the October 1941 anthology was a photojournalistic essay by the Takarazuka playwright, Utsu Hideo, detailing his fact-finding visit to Mongolia earlier that year. Utsu rhapsodizes about the natural beauty of the vast plains filled with abundant wildlife, but he seems equally enthusiastic about the modern factories dotting the landscape built by the Japanese for the production of butter and homespun. The rest of the article details the typical Mongolian diet of goat meat and fermented goat or horse milk—which, Utsu confesses, nauseated him—clothing, housing, festivals, folk dances, and various other aspects of material and ritual culture (Utsu 1941). Augmenting the colonial anthropology lesson of both the revue and the playwright's essay was an exhibition of photographs of Mongolia at the Takarazuka complex that continued through the play's one-month run.

European cultures and societies were also performed on the wartime Takarazuka stage. In the fall of 1941, for example, the Revue produced *New Flag* (*Atarashiki hata*), which glamorized the unification of Germany under the Third Reich. The play was described as the "staged performance" (*butaika*) of the information on Germany available in newspapers and magazines (Hasegawa Y. 1941:14). *New Flag* was published in a script anthology along with an article by the playwright, Hasegawa Yoshio, which supplied readers with background information on the relationship between Takarazuka and Germany; the geology and climate of Germany; German history, ethnic composition, agriculture, and industry; and a review of the consequences of post–World War I inflation—Hasegawa defines "inflation" for the readers—to which Hitler's rise is attributed (1941).

The revue and the Takarazuka complex as a whole may have functioned as a living archive, but on stage the concatenated fragments of cultural data often amounted to a fantastical vision of us-ness and (Japanese-inscribed) otherness. The Japanese audience was thereby able simultaneously to set itself apart from the rest of the world and to recuperate the rest of the world within its collective imagination.

CLAIMING "THE PEOPLE" THEATRICALLY

Revues, follies, and pageants have been deployed by various historical agents as "weapons" and not simply staged as fluffy, frivolous, and
fleshly entertainment. From the turn of this century in Europe, the
United States, and Japan, corporations—in collusion with the state, socialist labor organizers, and nationalists alike—utilized these theatrical forms to craft and claim both an audience ("the people") and a genealogy. What Linda Nochlin observes of the European pageant pertains
equally to its Japanese counterpart and the all-female revue theater:

> A combination of visual spectacle and dramatic performance,
> the pageant can weld together two seemingly disparate forces, the
> subject and object of dramatic metaphor. . . . For leaders of revolu-
> tionary movements, as well as for ideologues consciously or uncon-
> sciously intent on maintaining the status quo, the pageant was a
> potent weapon in forging a sense of communal identity for the
> hitherto inarticulate and unself-conscious lower classes. A pageant
> could function in the realm of participatory dramatic action . . .
> to forge a sense of contemporary purpose, self-identity and social
> cohesion out of a vivid recapitulation of historical fact heightened
> by symbolism.
>
> (Nochlin 1985:90, 91)[28]

State-sanctioned corporate theater programs in Japan, as in the
United States, were founded in part to counteract the growing popularity and effectiveness of leftist working-class theaters (Fukumoto
1942; Okamura 1942; Ōki 1942; Ōzasa 1993; Takagi Shin'ichi 1942;
Tsuchiya 1985:103; Tsubouchi Hakase Kinen Engeki Hakubutsukan
1932:395–98).[29] In both countries the increasingly visible proletarian
theaters were criticized harshly by rightists and nationalists with the
blessings of the state, which sought to appropriate the theater as a
supreme method of social engineering, since it was "the art, *par excellence*, of resolving the estrangement and conflict of social elements
into harmony" (Tsuchiya 1985:100, with 97, 104; see also Kitamura
1943; Miyazaki 1942; Ōyama 1941, 1943a, 1943b, 1943c; Ōzasa 1990,
1993; Sonoike 1933).

The effects that pageants and revues had on the performers were as
important as those they had on the audience, for the dramatic simpli-
fication and compression of events and issues made the performers
—who ranged from disgruntled farmers to striking factory workers

and even aspiring actors—conscious of the larger meaning of their actions and experiences, and cognizant of themselves as historical agents (Nochlin 1985:91; Tsubouchi 1921; Tsubouchi Hakase Kinen Engeki Hakubutsukan 1932:397). Japanese theater organizers of all stripes sought to form troupes of amateurs (*shirōto*) in their efforts both to claim "the people" and to instill in untutored women and men a sense of purpose, whether that be the embodiment of "Japanese spirit," the enactment of "correct" gender roles, or, until increasing militarization of the society made it impossible, the "empowerment of the proletariat" (Iizuka 1936:332–61; Kitamura 1943:43; Kobayashi 1961a:134–36; Sonoike 1933:2–6; Tagō 1941). Formally, the Revue was one such amateur outfit, and Takarasiennes have always been referred to as students and not as (professional) actors. Their amateur status constituted yet another "bridge" closing the gap between the stage and members of the audience; the Takarazuka students were cast and promoted as ordinary Japanese. As I discussed in chapter 2, Kobayashi was adamant in suppressing their extraordinary qualities.

The Japanese state acknowledged the social and political transformational power of drama and proposed several theater reform measures, including the centralization of theater groups in Japan and in the colonies. A film law enacted in 1939 set the precedent for a theater law formulated, but never formally legislated, two years later (Ōzasa 1993:243–72). This was not the first time that the state took the initiative to regulate theater performances. The Tokugawa Shogunate had strictly monitored both the form and content of Kabuki, beginning with a ban on female actors in 1629. At the turn of this century, the Meiji oligarchs may not have intervened directly, but they did pressure playwrights and directors to incorporate public morals into their dramas (Iizuka 1941:51). By the late 1930s and 1940s, however, the interference was much more calculated: the theater policies of Germany, Italy, Russia, and the United States were studied and adapted in an effort to claim the people through didactic entertainment that would catalyze the consolidation of a transcendent and unifying "citizens' culture" (*kokumin bunka*). Also, before and after the Axis Alliance, Japanese nationalists studied and were influenced by the Nazi use of theatrical forms to create a *Volk*, a national cultural body politic (see Gonda 1941:219; Niizeki 1940; Takagi Shin'ichi 1942). Theater, asserted one nationalist reformer, must become a "paragon of civic morality" (*kokumindōtoku to naru tehon*) that would turn audiences away from

Westernism (that is, individualism) and toward a collectivist New Japanism (Iizuka 1941:47, 50).

In an effort to "bring the theater to the people," Ōyama Isao and Iizuka Tomoichirō, both prominent theater historians and critics, inaugurated the Citizens' Theater Movement (*kokumin engeki undō*) in the mid-1930s as a component of "cultural administration" (*bunka gyōsei*).[30] They recognized the influential reach and wide appeal of theater as a manipulable artifact of everyday life (Fuwa 1941:2). "Citizens' Theater" was defined as "a theater in which the spiritual essence of the [Japanese] people is expressed and nurtured" (Iizuka 1941:45). The movement would facilitate the "advance of the Japanese race," a nationalist and imperialist agenda sanctioned by the military government. As the epitome of "wholesome entertainment," Citizens' Theater necessarily precluded dramas dealing with suicide, prostitution, and the grotesque, topics that were perceived to have deleterious psychological effects on popular audiences ("'Shinjū' no shibai kinshi" 1939; Terazawa 1943).

In his books and articles, many of which were published in the leading women's journals, Iizuka promoted a type of theater he called *shitsunaigeki*, or "indoor theater" (i.e., inside a room or a house). By "liberating performances from commercialism and specialized buildings" and by bringing the theater into the home or to the local community, this new approach could better "represent the lives of the people." Indoor theater, which could be staged in gardens, and in temple and shrine compounds as well, would "appropriate everyday talk as staged dialogues." By the same token, indoor theater actors should be not professionals but amateurs or "ordinary people"—family members and friends whose own furnishings and wardrobes would serve as props and costumes, and whose conversations would replace scripts (Iizuka 1922: 20, 24, 25).[31] Although Iizuka initially modeled his indoor theater plans after the American working-class-oriented Little or Community Theater Movement of the 1920s (Ōzasa 1986: 366–67), his interest in bringing the theater to the people eventually shifted, during the 1930s, from its basis in class struggle to an explicitly nationalist agenda.

Kobayashi, on the other hand, perceived the revue form as the ideal theatrical medium through which to impart the spirit of a new Japan. Unlike Iizuka, he advocated the construction of large "mass theaters" that could accommodate audiences of thousands and offer low-priced tickets (Kobayashi 1962:140–42, 194–95). Under Kobayashi's tutelage, Takarazuka directors were sent abroad to the United States and Europe beginning in the 1920s to study theatrical forms and stage techniques, which could then be incorporated into the Revue's own productions.

The definition and cultivation of a theatergoing audience as part of a general effort to mobilize people's wartime resolve preoccupied Kobayashi and the proponents of the Citizens' Theater Movement alike. Kobayashi believed that all of "the state's subjects" should work eight hours a day and spend four hours in the evening at rest and recreation. The Takarazuka Revue was promoted by him as "one of the most edifying forms of entertainment" and as a "basic life necessity" (1962:130). Audiences, he insisted, must comprise not individuals but entire households: just as the household was defined in the Civil Code as the smallest indivisible unit of society, so was it the smallest unit of spectatorship.[32] Writing in the daily *Osaka Mainichi Shinbun*, Kobayashi claimed that "what has been called entertainment for the masses has really been for males specifically. . . . Mass theater must cater to women as well as men. . . . A married couple should attend [the revue] together" (1935b). Promoted as "healthful family entertainment," Takarazuka was aimed at "the whole conjugal household (*katei*) over its constituent members (*kazoku*), the public (*kōkyō*) over the household, the masses (*taishū*)—and ultimately, the totality of the citizens (*kokumin*) of Japan—over the public" (Kobayashi 1962:130). Attending a Takarazuka performance was billed as tantamount to performing a patriotic act that affirmed the gender ideology encoded in the Meiji Civil Code. Appropriately, Kobayashi nicknamed the Tokyo Takarazuka theater the "palace of household entertainment" (*katei kyōraku no dendō*) (1962:125, 1935b).

Kobayashi often referred to the Takarazuka Revue as a "New Citizens' Theater" (*shinkokumingeki*), "new" in contrast to the valorization of "old" Kabuki by the proponents of the Citizens' Theater Movement. He derived this term from the expression "national theater" (*kokugeki*), coined by the eminent playwright and theater critic Tsubouchi Shōyō, who developed the concept during the "nation-minded" years of the Sino-Japanese War (1894–95). The war provided an impetus for efforts to consolidate cultural unity and fabricate a national identity based on symbols selectively drawn from Japanese history and non-Japanese institutions alike (Ōzasa 1986:104; Gluck 1985; Westney

1987). Tsubouchi was keen to reform the theater to better reflect contemporary sociopolitical realities as well as to symbolize Japan as a "civilized country" (*bunmeikoku*). In his 1904 book *Treatise on New Musical Drama* (*Shingakugekiron*), Tsubouchi writes:

> although imperial Japan is now equal in status to other civilized countries, we are not yet a civilized country, the hallmark of which is a national or state theater (*kokugeki*). . . . [Western] countries are alarmed by the Yellow Peril, and here in Japan, unwholesome (*fukenzen*) socialism is making inroads. . . . We must display Japanese ideals and refinements to the West, and we must transmit throughout all classes in Japan—upper, middle, and lower—an appreciation of the performing arts.
>
> (Tsubouchi, quoted in Ōzasa 1985:74)

Tsubouchi advocated the integration of Japanese and European musical idioms toward the creation of a new form of musical drama, a proposal eventually reformulated by Kobayashi and promoted as a New Citizens' Theater.

Not just theatrical forms but audiences too were at issue in the war years. Writing in 1942, theater critic Aoki Ryōichi observed that although much attention had been paid to the theoretical and practical sides of wartime theatrical developments, a dearth of information existed on audiences. In referring to them Aoki used the terms *kankyaku* (viewing clients) and *kyōjusha* (recipients) interchangeably, reflecting his position that, ideally, the individual members of an audience should exercise no agency, and that collectively they should be passive recipients of the singular, dominant text—the official story—of a play (Aoki R. 1942).

A year later, in 1943, Takaoka Nobuyuki published a book on Citizens' Theater that included a chapter on audiences—their constitution, organization, psychology—and the conditions of theatergoing. Takaoka was keen to mobilize the people through a theatergoers' association managed by a nationwide network of large-scale theaters seating thousands, which, like Kobayashi, he regarded as more didactically effective than smaller theaters. Although the state recognized the value of theater as a technology of imperialism, Takaoka argued that it was imperative to identify in detail, analyze, and consolidate theater audiences if the Citizens' Theater Movement was to succeed. According to Takaoka, spectatorship was a key disciplinary site where the pleasure (*iraku*), education (*kyōyō*), and assimilation (*dōka*) of an audience could be achieved through etiquette (*girei*), social inter-course (*shakō*), and friendship (*shinwa*) (1943:194). These principles or values were necessary in order to prevent the theater experience from degenerating into a hedonistic event, "like a garden party or a visit to a brothel" (195). Takaoka conjured up the image of the Western fe-male spectator—spectators were generically cast as females in need of discipline—for whom the theater was an extension of the beauty salon, providing an opportunity for conspicuous display. The closest Western equivalents of the beauty salon in Japan were, Takaoka de-clared, the Kabuki theater and the all-female revue, the latter of which he likened to a department store, with its displays of exotic miscellanea.

Changes in the composition of theater audiences informed Ta-kaoka's prescriptions for theatergoers in wartime Japan. In the emer-gency climate, the revue theater was one of the few forms of mass entertainment available, and increasingly men and women of the working class, military personnel, and whole households—"the people"—filled auditoriums to capacity (Takaoka N. 1943:196, 200–201; Hijikata 1944). One critic observed that theater was no longer the domain of the leisured upper classes (Hijikata 1944). Theater audi-ences came to represent a broader spectrum of Japanese society in large part owing to the state's investment in the mass organization of recreation and entertainment. For Takaoka the provision of organized pleasure and education were strategies of, in his words, assimilation (*dōka*). The cultivated values of decorum, sociality, and friendship that characterized "traditional" and more elite audiences were redefined by Takaoka as constituting both the ideal behavioral parameters and the interpersonal consequences of Citizens' Theater spectatorship (Takaoka N. 1943:194, 196, 200–201, 208). He and his contemporaries acknowledged the positive influence of theater on worker produc-tivity: "it is relaxing and reduces stress—provided one does not be-come addicted to entertainment" (207).

Similarly, in an article on theatergoing and productivity, the head of International Steamship (Kokusai Kisen) further insisted that the theater experience should be improved and controlled to ensure that the didactic content of wartime productions was conveyed in per-formance. Decorum and sociality figured strongly in his suggestions: "Children should be kept from crying and people should be dis-couraged from wearing hats or interfering with the audience in other ways so as to maintain an upbeat mood in the audience throughout a performance. Theatergoers should be provided with a good meal during intermission, and music should be played as they eat in an effort to raise their spirits" (Sumida 1944).

Like audiences, theater directors were singled out for attention. To a certain extent, the Citizens' Theater Movement represented a viable but informal theater law, one that was to be implemented "spontaneously" and "voluntarily" by commercial theaters such as the Takarazuka Revue. Theater directors were required by the Ministry of Education to pass an examination to qualify for their profession. It was widely recognized that this prerequisite was a form of thought control (*shisō tōsei*); leftist or Westernized personnel were not welcome to exercise influence in the New Japan. Similarly, in a move designed to sever the ties between theater performances and uncensored theater criticism, the five main drama journals remaining after an earlier purge were consolidated in 1940 under one publisher and reissued under two titles over which the powerful Cabinet Information Bureau (Naikaku chokuzoku jōhōkyoku) exerted complete editorial control (Toita 1956 [1950]:274–75).[33] These developments were matched by the state's admonitions to Japanize mass entertainment.

JAPANIZING THE THEATER

The Japanization of mass entertainment in Japan corresponded to the state's Co-Prosperity Sphere agenda for Asia and the Pacific ("Asu no shōjo kageki" 1940; Toita 1956 [1950]:243). *Only One Ancestral Land*, for example, a revisionist allegory of the 1940 Thai offensive on Cambodia and Laos, illustrated the emphasis on Pan-Asian linkages, including the specious claim that Japanese and Thai were "blood relatives" who, moreover, shared a common Buddhist heritage (Reynolds 1991:94).[34]

The Japanization of the theater also entailed, from September 1940 through April 1944, the government-mandated substitution of Japanese equivalents for foreign loanwords (especially English). Nevertheless, English was retained as a lingua franca in many territories under Japanese control—pending the inhabitants' mastery of Japanese—and as an important propaganda tool, in the form of radio broadcasts and colonial newspapers. In Japan, however, *rebyū* (revue) and *opera* (opera) were replaced with *kageki* and *ongakugeki*, and

Figure 15.   *Peking* finale. The finale of this 1942 production featured the "Dance of the Five-Color Flag," which symbolized the unity of north and central China under Japan. From Takarazuka Kagekidan (1943:15).

myujikaru komedei (musical comedy) with *kikageki*.[35] New categories of dramatic production were created to promote a paternalistic ethos of emergency-mindedness, such as "social welfare dance" (*kōsei buyō*); "citizens' songs" (*kokumin kashō*); "mirror of women's morality" (*fudō no kagami*); "culture dramas" (*bunka kageki*); and "onward, Japanese products" (*yuke Nipponhin*) (Hashimoto 1993:51; Hagiwara 1954: 240–43).[36]

Advance, Naval Ensign! (*Susume kaigunhata*), staged in 1941 with the support of the Navy Office, was "intended to make the public conscious of the importance of submarines in the defense of the Island Empire." The play, one of the several multimedia "cinema-dramas" (*kinodorama*) produced at this time, included footage from a French motion picture to show "how a submarine submerges and rises" (N. Matsumoto 1941b; "Takarazuka eiga no senku" 1938). Other plays, such as *Made in Japan* and *Ears, Eyes, and Mouths* (*Mimi to me to kuchi to*, 1941), included songs that emphasized, respectively, the virtues of recycling everything from old watches to cigarette butts ("to ensure the production of superior airplanes") and the necessity of antiespionage precautions in everyday living ("for spies are lurking everywhere, in trains, buses, coffee shops, barber shops, public baths, and movie theaters") (*Sekai no ichiba* 1941:77; *Mimi to me to kuchi to* 1941:26). The didactic purpose of the latter revue was underscored by an emcee who, from the silver bridge, explained the dominant, unequivocal meaning of the play, contextualized the episodes, and delivered self-evident summaries for the audience.

The concept of Japanization also included the strategic effect that the Takarazuka Revue, for one, was to have on peoples subjected to some form of Japanese domination or direct colonial rule. Radio broadcasts of some Takarazuka performances were transmitted to Mongolia, China, Thailand, India, and Burma with the aim of "introducing Japanese theater culture to the peoples living within the area of the Co-Prosperity Sphere." Multiple ironies framed the transmission of the play *Peking* (*Pekin*, 1942) to Mongolia and China on June 5, 1942 (figure 15). Chinese listeners were treated to a Japanese musical representation of Beijing and its apparently bilingual inhabitants, who spoke and sang in Japanese and Mandarin (rendered in the Japanese syllabary) about their "love" (*ai*) for Japan and the benefits of colonial rule, which included "progress and prosperity" (Hagiwara 1954:141).

Another component of the Revue's Japanization policy involved having actual "natives" in the audience vouch for the cultural authenticity of plays set in their respective countries. After watching *Peking* at the main Takarazuka theater, the Chinese ambassador to Japan remarked, "*Peking* is superb. It weaves together skillfully the establishment of the Greater East Asia Co-Prosperity Sphere and the awakening of Asian peoples. For us Chinese, what really clinches the play is the Pan-Asian unity of the dancing and acting techniques. Whether staged in Hong Kong, Nanking, or wherever Asian peoples live, *Peking* will generate appreciative applause" (quoted in Takarazuka Kagekidan 1943:37). Likewise, the (Thai) director of the Thai Monopoly Bureau, who attended *Return to the East*, discussed below, declared publicly that "the stage sets, acting style, and choreography were redolent with the aura of Thai culture . . . I felt as though I had actually returned to my country" (quoted in Takarazuka Kagekidan 1943:37). In fact, the play itself returned to the East, staged as it was in Thailand, India, and other Asian countries (Saburi 1942a:70).

ORIENTALISM: MADE IN JAPAN

The symbolically titled revue *Return to the East* (*Higashi e kaeru*, 1942) was the third drama in the Greater East Asia Co-Prosperity Sphere series. The series reflected, in part, Kobayashi's efforts as minister of commerce and industry in the period 1940–41 to consolidate the newly conceived Co-Prosperity Sphere.[37] Based on a novel by a Thai official, *Return to the East* promoted a vision of a Japan-centered New World Order.[38]

The fifteen-scene play focused on the short life of Rambha, the beautiful daughter of the deposed maharaja of Misapur.[39] Concerned for his infant daughter's safety, the maharaja had entrusted her upbringing to his best friend, the Thai ambassador to France, and his wife; the girl, unaware of her royal lineage, was educated at an elite French school. (The play opens with a formal reception at the school.) When she comes of age, the ambassador recounts her biography and urges her to return to the East and devote her life to restoring her late father's kingdom in Misapur. She travels to Japan, Thailand, and India in order to learn more about her ancestral domain and soon finalizes plans to transform Misapur into "a strong country like Japan" (*Higashi e kaeru* 1942:51).

While still a student in France, Rambha had fallen in love with Paul Roy, like her an "Oriental" (*tōyōjin*) but unlike her raised in a Bombay orphanage. Paul was later adopted by a wealthy Indian who moved to France where the boy was educated. The two teenagers shared a sense of alienation from their Asian roots and bemoaned the fact that they knew little about "the East." When she is bitten by a poisonous snake in Thailand, Paul rushes to her side to spur her recovery. Rambha has already decided to choose her country over Paul, but just as she is about to break her decision to him, the two discover that they are siblings. Rambha, recovered and relieved, journeys to Misapur, whose residents are being ravaged by a cholera epidemic, and, as planned, manages to win the heart of the current maharaja, Ravana, son of the usurper (figure 16). She poisons the cruel Ravana and then commits suicide by swallowing poisoned tea. Paul ascends the throne as Bhumindra, the rightful maharaja of the now liberated Misapur (*Higashi e kaeru* 1942:40–68).

The intertwined themes of Western colonialism, patriotism, duty, imperialism, sibling incest, murder, and suicide form an allegory of

Figure 16.   Royal Court of Misapur in *Return to the East*. The cruel Ravana and Rambha. From Takarazuka Kagekidan (1943:17).

Pan-Asian history and co-prosperity shared by Japan, Thailand, and India.[40] The relationship between Rambha and Paul/Bhumindra is a romanticized reading of the "family" relationship between Asia and Japan. And like Japan, both Paul and Rambha are cultural hybrids. Rambha signifies a feminized Orient whose duty is to clear the way of obstacles (i.e., Western imperialists and local anglophiles) in preparation for the emergence of a Pan-Asian New Order spearheaded by Japan. Like Paul and Rambha, Japan was orphaned by the West and alienated from its Eastern roots. The nation, like Paul/Bhumindra, was able to regain its spiritual identity and regional preeminence through the extreme sacrifices made by non-Japanese Asians who were part of the paternalistic, imperial family system. In this respect, *Return to the East* shares key motifs with the folktale "Peach Boy" noted earlier. The review published in the Japanese press recommended that *Return to the East* be presented throughout Asia, which it was, as well as in Germany and Italy, where the Takarazuka Revue toured in 1938 and 1939 (N. Matsumoto 1942).

IDENTITY AND ASSIMILATION

Let us review the relationship between Japanese national cultural identity and the colonial doctrine of assimilation. As discussed earlier in this chapter, the integrity and stability of this identity are premised on a protean ability to assimilate difference and to absorb perceived otherness. The wartime state also recognized that while the protean character of the Japanese nation guaranteed its resilience, the same character also had the potential to compromise the nation's purity. For if Japanese could masquerade as Chinese, Mongolians, and Southeast Asians, then the reverse was also possible: "others"—who were, after all, subjected to Japanization—could pass as Japanese. A similar anxiety was provoked by the Takarazuka *otokoyaku* and other masculine females, as we saw in chapter 2. Whereas Kabuki *onnagata* were celebrated as the essence of femininity, the *otokoyaku* was not to become too successful or convincing in her appropriation and performance of "male" gender. Both cross-dressing and cross-ethnicking are unequal and asymmetrical operations. Passing as Japanese is expected of Chinese and Korean residents of Japan today, who are strongly encouraged by the state to adopt "Japanese-style names" when applying to be naturalized as citizens. But despite an official policy of Japanization, successful passing was looked on by the xenophobic military state in the late 1930s and early 1940s as a serious threat to national cultural integrity.

This dilemma was highlighted in the Takarazuka revue *Ears, Eyes, and Mouths*, a play categorized as an "antiespionage primer" (*bōchō tokuhon*). In one vignette, titled "Guarding each word is the most immediate national defense," a young boy is approached by a friendly man, identified as a "Japanese uncle" (*nihon no ojisan*), who is interested in extracting information from him. Later, when the "uncle" is arrested for espionage, a police officer warns the boy that enemy spies often masquerade as Japanese (*Nipponjin ni misekake[ru]*). The allegedly Chinese ethnicity of the spy is never explicitly identified; rather, the character utters Chinese expressions and also English loanwords, the everyday use of which among Japanese offstage had been censured since 1940 (*Mimi to me to kuchi to* 1941:29–32).[41]

Some forms of previously assimilated difference and otherness were newly coded as pathogenic in the rhetorical climate of war, and a number of wartime revues accordingly alluded to things Anglo-

American in terms of dangerous "germs" (*baikin*). These germs had to be destroyed before they irrevocably weakened individual Japanese and the "national body" (*kokutai*) alike. The lead song in the "comic opera" *The Battle Is Also Here* (*Arasoi wa koko ni mo*, 1943), for example, dwelled on the need to eradicate "the much-dreaded germs called Anglo-Saxon ideologies" from within one's body and mind (N. Matsumoto 1943a; *Arasoi wa koko ni mo* 1943:18). The preface to the script makes it clear that the play is directed particularly toward "all females" (*subete no josei*), who, exempted from military service, were the main target of the state's "spiritual mobilization" campaign (*Arasoi wa koko ni mo* 1943:18):[42]

>   Attack and destroy the germs
>   The germs in our heart-minds
>   Get rid of them now
>   Quick, quick expel them
>   Attack and destroy the germs
>   The Anglo-American[isms] in our heart-minds[.]
>   (*Arasoi wa koko ni mo* 1943:19)

Expunging "degenerate and corrupt" Western artifacts and ideas, especially individualism, from everyday life was part of the state's mass surveillance campaign to search, locate, and destroy the enemy within from within. It was a battle every bit as strategically crucial as those fought with guns, a battle in which the ambivalence and ambiguity of national cultural identity was, temporarily, turned into a "neat division" (Bauman 1991:174). It was also a battle in which the erotic allure of the Revue was invested with sadomasochistic nuances, for the expulsion of Chinese-isms and Anglo-Americanisms simultaneously implied an identification with and a repudiation of the historical and contemporary "other" within.[43] The inversion of imperial expansion is imperial implosion, whereby political power and eroticized domination are compressed and interiorized. As I have emphasized, the theatrical space of Takarazuka was not an inert area: rather, it interacted with social and psychological space, creating a site where ambiguous gender and protean ethnicity were linked to, and at times unlinked from, the ambivalent status of Japan as an anticolonial colonizer.

Even as the state embarked on an imperialist campaign to Japanize Asia, Kobayashi promoted the Takarazuka Revue as epitomizing the nationalist slogan, "Japanese spirit, Western skills" (*wakon yōsai*) (cf. Kobayashi 1962:130–33). The actors, selectively recruited for their "naturally long legs" and "straight, white teeth," were lauded as fulfilling the Western ideal of physical beauty better than their Euro-American counterparts (Hata 1948:133–34). Here too we see the ambivalent appropriation of both female bodies and "the West" as necessary components of modernity and national identity formation. The evocation of the West through the female figure was less about Euro-American societies than about social transformations in Japan since the turn of this century. The West and its locations in Japan, such as the revue theater, were targeted by competing parties as sites for animated cultural and political critique (cf. Chen 1992:688). Kobayashi sought to use the stage as a showcase not just for the ideal man but for his version of the New Woman: namely, a female who was a cultural hybrid though of "pure" Japanese and not "mixed" ancestry ("blood"), who looked Euro-American from the outside but was filled with the ineffable Japanese spirit and symbolized the New Japan.[44] However, as I argued earlier, the Revue and its actors were never really an unambiguous and stable symbol of the New Japan.[45]

Applied to the Takarasiennes, the slogan "Japanese spirit, Western skills" signified not a clear-cut division but a doubling—an epistemological condition that makes it possible to be in at least two places or mental spaces or bodies at once (Bhabha 1990:187). Takarasiennes were recruited for their allegedly atypical bodies and displayed as homegrown cultural hybrids—they embodied difference, but their Japanese ancestry was not compromised by "foreign" blood. Their outward appearance may have scrambled the received markers of gender and ethnicity, but spiritually and genetically, according to Kobayashi, they retained the essential dichotomy that distinguished "us" from "them." In this sense, the actors could also be described as body doubles, or bodies that double as their other(s).

Writing in 1942, culture critic Saburi Yuzuru asserted that Japan constituted a unique, composite culture enhanced by the assimilation and absorption (*kyūshū*) of foreign (*gairai*) cultural products and practices. Saburi highlighted the so-called Nagasaki "Maria Kannon" of the sixteenth and seventeenth centuries as an example of cultural hybridity. A fusion of both the Asian Kannon (Bodhisattva of Mercy) and the Catholic Madonna, the "Maria Kannon" represented an aesthetics of exoticism. Similarly, he maintained, the cultural exchanges (*bunka kō-*

ryū) occasioned by the Co-Prosperity Sphere agenda contributed to the "wholesome exoticism" and uniqueness of Japanese culture. I mention his views specifically because they were shared by Kobayashi as well. For Saburi, the montage-like Revue was the ideal means of communicating the glory of a unique Japan and dreams of empire to the Japanese people (Saburi 1942b). The Takarazuka Revue and its hybrid actors, like Japanese culture in general, possessed, in Saburi's words, the captivating charm of "wholesome exoticism" (*kenzennaru ekizoteizumu* [*sic*]) (25). But when necessary, that exotic self could be cleansed by uprooting the suddenly pathogenic forms of internalized otherness, whatever their provenance (cf. Dower 1986:203–33).

MON PARIS, MON JAPON

In 1987 Takarazuka celebrated the sixtieth anniversary of *Mon Paris* with a production titled *The Revuescope*. A slide show summarizing Takarazuka's history was shown followed by "Mon Paris Express 60," a segment featuring the trademark train dance. But, significantly, Asia was nowhere to be found: *The Revuescope* was constructed as a montage of scenes from New York, Vienna, and Rio de Janeiro (*Za Rebyūsukōpu* 1987:43–50).

The disappeared Asia resurfaced in 1990 and again in 1994 in the revues *The Modern* (*Za Modan*) and *Jump Orient!;* like their predecessor, *The Revuescope*, they were pastisches of exotic otherness. *The Modern* blended together art deco interiors, tropical birds, chandeliers, Josephine Baker, Maurice Chevalier, and "golddiggers." *Jump Orient!,* introduced in chapter 1, offered the audience a whirlwind tour through Babylonia, Ming China, present-day Hong Kong, and opulent palaces elsewhere in Asia where "Mandarin festivals" and "Garuda dances" are staged. Japan and the Japanese are all but absent. Included among the many scenes in *The Modern* that celebrated different modes of modernity, such as "Tropical Modern," was a particularly telling sequence titled "Exotic Modern," which featured an "Oriental lady" in 1920s Paris who is scrutinized by Westerners. As in *Mon Paris,* Japan is positioned within European modernity; but in a doubly reflexive, orientalist moment, "Europeans" evaluated the "customs of modern Japan" symbolized by an "Oriental lady." The accompanying song mused about strange worlds and unrequited love (*Za Modan* 1990:47–53).

Figure 17.   Europeans and Samoans in *Papalagi*. A *papalagi* (European) couple in striped outfits dancing with Samoans in grass skirts. From *Paparagi* (1993:7).

By contrast, in the 1993 revue *Papalagi* (*Paparagi*), Japan is absent and the critical gaze has shifted hemispheres. *Papalagi* is the Samoan term for foreigner (Westerner), and the revue constituted a sustained examination of "Europeans" through the eyes of "Samoans." Colonizer and colonized alike are performed by the Japanese actors (figure 17). The white-skinned *papalagi* become accustomed to life on the sunny island, which contrasts with their sunless homeland, and opt to stay. A gathering of Polynesian peoples fuels the high-octane finale (*Paparagi* 1993:66–75). Whereas European colonialism is an almost overdetermined subtext of *Papalagi*, Japanese colonialism—both its history and postwar reincarnation as tourism and trade—is unaddressed and invisible. One need only recall *Saipan-Palau: Our South Seas* (1940) and the South Seas Dance performed by Japanese soldiers in Burma in 1943 to revive the dormant irony of *Papalagi*. Collectively, these postwar revues manage to circumvent history and diffuse imperialist agency in alluding to the strategic ambivalence of Japan as an anticolonial colonizer.

During the wartime period, a Japanese actor (or soldier) embodying a Thai, Indian, South Sea islander, Malay, or Mongolian simultaneously represented both the utopian and the dystopian politics of Pan-Asianism. The utopian idea involved unity in diversity; the dystopian idea, the refracted, hierarchical relationship between Japanese and non-Japanese. Japanese soldiers caricaturing South Sea islanders, Asian peoples subjected to Japanization, and Revue actors performing gendered, ethnic characters were all participants in the dramatic process of body montage or body doubling. Aroused in these oscillating roles—colonizer and colonized, man and woman, Japanese and non-Japanese—was the erotics of the exotic, or what might be called the libidinal economy of imperialism.[46] Of course forms of entertainment, together with the erotic dimensions of the colonial encounter, were visibly central concerns of the Japanese state, which attempted to manipulate scopophilia, or pleasurable viewing, as both a powerful trope and a tool of imperialism. But in a manner homologous to the antipodal operations of Japanese orientalism, the ambiguous gender and ethnic symbology of the Takarazuka Revue rendered that spectacular theater simultaneously as the representation of New Japan and as the antithesis of a pure Japan. The montage-like Takarazuka Revue, with its allegorical concatenations of meaning and oscillations between text and subtext, both epitomized and extended a dominant Japanese national cultural identity that was premised, ambivalently, on a protean ability to assimilate difference and absorb otherness. Although these tendencies were especially tangible during the wartime period, their reverberations are perceptible today in the Revue's trademark spectacles of cultural difference.

Mobilized by the wartime state as a technology of imperialism, the revue theater helped bridge the gap between perceptions of colonialized others and actual colonial encounters; it was one way of linking imperialist fantasies and colonial realities. Takarazuka thus serves as a type of archive—a veritable "human relations area file"—that, along with census reports, maps, photographs, ethnographies, statistics, and newsreels, continues to create and naturalize a pleasurable vision of other worlds and old world orders. The difference represented and embodied by the Takarasiennes is the Revue's key attraction, an attraction that has served diverse and often contradictory ends simultaneously. At the very least, wartime revues invited a vicarious, fantastical experience of foreign travel and exotic romance, while at the same time sounding a call to cultural arms and the shared work of empire. Today, that particular call may be muted; but the eroticized allure of transgression and ambivalence, whether sexual, ethnic, or cultural, continues to invite dreams of what was and could be.

4

Fan Pathology

The cartoon: A young woman, a Takarazuka fan, lies in bed, crying. Her worried mother, wearing a kimono, stands next to her, and a mustached doctor looks on. A heart-shaped thought-bubble above the bed contains the image of an angelic *musumeyaku* on the silver bridge. The fan reaches out to touch her idol's shoe.

Mother: Your fever is really high. Let the doctor examine you.

Daughter: No! I'm feverish because yesterday I touched the Waltz Princess![1]

"Takarazuka manga" 1935:59

The cartoon: A Takarazuka finale. A young couple is sitting in the audience; the woman is clapping wildly. Her boyfriend mutters: "There she goes again. I wish she were even half that excited with me."

"Takarazuka manga" 1935:62

FANDOM

The discourse of fandom and its perceived pathology has a long history in Japan, and in this century it has emerged most notably in public debates about the relationship between sexuality and modernity. I shall trace the jagged contours of fandom in Japan since the 1910s, when the loanword "fan" (*fuan*) entered popular parlance. Others have written about Kabuki devotees in the Edo period (Matsudaira 1984; Raz 1983); but female fans in particular were a prominent site for and target of social criticism in the early twentieth century.

We have already seen how the return of females to the public stage prompted several contradictory but overlapping arguments about gender and sexuality whose core themes included the masculinizing influence of the all-female revue on Japanese girls and women, on the one hand, and the national vigor represented by the all-female revue on the other. We shall now consider the conditions and patterns of spectatorship that provoked such heated debate. When useful and relevant, I shall draw connections between the Japanese and Euro-American analyses and theories of pathologies of fandom for the purposes of comparison—many Japanese writers themselves, past and present, have done the same.[2]

The operations of fandom have been described by John Fiske in terms of the semiotic productivity of fans, whereby new meanings, knowledges, texts, and identities are produced, accumulated, and circulated among fans as a form of popular cultural capital (see Fiske 1989, 1992). To paraphrase Henry Jenkins, revue fans are consumers who also produce, readers who also write, and spectators who also perform (Jenkins 1992a:208). I shall return to these observations in the next chapter, where I discuss fan letters and magazines, but the semiotic productivity of fandom is not limited to closed communities of fans. The history of the Takarazuka Revue has been marked by a constant struggle between competing parties of fans, Revue administrators, state ideologues, and social critics. Whereas the Revue has attempted to contain, neutralize, and incorporate the desires of fans, fans have attempted to release, recontextualize, and "excorporate" the Revue's many registers of symbolic and allegorical meaning (Fiske 1992:47).

DISCIPLINING AUDIENCES

In 1916, two years after Takarazuka's inaugural stage show, an article was published in *Fujin Zasshi* (*Women's Magazine*) on theater etiquette for women. The author, Matsumoto Haruko, resurrects the theater as a legitimate social space for women but decries the rude behavior of female theatergoers, a theme echoed over the next several decades by social critics, some of whose commentaries we examined in the previous chapter. While lauding theater attendance as an efficacious way for Japanese women "to expand their interests, soften their emotions, and cultivate character," Matsumoto sharply criticizes these women for their "shameful manners":

> Today, the most obvious bad habit of female theatergoers is how often they leave their seats during a performance. To be sure, they may be leaving to take care of an urgent condition; nevertheless, they block everyone's view when they get up and walk brazenly across the stage. This is extremely rude both to the actors, who are deeply involved in the performance, and to the director. . . . When Westerners cross in front of someone they always excuse themselves . . . ;

Japanese women never utter a word of apology. . . . Just because
someone has bought a ticket does not mean that she has a right
to do whatever strikes her fancy. The theater is a society in its own
right whose social order cannot be maintained unless members of
the audience practice self-respect and show some concern for others.
(Matsumoto H. 1916:131, 133)

Like many of her contemporaries, Matsumoto regarded the theater as both a microcosm of society and an arena for representing the
"civilizing process" and propagating social norms, concepts that were
further developed thirty years later by proponents of the Citizens'
Theater Movement. She nonetheless complains that theater's normalizing potential is lost on Japanese women, who have no peers in
rudeness and inconsiderate behavior.

As soon as the curtain closes, several hundred women dash into
the hall and head for the bathroom; the sight of women fighting to
get in line is a far from pretty scene. Western women never use toilets
outside their homes, and, if necessary, will refrain from urinating for
half and even an entire day. But Japanese women are overly attached
to the bathroom; some rush just to wash their hands and dab on
perfume. . . . Most women leave the theater before the performance
is over even if there is no reason to hurry—they save five or ten
minutes at most. This is thoughtless behavior. In rushing out, they
often leave behind their personal belongings or injure themselves. . . .
Some women go to the theater just to show off to others; they are
the types who grow restless during the performance and spend their
time gawking at other women's kimonos.

(132)

Matsumoto contrasts Japanese women unfavorably to their Western counterparts with regard to theater protocol and bathroom practices. Of course, the "Western women" invoked do not really exist but
rather constitute a fictitious foil—a local invention—against which
Japanese women's poor spectatorship is measured and criticized.[3]
"The West" in general appears again and again in Japanese theater
criticism of the early twentieth century, invoking not particular countries and cultural areas but rather a metaphor for both desirable and
undesirable social precedents and cultural transformations in Japan
(cf. Takaoka N. 1943). Unlike Matsumoto, other social critics reacted
negatively to what they interpreted as the "masculinizing" effect of
Western institutions on Japanese women (e.g., Tachibana 1890). And

as we read in chapter 2, one sexologist claimed in a newspaper interview that Japanese women's recent interest in assuming a masculine guise was fostered and reinforced by the revue theater and foreign films (Hori Kentarō, quoted in "Dansō hi ari" 1935). Whereas Matsumoto perceived Japanese women to be unfeminine theater spectators compared to those in the West, some of her contemporaries believed that the Western-style theater compromised the traditional femininity of Japanese women. These diametrically opposed opinions characterized the dynamics of the larger debate in which they were cast: namely, the controversy about gendered social spaces that accompanied the formal return of females to the public stage. Although Matsumoto did not single out a particular type of theater, her critique of female spectatorship was echoed in the rash of satirical reporting a few years later on zealous fans of the all-female revues.

FANNING DESIRE

The cross-dressed Takarasiennes clinched the popular appeal of the avant-garde Revue among a very broad, multigenerational, mixed-sex audience in the first half of this century. Since the 1950s and especially today, in large part due to competing forms of mass entertainment, the Takarazuka Revue has attracted a much more specialized audience—the majority now are adult women, married and in their thirties or older. But even in the 1930s not a few revue reporters observed that "the majority of Revue fans range in age from forty to fifty years of age, and include widows and affluent married women" (Haruno 1936:242). This information about the Revue's audience calls into question the prevailing but unsubstantiated notion that the all-female revue from the start has appealed exclusively to young, unmarried women, and especially to teenage girls.

Social critics regarded young women and teenage girls as the most visible and problematic of theater audiences. They were categorized under the rubric *shōjo*, which, as discussed in chapter 2, was the term for girls and women between puberty and marriage. In my view, the novel spectacle of the players of men's roles and not actual fan practices has shaped the popular (and mistaken) perception that the all-female revue is attractive to *shōjo* exclusively. The benign rationale for this "fact" was that the all-female revue theater provided a safe outlet for the budding passions of teenage girls and young women until they were older and their sexual desires had matured and shifted "naturally" to anatomically correct men. This rationale has persisted into the postwar period among writers sympathetic to the Revue. Obviously, it was and remains more difficult for critics who take for granted both heterosexuality and the "natural" alignment of sex, gender, and sexuality to even conceive that, much less explain why, adult—and especially married—females should be attracted to the *otokoyaku*. Their narrow, ideological assumptions about sexuality also preclude recognition of the "subversive" erotic potential of the *musumeyaku* and the female (often feminine) fans attracted to them.[4]

Married women themselves have been more forthcoming about their erotic and sexual desires. A fan provides the gist of one type of explanation I have heard repeated over the past decade from married and unmarried fans alike: "Japanese men are boring, so of course women love Takarazuka. The husbands work so hard that they have no time for their wives, and Takarazuka is a place for wives to go that doesn't threaten their husbands. At Takarazuka, women can express the emotion they can't show their coldhearted husbands. Takarazuka never disappoints them" (quoted in Sischy 1992:93–94).

This particular rationale is typical in collapsing—whether consciously or unconsciously—several different, even contradictory statements: a critique of the "company as family" model of Japanese capitalist enterprises; a critical assessment of marriage as an institution and a relationship; a subscription to the notion that sex and sexual attraction are heterosexual by definition; and a recognition, albeit inchoate and undeveloped, of the unstable relationship of sex, gender, and erotic desire, and, concomitantly, the flexibility of one's own sexual affinities.

MISS DANDIES

A digression at this juncture on the simultaneous expression of sexual rigidity and sexual plasticity may provide additional insights into Japanese erotic practices. Capitalizing on (hetero)sexual ennui are several clubs for women staffed by "Miss Dandies," or female cross-dressers. Some friends and I visited one such club, Kikoshi (Young Noble), in August 1987, as a fitting cap to that evening's Takarazuka revue, *Me and My Girl*.[5] Kikoshi, now defunct, was a basement bar located in Roppongi, a mecca of discos and nightclubs surrounding the blocky and grim Self-Defense Force Headquarters, the Japanese equivalent of the Pentagon.

Not knowing quite what to expect, our party was taken aback by the sight of the closely cropped businessman who opened the heavy door, and thought we had landed at one of the ubiquitous bars for "salary men" (*sarariiman*, or male white-collar workers). As it turned out, the "salary man" was the club's manager and one of the several Kikoshi hosts, all wearing suits and ties. The manager declared that knotting a tie made her feel that she was really at work. The few (female) guests present were all stereotypically feminine, and appeared even frillier in contrast to the suited hosts and Kikoshi's dark, wood-paneled, masculine ambiance. As we munched on peanuts washed down with beer—for which we were charged a small fortune—we learned from our attentive hosts not only that they were Takarazuka fans, but that Takarasiennes had been regular guests at the club until recently, when, in a throwback to its wartime policy, the Revue imposed strict guidelines regulating the offstage activities of the "students." The Revue's perennial fear of behavior that would compromise its ethos of chaste, wholesome entertainment erupted anew, and Takarasiennes were reminded that their primary loyalty was to the company, which they were to serve in good faith.

New Marilyn is another Miss Dandy club located in Kabukichō, Tokyo's infamous gay district. As in the case of Kikoshi, the club's regular customers include off-duty nightclub workers, students, housewives, and OLs or "office ladies" (*ofuisu redei*), as female clerks are called, mostly in their twenties and thirties. The hosts, some of whom apparently receive injections of androgens, are basically offstage *otokoyaku* who live their daily lives as men. Echoing the Takarazuka fan cited earlier, one New Marilyn dandy, with the professional name of "True Lavender" (Mamurasaki), explained why the club is successful: "Many of our customers crave a kind of attention that actual males rarely provide. . . . We look and act like men, but we are always kind and gentle. We understand what women really want" (Jun'ichi Mamurasaki, quoted in Haworth 1995). A customer confirmed this explanation, admitting, "I can talk to them about anything because they are females underneath, yet I can flirt with them because they are also men" (quoted in Haworth 1995).

The fluid negotiation of the disjunction between sex and gender here recalls the politics of androgyny discussed in chapter 2. Generally speaking, as long as an individual's sexual practices do not interfere with or challenge the legitimacy of the twinned institutions of marriage and household, Japanese society accommodates—and in the case of males, even indulges—a diversity of sexual behaviors. Human reproduction need not be synonymous with social reproduction, but the latter must not be compromised by a politicized sexual identity that interferes with the former. As for the Takarasiennes, they may inspire unaligned erotic play and sexual relations, but they themselves are not free to partake in the wider, looser, "after hours" society until their retirement, and sometimes not even then.

Two of the most tenacious of the mistaken assumptions that need to be dismantled if any progress is to be made in understanding sexuality and its theories are the willful elision of "unaligned" sexual relations by persons not already discounted as unconventional—or worse, as "deviant"—and the easy equation of marriage with sexuality and heterosexuality in particular. In Japan, simply examining the Meiji Civil Code alerts us to the role of the state in regulating gender and sexuality, and in making marriage and motherhood virtually compulsory for women. For females (but not males), sex was to be limited to procreation and practiced under the auspices of marriage, which, along with motherhood, continues to mark both adulthood and gender- and sex-role maturity, demonstrating the relative staying power of state-sanctioned conventions—for the time being, at least. One need not be misanthropic to realize that many Japanese women continue to marry neither for love nor as an expression of their sexuality but rather, as is common knowledge, to survive economically. Even in the slightly more accommodating social space of today, few women can afford the financial strain of being unmarried and independent given the prevalence of sexism and ageism in the workplace (see Atsumi 1988; Jackson 1976; T. Lebra 1985 [1984]; Shida and Yuda 1987:114). It is therefore not difficult to understand, by extension, why many female fans, young and old, married and unmarried alike, are attracted to the Takarazuka *otokoyaku*. As I have noted, the player of men's roles represents an exemplary female who can negotiate successfully both genders and their attendant roles and domains without—theoretically, at least—being constrained by either.

FANDOM AS SOCIAL DISORDER

Same-sex crushes and relationships were sanctioned among *shōjo* provided they did not extend to actual lesbian practices, particularly of the *ome*, or "butch-femme," type, as discussed in the last chapter. But the longer the gap between puberty and marriage, the greater the potential among *shōjo* for disorderly conduct. Critics distressed by the Revue and its "modern" culture argued that Takarazuka attracted *shōjo* exclusively and linked the theater and fandom to the emergence of "abnormal" or "deviant" sexual desire: namely, sexual relations between females.

By the mid-1930s, revue fandom, in the case of women at least, was identified in the press as an illness symptomatic of social disorder. For every one of the literally hundreds of articles on either Takarazuka or its contemporaries, there was also an article on female fans, who were treated collectively as both a potentially exploitative and an exploitable group of *shōjo*. On the one hand, fans were criticized for spoiling their Takarazuka idols for ultimately selfish ends—for example, boring the stars with tea parties and pointless conversations (e.g., Fujioka 1937:49; Kobayashi 1935a:11). On the other hand, fans were warned about the pathological, "perverting" (i.e., "homosexualizing"), and even suicidal effects the all-female revues had on their nubile hearts and minds (e.g., "Dansō hi ari" 1935; Yoshiwara 1935:187).

Articles addressing the general subject of fan pathology appeared frequently in popular magazines. The author of one such article worried about the trend toward

> excitable, infatuated fans who buy photographs of their favorite revue stars or cut their pictures out of magazines. [Girls' school] students hide the pictures in their textbooks where they can sneak looks during class. Fans will wait in front of the dressing room entrance [before and after a performance] to collect autographs, pushing and shoving to get to the stars when they emerge. The most popular stars are the *otokoyaku*. . . . Against their parents' will, fans cut their hair in imitation of the masculinized performers.
> ("Hogosha wa kokoro seyo" 1935)

The short, or "masculine," haircut especially was interpreted by critics as a symbol of lesbian sexuality to which *shōjo* were all too susceptible. "Since the age of marriage is much later these days than it was in the past," the author continued, "fans' infatuation with cross-dressing [and with the *otokoyaku*] can be viewed as one form of amusement before marriage." It was, however, an amusement with sexually, and therefore socially, subversive possibilities, and the author went on to advise that

> parents and teachers must explain to the young women what the revue is all about and exercise prudent guidance; parents should even accompany their [nubile] daughters to shows. . . . True same-sex love (*dōseiai*) is not a self-limited phase; rather, such females despise males and consequently are unable to lead a married life. This pathological condition is virtually incurable. . . . Therefore, [girls and young women] should be encouraged to pursue interests other than the all-female revue—hiking, for example.[6]

Most Japanese sexologists quoted in the mass media of the 1930s blamed the players of men's roles for provoking the supposedly increased incidence of lesbian practices among girls and women. A few disagreed, noting the "long history in Japan of true same-sex love (*shinsei no dōseiai*)," and suggested that "there has not necessarily been an increase in such practices among women today." Rather, in the past "same-sex love affairs were associated with lower-class females. Today, the homosexual love affairs of upper-class girls and women are making headlines" (Hori Kentarō, quoted in "Dansō hi ari" 1935). Such women were to epitomize the Good Wife, Wise Mother ideal and to serve as living repositories of Japanese tradition. Thus, passing as men was associated with sexual deviancy only in the case of affluent, city-dwelling girls and women who, it was argued, wore masculine attire not to secure a livelihood, like their working-class sisters, but to flaunt their "moral depravity" (Tomioka 1938:103; Yasuda 1935).

Although estimates suggest that during this period roughly half the audience members at Takarazuka performances were boys and men (Kawahara 1921), female fans were singled out as individuals in need of (re)socialization. In the mid-1930s especially, but even as early as the 1920s, public attention was riveted to splashy accounts of the lesbian sexuality of Takarasiennes and their fans. The players of men's roles were depicted both as corrupted *shōjo* and as exerting a corrupting influence on *shōjo*. But young women themselves were the first to rebut these polemical allegations, as we shall see.

PROFILES IN FANDOM

In 1935 a leading women's magazine, *Fujin Kōron* (*Women's Central Review*), published a transcript of a roundtable discussion (*zadankai*) between mothers and daughters on the all-female revue theater. Their comments suggest ways in which the subtextual elements of theatrical performance are extracted, reinterpreted, and reinvested with new, even subversive, meanings. Indeed, the roundtable discussion format was (and remains) a major narrative device through which individual fans and stars—or both together, depending on the occasion— were publicly presented in an apparently informal, unrestrained, and personal setting. Such media events aimed at putting a "real," human face on phenomena (in this case, the revue theater and *shōjo* fandom) otherwise subject to speculation, dire diagnoses, and mystification.

Typical of the daughters' impressions was the observation that "Tākii [Mizunoe Takiko, the leading *otokoyaku* of the rival Shōchiku Revue] is a real man . . . she is full of self-confidence and is not afraid to perform in public" ("Shōjo kageki o kataru" 1935:289) (figure 18). One young woman joked about how even a blind masseuse initially thought that the masculine Tākii was a male (290), a comment indicating simultaneously the disjunction and perceived fusion of sex and gender. Others described Takarazuka *otokoyaku* Sayo Fukuko as "abrupt and brusque, like a man," and, like other players of men's roles, "not suited for marriage or domestic life" (291) (figure 19). And why should they marry, insisted the daughters, when they are doing so well on their own? Moreover, marriage will only lose them fans (292). Contradicting Kobayashi's plans for his students, not a few Takarasiennes themselves publicly eschewed wifehood and motherhood: three years earlier in 1932, for example, Tachibana Kaoru declared that "marriage was the vocation of boxed-in gals" ("'Watashi' wa 'boku' e" 1932). Such comments by (or at least attributed to) fans and actors alike are among the many instances of contested interpretations of the Revue's social ramifications.

The mothers, perhaps more outwardly invested in the sanctioned gender role of Good Wife, Wise Mother, were somewhat more guarded in their impressions of the all-female revue. Whereas one mother declared that the performances made her "feel youthful all over again," another stated that she did not want her daughter watching plays with erotic content ("Shōjokageki o kataru" 1935:293).

Figure 18.   Mizunoe Takiko (Tākii) of the Shōchiku Revue. From
Ikita koishita onna no 100nen (1988:44).

Yet several others confessed to liking the players of men's roles in particular (296).

The transcript of the roundtable discussion was punctuated by
framed minireports on Takarazuka rituals and stars that alluded to
the association between lesbian practices and the Revue. One such
box, containing a brief profile of *otokoyaku* Nara Miyako, mentioned

Figure 19.   Sayo Fukuko. From *The Takarazuka: Takarazuka kageki 80shūnen kinen* (1994:114).

her alleged same-sex love affair in 1929 with Shinpa actress Mizutani Yaeko (297). Nara was performing as the prince in *Cinderella* (*Shinderera*, 1929) at the time. The press reported variously that "Nara has the charisma to attract women"; "even married women tell their husbands that they are more attracted to Nara"; and "widows find Nara most attractive" ("'Dōseiai' to ieba okoru" 1929; "Onna to kekkon suru uwasa" 1929; "Takarazuka bijin hensenshi" [5] 1930).[7] In short, although a lesbian presence within the Revue was not categorically denied by the management and its sympathizers, it was safely contained either within the sanctioned space of the *shōjo* period of the female life cycle or within the guise of scintillating and unsubstantiated (but not insubstantial) gossip.

The veiled account of the Nara-Mizutani affair in *Kageki*, one of the three official Takarazuka "fanzines," assumed a stand diametrically opposed to that of the newspaper stories. Although she was not mentioned by name, Mizutani was likened to a vamp preying on naive and impressionable "students," who were cautioned to maintain a "respectable distance" (*resupekutaburu jisutansu*) from the likes of her (Aoyagi 1930). Whereas Nara was portrayed in the mass media as the aggressive, masculine seducer of ordinary women, Mizutani as depicted in the official fanzine was the aggressive, feminine seducer of charming *otokoyaku*. The difference in agency reflects the different constituencies represented by these media. *Otokoyaku* may have been under fire in the newspapers for their deviant psychology, but the Takarazuka management, in seeking to protect the reputation of the Revue, depicted the players of men's roles as victims of unrestrained female desire, an ironic twist on the mythic theme of the insatiable sexual appetite of unattached (unmarried and widowed) females.

Significantly, in 1933, four years after the publicity surrounding the Nara-Mizutani affair and a year after a leading player of men's roles (Kadota Ashiko) got herself a masculine haircut, Kobayashi coined a motto for the Academy and the Revue: "Purely, Righteously, Beautifully" (*kiyoku, tadashiku, utsukushiku*). This was an apparent public relations move to emphasize his honorable aspirations for the Takarasiennes (Sakada 1984:317–18).

Just as the Takarasiennes were assigned specialty roles, fans too were categorized by type. An illustrated article on Takarazuka fans published in 1935 in *Kageki* identified five different types of Revue fans within the general category of *shōjo* (figure 20). Most fans probably were then, as they are today, an eclectic and fluid mix of these and other types. Yet this caricaturing typology nevertheless is informative about stylistic and behavioral differences among fans that tended (and tend) to be glossed over in the popular and serious literature alike. The "courtesan"-type (*onnataiyūkei*) fan was trustworthy and dedicated to looking after every need of her favorite Takarasienne. The

Figure 20.   Five types of Takarazuka fans. From left to right: "courtesan," "early bird," "poetic," "bodyguard," and "copycat." From Hirabayashi (1935).

"early bird"–type (*shohatsukei*) fan was faithful and devoted to the Revue, always rushing to performances on the first available train. An infatuated fan overwhelmed by romantic nostalgia was the "poetic"-type (*wakarankei*), and "bodyguard"-type (*goeikei*) fans walked in a protective group behind their favorite Revue actor. Finally, "copycat"-type (*sōjikei*) fans imitated their favorite Takarasiennes, from clothing fashions to body language (Hirabayashi 1935).[8]

This last type of fan was perhaps the most problematic in terms of the potential for cross-dressing and, by association, a lesbian orientation, as is made explicit in the articles at the time on fan pathology. The courtesan and poetic types were depicted wearing kimonos, the early bird type was sketched in a skirt and blouse, and the bodyguard and copycat types were drawn wearing both kimonos and Western-style dresses. Perhaps the absence of representations of fans in short hair and trousers was purposeful in order to deflect negative associations linking the Revue and the masculinization of impressionable *shōjo*. All five types were rendered with their faces flushed with the feverish passion of fandom. The mix of clothing styles is suggestive not only of the Japanese and Western-style productions staged by the Revue, and the offstage appearance of some Takarasiennes, but also of the historical fact that Takarazuka fans represent a cross-section of social classes and backgrounds. The implication was that no woman—from the Good Wife, Wise Mother in the making to the Modern Girl—was immune from the all-consuming influence of the all-female revue theater. (A negative interpretation would stress the disruptive pathology of that

influence.) Similarly, Kobayashi maintained that vicarious or otherwise, consumerism effaced or at least transcended class differences.

CLAIMING A FEMALE AUDIENCE

The Takarazuka Revue was one component of Kobayashi's capitalist project to develop a mass theater that would facilitate the shaping of girls and women into seasoned consumers. The railroad terminal department store was another, and official fan clubs and shoppers' associations were yet a third component. For the first forty years of its existence, Takarazuka audiences were fairly evenly divided between females and males, although Kobayashi strategized ways of attracting women, and married women especially, to the nascent theater and amusement park. Even before Takarazuka's first performance in 1914, he organized a Women's Exhibition (*fujin tenrankai*) of consumer goods at his Paradise spa (Kumano 1984:6–7). In his efforts to capture the interest and loyalty of female consumers, Kobayashi went so far as to lower the floors of Hankyū trains to make boarding and exiting less awkward. He also staged a contest in which women nominated and voted on a color for Hankyū trains ("Fujin muki no shinshiki densha" 1923). The winning color was the deep maroon that distinguishes the trains today. A decade later, in 1937, Kobayashi installed a modern beauty salon, beauty school, and women's center in the Nippon Theater, one of the several Tokyo theaters under his banner. Apart from consolidating a female clientele, his motive was to nurture among theatergoing women a bewitching stage presence of their own: every woman could be a well-coiffed star, so long as she shone on the home stage ("Nippon gekijōnai biyōin" 1937).

The revue theater and the theater of capitalism merged in the lobby of the Takarazuka Grand Theater, completed in 1924 and rebuilt in 1935 after a devastating fire earlier that year. Lining both sides of the mammoth structure were restaurants and souvenir shops. Not surprisingly, several social critics drew analogies between the revue theater, with its juxtaposed images and events, and the miscellaneously stocked department store, where publicity campaigns emphasized the spectacular dramaturgy of shopping (Iizuka 1930:44; Takaoka N. 1943:195). Kobayashi demonstrated how a place of production was also a place of consumption.

Inside the auditorium, the sumptuous sets and exotic foreign and historical settings provided spectators with an enticing and accessible vision of what capitalism and commodity culture could mean in terms of entertainment, pleasure, and desire. The "masses," and female aficionadas especially, were recast as consumers, and the commodities on sale, from Revue performances to souvenirs, became part of the machinery of modern Japanese citizenship (cf. Evans 1993:5; Iwahori 1972). Kobayashi's attempts to claim a female audience for his shopping and entertainment complexes capitalized on the trend toward female consumership, and he doubtless played some role (perhaps a large one) in establishing the tenacious connection between women and commodity culture (Silverberg 1991). We therefore should not be surprised to learn that by 1940, when civilians began to experience firsthand the dire ramifications of war, the state initiated an antiluxury movement—"a spiritual mobilization of the people"—directed at reforming women's alleged penchant for conspicuous consumption ("New Order of Living" 1940). Similarly, a timely Takarazuka revue, *The Battle Is Also Here* (1943), introduced in the previous chapter, presents girls and women as incorrigible materialists—the result of their infection by Anglo-American "germs"—who must reform their selfish ways if Japan is to win the war.

Contemporaneous with Kobayashi's interest in tapping the consumerist potential of girls and women was the push by feminists for progressive changes, despite the defeat of a legislative bill for female suffrage in 1931 and the steady militarization of the society. An anonymously authored article representative of the mainstream feminist position appeared in the women's newspaper *Fujo Shinbun*, and it can be paraphrased as follows:

Women (*fujin*) are not included in the official definition of citizen (*kokumin*). Not only are women prevented from voting and from running for public office, but collectively they receive only 1 percent of state funds earmarked for public education. Consequently, most girls' and women's schools are privately owned and operated. Moreover, "female" is a marked category: unless prefixed by a word for "female" (such as *fujin*, *joshi*, or *onna*), terms such as physician (*ishi*), reporter (*kisha*), and clerk (*ten'in*) refer to males exclusively, despite the theoretically genderless meaning of these words and attendant occupations. Therefore, if the keepers of the male-centered (*danshi hon'i*) status quo are not going to distinguish between citizen (*kokumin*) and female citizen (*joshi no kokumin*), then they should make it absolutely clear that at least half of the total number of *kokumin* are female, and that women give birth to all citizens.

> ("Kokumin no hansū jogai" 1935)

Kobayashi was no feminist, but he did criticize the male-centeredness of the dominant discourse of citizenship as well as that of consumerism and popular entertainment. He was less interested in women's civil rights than in creating a patriarchal framework in which women could evolve as visible and sophisticated consumers. For him, marriage and consumerism were tropes for female citizenship. Theater offered an ideal means of connecting Kobayashi's social prescriptions and the wider society. Thus, he argued that "mass theater must cater to women as well as to men" (Kobayashi 1935b). In so saying, Kobayashi was not making an argument for female-centered and-identified entertainment; rather, his professed ideal was a family-oriented show whose audience consisted of married couples. Just as the patriarchal household was the smallest legal unit of society, so it was the ideal unit of spectatorship and consumption, which were regarded as activities that married women should coordinate. According to the dominant ideology of complementarity dictating household relationships, males were responsible for modes of production, and females were in charge of modes of consumption. Whether as actors or audiences, females acting on their own behalf outside the household were regarded by the state as socially disruptive and anomalous (Nagy 1991; Nolte and Hastings 1991; Sievers 1983). The Peace Police Law enacted in March 1900 (and modified in 1922 and 1926), which was aimed primarily at antigovernment groups, included a ban on political activity by women, for whom "political" was broadly and loosely defined.

But whereas Kobayashi sought to use the actor as a vehicle for introducing the spectacular artistry of the theater into the home, some Takarasiennes and their fans used the theater as a starting point for an opposing strategy, which included the rejection of gender roles associated with the patriarchal household.

ENTER THE *SHŌJO*

All women in public were problematic, but the *shōjo* period in particular was perceived by some as a downright dangerous phase of unstructured social interaction. Some critics active in the 1930s blamed not only Western-style entertainments but also the government's revised education policy for further exacerbating the delinquency and masculinization of *shōjo*. The new sports curriculum was singled out for "fostering a spirit of opposition to males" (Sugita 1935:277; see also Yamawaki 1914). School sports, one critic worried, which were newly introduced and promoted by the proeugenics Ministry of Education, are not a means to health; rather, "the pursuit of sport is forcing girls and young women to forgo the elegance of Japanese customs and to act independently, partly to keep males from being attracted to them." Sports, the revue theater, and cross-dressing, he summarized, "are Western imports that play a central role in the progressive masculinization and independent-mindedness of Japanese girls and women" (Sugita 1935:278). The critic's comments, which clashed with the objectives of the eugenics movement, are illuminated by our earlier discussion of the use of "the West" as a foil and by the negotiated alignment of sex and gender. He suggested that one's body (sex) is not a necessary condition for one's gender—thus the advent of untraditional girls and women—but he also implied that certain bodily practices (such as sports and acting) can impart a gendered state of mind contrary to the traditional social norms for one's sex.

Like sports, the redesign of girls' school uniforms in 1940 as a wartime austerity measure rekindled anxiety about the loss of femininity. The Ministry of Education introduced a single style of uniform nationwide, and the state promoted—temporarily—the adoption of "citizens' clothing" (*kokuminfuku*), which for girls and women included Western-style trousers and Japanese-style baggy pants (*monpe*). The initial worries voiced by the Osaka government administrators about how girls would lose their "schoolgirlish cuteness" (*jogaku-*

seirashii kawaisa) should the existing sailor-type blouse-and-skirt uniform be discontinued, coupled with the anxieties expressed by other pundits about the state's contribution to the masculinization of females, led to the repeal of the new dress code in 1943. The state continued to encourage the physical development of girls and women through exercise, and also urged them to cultivate their "feminine beauty" by wearing kimonos or Western-style skirt-suits made out of kimono material (*Joseitachi no Taiheiyō sensō* 1994:68–69; "Sērā haishi" 1941).

The seemingly contradictory ideas about the relationship of sports, uniforms, and female-embodied femininity are linked to the image of the *shōjo*, which includes revue fans. The *shōjo* was reified and scrutinized by critics as a barometer of decadent, un-Japanese social transformations. Thanks to various Western or modern (depending on the rhetoric) masculinizing apparatuses, *shōjo* were "no longer discreet, obedient, or domestically inclined" (Sugita 1935:274). Statements such as these were in themselves anachronistic and misleading since the category of *shōjo* was created in the early 1900s specifically to designate potentially disruptive girls and women between puberty and marriage.

The author of the *Lifestyle Guide for Girls* (*Shōjo no tame no seikatsuron*), published in 1932, hints that the "warmth, gentleness, and nurturance for which Japanese women have been known through the ages" were not likely to be reproduced in contemporary young women on account of their exposure to things Western, including the revue theater. He was especially worried about the consequences of their maverick tendencies, since "*shōjo* are the wombs of Japan's future," repositories of a living history and authentic traditions (Furuya 1932:1). In part, his logic presaged Carroll Smith-Rosenberg's observation about criticism directed toward the New Woman in Victorian America: namely, that "the control of literal sexual behavior at all times constitutes a secondary goal. [Critics] were obsessed not with sex, but with imposing order through the elaboration of categories of the normal and the perverted" (1985:268).

It is not that *shōjo* were once—prior to the influx of ideas and things Western—discreet, obedient, and domestically inclined. Rather, the interpretation of *shōjo* and fandom as pathological provided a code for a more fundamental and elementary discourse of national cultural identity at a time when the Japanese state was both opposing Western imperialism and pursuing colonial projects of its own in Asia and the Pacific. Pundits were also conscious of the possibly irreversible cultural transformations catalyzed by national processes of hybridity and by the people's fanlike infatuation with Western commodities and institutions. The Takarazuka actor, the revue fan, and the *shōjo* in general constituted a single, anomalous body in the eyes of patriarchal critics, which was co-opted as a site where a discourse of national identity was played out through allegorical associations. The social disorder associated with the revue and its fans reflects the instability and ambiguity of both the *shōjo* and the New Japan. Official attempts to "straighten out" the convoluted meanings of the *shōjo* and to push her toward complete femaleness and symbolic adulthood were emblematic of attempts to resolve some of the more problematic aspects of the strategic ambivalence characterizing the New Japan. The *shojō*— and all categories of female under that rubric—was an ideal test site for this partial resolution: controlling her was desirable because she was fascinating, attractive, and weak, and it was necessary because she was powerful, threatening, and different (Kiernander 1992:187).

Since at least the 1980s, the *shōjo* has been reconceptualized as both a dominant icon and an index of Japanese consumer capitalism in the guise of popular and mass culture: comic books and cartoons, television commercials, fashion magazines, pop songs, "cute" paraphernalia,[9] brand names, fast food, and so on. Whereas sixty years ago, some pundits cast the *shōjo* or zealous revue fan as the analogue of a nation infatuated and preoccupied with the West, several "celebrity" critics today have extended the image of the now relentlessly cute *shōjo* to all Japanese in light of their "compulsory and excessive consumerism" (Horikiri 1988:114–15; see also Treat 1993). Its referent no longer limited to girls and women, much less revue fans, some (male) critics suggest that "*shōjo*" today is synonymous with citizenship— irrespective of age, sex, or gender—in the new, conspicuously affluent "post-postwar" Japan. Ōtsuka Eiji, whose "ethnographic" analysis of *shōjo* has received wide media play in Japan, suggests that *shōjo* has replaced *jōmin* as the term for the Japanese people collectively (1989:14–21). *Jōmin*, or "ordinary, abiding folk," is, as I discussed in chapter 1, the nativist neologism coined by Yanagita Kunio to unify all Japanese in opposition to Western societies. Ōtsuka's claim is not a little glib: whereas both *shōjo* and *jōmin* are reified categories, albeit of very different origin, into which actual people have been placed, the former is an explicitly gendered term for problematic girls and women, while the latter is an ungendered term (that is, not about females specifically) for an ideal, quotidian folk.

What Ōtsuka and his contemporaries seem to be describing is the emergence in the late 1970s of a "middle-mass" society of consumers —"middle mass" because opinion polls suggest that 80 to 90 percent of the Japanese people identify with the "middle class," thus rendering class and class identity meaningless measures of social differentiation and complexity. It is this "mass" that is effectively feminized by Ōtsuka and others in their postmortems of the very consumer capitalism that has occasioned and inspires their own work. And as I suggest in the next chapter, some men today have even co-opted the *shōjo* image in their quest for psychosocial autonomy.

The problem remains that then and now, the *shōjo* has been portrayed by fearful and pessimistic critics—mostly male—as synonymous with "the masses" who had to be prevented from massing except at sanctioned sites and in prescribed numbers. Actual girls and women have countered these semiotic moves by demonstrating that the universal *shōjo* is but another patriarchal, even misogynist, invention and by claiming a different categorical significance as a body politic. Thus some Japanese feminists now use the term "ultra-*shōjo*" (*chōshōjo*) in reference to adult females who eschew heterosexism and believe in the power of sisterhood (Takano 1987). The emergence of *shōjo* fiction in the 1920s, the formation of private Takarazuka fan clubs, and the recent maturation of a *shōjo* script (discussed later) further attest to the powerful salience and social ramifications of the sex-gender ambivalent *shōjo*.

FAN CLUBS

Let me reiterate here that contrary to so-called common sense, Takarazuka fans are not limited to *shōjo*, although females categorized as *shōjo* have been represented as the most problematic fans (later, I shall review the attitudes and activities of male fans of all-female revues). Common sense, or the everyday articulations of the dominant ideology, tends to be associated with a practical consensus at the core of social reproduction (Fiske 1989:118; Thompson 1984:62). In the early 1900s, the popular representation of girls as both daughters and juvenile delinquents made the Janus-faced category of *shōjo* particularly compelling. This was especially true in the context of fandom associated with all-female revues at a time when the "woman problem" attracted the attention of sanctimonious social commentators. However, my field and archival research leads me to suggest that there actually was and is a *lack* of consensus about the sexes and genders of Takarazuka fans. The *shōjo*, especially in the narrowest sense of the term (i.e., teenage girls), remains the quintessential image of the Revue fan despite a history of evidence to the contrary largely because knowledge of other types of fans has not produced a coherent alternative view or understanding of fandom. Consequently, the image of the all-female revue fan as an impressionable *shōjo* remains paramount, leaving older female fans underacknowledged and male fans of all stripes invisible to the public eye. How the ideology of common sense works in the case of fandom is one of the key questions underlying this chapter, which focuses on the complex series of mechanisms whereby the meanings of all-female revues and their fans are activated for both the maintenance and the subversion of the status quo, making visible the concomitant relations of domination and subordination.

In 1935 the essayist Dan Michiko wrote an article on fans of all-female revues in the form of a letter to *shōjo* who wanted to become actors. In using the epistolary format, she acknowledged the primacy of letters as fans' favored mode of expression and communication.[10] Dan notes that despite the exposure in the mass media of the "unglamorous backstage of the glamorous revue stage," *shōjo* remain lost in a dreamworld and continue to apply to the Takarazuka Music Academy in ever-multiplying numbers. She begs the girls and young women to rethink their decision to pursue a career in the theater lest their dreams be crushed or they grow conceited despite their best intentions. Here and elsewhere Dan phrases her admonishments in a friendly but firm, almost cajoling fashion. "Although much in the all-female revues is unsavory (*iyarashii*) and calls for an averted gaze," she continues, "even refined young women (*ojōsama*) have managed to aestheticize the dubious content of the plays and weave romantic scenarios into their daydreams" (1935:280–81). An unstated theme informing Dan's epistolary article is the sexological "finding" that girls' and women's "naturally arising" (*shizen ni moriagatte kuru*) melancholy and passivity makes them particularly susceptible to same-sex love affairs.

Dan expounds at length on the problems associated with fans. Fans are characterized as vexatious and the life of a revue actor is portrayed as fraught with hardship and chicanery.

> [The all-female revue] is like a beautiful but poisonous flower. . . . Popularity is an occupational hazard faced by revue actors. "Fan" has a slightly vulgar (*gehin*) nuance. Fans are attracted to an actor's popularity alone and, consequently, are fickle. Actors, therefore, must make sure that their popularity is based on artistic talent if they are to avoid feeling vulnerable around fickle fans. Actors should be grateful for their acquired (*mi ni tsukete iru*) talent and avoid the capriciousness of popularity and adulation. Popularity comes unexpectedly and can leave unexpectedly. Only one in a hundred, one in a thousand actors have the good fortune to remain popular throughout their careers. . . . From the outside, a career in an all-female revue seems paradisiacal; from the inside, it is hellish.
>
> (283, 285)

Dan addresses revue fans as if they themselves were revue stars facing the trials and tribulations of popularity. The narrative strategy operating here seems to be one designed to encourage empathic reflexivity, a twist on the fused identity of fan and idol. It acknowledges that from one vantage point, there really was no difference between fans and actors: applicants to the Takarazuka Music Academy were all Revue fans, and the junior actors were fans of their seniors. Moreover, many Academy instructors were fans prior to joining the staff, and not a few Takarazuka employees were recruited on the basis of their participation in official fan clubs (Matoya 1937:229). The dynamics of fandom provided—and continue to provide—an important emotional catalyst within the Revue's strict vertical and self-contained social structure, as well as in the wider society.

Complementing Kobayashi's concern to resocialize potentially wayward *shōjo* and to assert his authority over the actors, the management of the Takarazuka Revue established official clubs primarily for female fans as a way of controlling the interaction between Takarasiennes and their admirers; a secondary purpose was to better mobilize women as informed consumers. The specter of "abnormal sensations" haunted Kobayashi; and because such conduct could not be sanctioned, it had to be contained. Significantly, the first official fan club, the Takarazuka Friendship Club for Females (Takarazuka joshi tomonokai), was founded in December 1934 at a time when scandalous stories on the relationship between all-female revues and lesbian practices were regular media fare.[11] ("Female" [*joshi*] was dropped from the name in 1951, making the club a coed organization, at least nominally.) The Revue management sought to appropriate fandom as a vehicle not only to ensure the commercial success of the Revue but also to impose on female fans a dominant gender script and associated roles.

Within three years of its establishment, the Takarazuka Friendship Club had grown to 2,000 members, each of whom paid a small membership fee and enjoyed tea parties and hikes together, sometimes with their stage idols (Matoya 1937:233). In 1979 the club boasted 80,000 members. Originally housed on the sixth floor of a "famous Tokyo restaurant," the club in its early years published a monthly newsletter, *Midori* (*Green*, which is also the official Takarazuka color), with such regular features as pictures and drawings of Revue stars, members' essays and poems, photojournalistic accounts of visits to the dormitory rooms and houses of Takarasiennes, and a question-and-answer column ("Gendai no ōoku" 1979:22). Today, three "fanzines" are published by the club: *Kageki* (*Revue*, founded in 1918), *Takarazuka Gurafu* (*Takarazuka Graph*, 1936), and the pamphlet *Takarazukadayori* (*Takarazuka News*, 1966). Each of these magazines corresponds to a different membership option.[12]

As a rule, but one not always followed, the Revue management does not permit the actors to give interviews to reporters from the mainstream press without a chaperon present. The official fan magazine is regarded as the safest venue for Takarazuka information brokering today, in contrast to the Revue's somewhat looser relationship with the mass media in its early decades. In terms of financial arrangements and sponsorships, however, Takarazuka continues to enjoy a close relationship with the press. Kobayashi was a close friend since his college days with the publisher of the *Ōsaka Mainichi* newspaper, who organized a fund-raising "club" for the nascent Revue in 1914 that remained operational for about ten years (Iwahori 1972:104–7; Kobayashi 1961b:545; Tsuganesawa 1991:46–50). Generally speaking, Takarazuka and the mass media have cultivated a symbiotic relationship: the Revue has been regularly reviewed in newspapers and magazines, and, during the wartime period in particular, was envisioned by the state as a "living newspaper" instrumental in the mobilization and indoctrination of the people.[13] The sensationalism that sometimes characterizes the mass media does not negate their value as ethnographic, sociohistorical resources, as this book demonstrates. In fact, sensationalism probably facilitated the process by which many popular perceptions of Japanese and other societies were obtained, absorbed, and naturalized (cf. Shephard 1986:95).

During the wartime period, newspaper interviews with leading Revue actors, such as Harue Fukami, constituted direct attempts to link Takarazuka with the military and state policy. In a 1939 newspaper article with the headline "A Fan of the Gallant Hitler," Harue, who had recently played the role of an officer in *The Black Rose of Spain* (*Supein no kurobara*, 1939), was asked what she thought of the "European War" (*ōshūsensō*):

> Hmm, that's a difficult question. Since Japan is neutral I can't really judge one way or the other. My personal feelings? Well, I really like that gallant and dashing Hitler.
>   What about Chiang Kai-shek?
>   He's detestable! . . .
>   Who in Japan do you like?
>   I like soldiers who've become politicians—that's why I like Prime Minister Abe.[14]
>   ("Sassō Hitora fuan" 1939)

The interview ended with Harue, identified as a "daughter of the military state" (*gunkoku no musume*), expressing her desire to tour the war front in China, "especially since I just played the role of an officer." Disingenuous comments about Japan's "neutrality" aside, the actor acknowledged the emerging Axis Alliance; she also made a symbolic correspondence between wartime theater and theaters of war, blurring the distinction between actors and their stage characters.

The issue of press coverage centers on control, and one of the most important functions of fan magazines is the production and circulation of information and knowledge. Managing impressions has always been a major preoccupation of the Takarazuka administration and one of the initial reasons for the establishment of the Takarazuka Friendship Club. Editorials by Kobayashi in the early issues of *Kageki* laid out the official ethos of the Revue and helped mediate the transmission of topical data and their interpretation. The official fan magazines, assisted in part by the mass media, have worked to maintain the Revue's public profile as wholesome family entertainment. Some fans, discussed below, formed private fan clubs and have reread and redeployed the master text in ways that accommodate their own interpretive needs and desires.

In 1939, when media criticism of the "deviant and ostentatious" lifestyle of the Takarasiennes rose to a crescendo, the actors were forbidden either to socialize with their fans or to answer fan mail ("Takarazuka fuan ni tsugu" 1940). The critics' shrill attacks were matched by the boisterous shouting and clapping of Takarazuka audiences—fan clubs would attend en masse and applaud and yell vigorously whenever their favorite star appeared—until finally, decades later in the fall of 1964, shouting was prohibited by the Revue administration (Ōhara Kaori 1992 [1991]:284). Whereas the mass media warned parents of the pernicious effects all-female revues had on their daughters, the Revue perceived that some fans were themselves disruptive and undisciplined, and thus sought to isolate them from the impressionable Takarasiennes and to control their behavior.

The relationship between Takarazuka fans and actors has remained one of interdependency. From the time they are enrolled in the Music Academy, the Takarasiennes indulge fans who wish to indulge them. Theatergoers today are familiar with the hundreds of animated girls and women who line the sidewalk outside of the main and Tokyo Takarazuka theaters, chatting as they wait for a glimpse—and if they're lucky, a snapshot—of the stars as they arrive or leave (figure 21). In a throwback to the fan typologies published in 1935, Riko Umehara—founder and editor of the private fan club and magazine called *Silk Hat* (*Shirukuhatto*), and author of a recently published fan-oriented guidebook to Takarazuka—draws critical attention to the "guard" (*gādo*) fans, outfitted in training wear, who recall the "bodyguard"-type fan. These sometimes intimidating young women form a phalanx ostensibly to protect their idol as she arrives at and departs the theater, but also to secure for themselves exclusive claims on the best spots from which to stargaze (Umehara 1994:150). Depending on the rank of the actor (and the presence or absence of "guards"), she will be cheered either by a small group of fans or by the crowd as a whole; a top *otokoyaku* will often be overwhelmed with offerings of cut flowers and stuffed animals.

There are not only kinds but degrees of fandom: an actor's longtime fans will chauffeur her to and from the theater, prepare her meals, provide secretarial services, and collect the presents offered by other fans; when she retires from the Revue for a career in show business,

Figure 21.   Shion Yū and her fans. The Star Troupe's top *otokoyaku* is greeted by her fans as she arrives at the main theater in Takarazuka. From *Fushigi no kuni no Takarazuka* (1993:103).

they will attend whatever productions in which she appears. Should an actor retire from show business altogether and open a bar or a restaurant, as many do, the fans will often provide the collateral and voluntary labor necessary to make the venture a success. Not all fans are equally selfless, nor are all Takarazuka actors equally considerate of their fans, but for the most part their relationship is one of mutual dependence and reciprocity.

Private fan clubs have been established by a variety of constituencies, and from what information I have been able to gather, these clubs are usually organized as exclusively same-sex (male or female) associations. The Waseda University [We] Love the Takarazuka Revue Club (Waseda daigaku Takarazuka kageki o aisuru kai) is one of the few prominent private fan clubs that is coed, although males constitute a small minority. The club publishes a quarterly fanzine, *Yume no Hanataba* (*Bouquet of Dreams*). Takarazuka fans are known for their loyalty and tenacity, and not a few "old fans" have formed their own private clubs, such as the all-female Green Praise Club (Ryokuhōkai). In 1981 it was under the direction Ashihara Kuniko, a top player of men's roles in the 1920s and 1930s, and Sayo Fukuko, another leading *otokoyaku* in that period, served as vice-director. Like other fan clubs, Green Praise schedules tea parties and regular meetings where members decide which actor should be awarded the annual Green Prize (*midorishō*). Past winners of that prize are eligible for the Special Prize (*tokubetsushō*) awarded to a Takarasienne whose performances have been superior over the years (Sugawara 1981:56). In a clever pun on *patoron* (patron), Takarasiennes refer to their devoted and distinguished "old [female] fans" as *apuron* (aprons) ("Gendai no ōoku" 1979:24).

Inspired by the Waseda club's publication, Riko Umehara founded Silk Hat for two reasons: to promote an appreciation for the entire Revue, as opposed to individual Takarasiennes, and to combine her interest in writing and editing with expanding her social network (Umehara 1991:1). The majority of private fan clubs, however, are organized around individual Takarasiennes. The Kaoru Club (Kaoru no kai), for example, is devoted to Star Troupe's top *otokoyaku* Hyūga Kaoru, who retired from the Revue in 1992 and is now pursuing a career as an actress. According to the Kaoru Club's informational flier, members are guaranteed tickets to Takarazuka performances at the main, Tokyo, and regional theaters; can enjoy the company of Nessy (Hyūga's nickname) at several tea parties (*ochakai*) throughout the year; will receive *Hyūga*, the seasonal fan newsletter "chock full of information about Nessy"; and can purchase Nessy-brand T-shirts, sweatpants, and votive papers (*senjafuda*).[15]

In the past two years, the Revue has reversed its usual policy of not promoting individual stars; it now markets "official goods," such as T-shirts, scarves, shopping bags, mugs, stationery, memo books, and diaries, emblazoned with a picture of the top *otokoyaku* of each troupe. A black T-shirt in honor of Asaji Saki of the Star Troupe, for example, is printed in gold letters with the caption: "Her embracing power and untamed spirit project real masculinity into her male roles" (figure 22) (Takarazuka Goods Selection 1996:94).

MALE FANS

There is comparatively little mention of male fans in the popular press or the literature on all-female revues, although they did and do exist. Some authors have noted Takarazuka's popularity among males of

Figure 22.   Asaji Saki. The Star Troupe *otokoyaku* in her offstage
clothing. From *Takarazuka Gurafu* (1987).

all ages in the 1920s and 1930s, when it was one of the few avant-garde musical theaters catering to a mass audience (Suzuki T. 1975 [1974]:83). Not a few patrons of the Takarazuka Revue, mostly established businessmen, lavished money and gifts on their chosen stars. One notorious patron of Takigawa Sueko, an original member of the Takarazuka Revue, was the loan shark Ishii Sadashichi, who reportedly bought his idol expensive kimonos. Others wined and dined their favorites several times a month, and some tried to persuade the actors to become their mistresses—a situation that reinforced some critics' equation of a theatrical career to a life of prostitution ("Ishii shakkin'ō" 1925; "Joseito no matsuro" 1925).

Many, if not most, Takarasiennes initially were fans of the Revue, and in the first half of the twentieth century, a number of male fans similarly aspired to the Takarazuka stage. As early as 1919, when the Takarazuka Music Academy was established, Kobayashi sought to recruit about twenty young men to a newly founded troupe, the Takarazuka New Revue (Takarazuka shingekidan). He appointed the famous playwright and theater historian Tsubouchi Shikō as its director. The outfit folded within a year, allegedly because the female students enrolled in the Takarazuka Music Academy refused to perform with their male counterparts. Among the most promising of the young men were Hori Masahata and Shirai Tetsuzō; Hori subsequently was appointed to the editorial staff of *Kageki* and later directed revues, and Shirai joined the directing staff of an opera company, only to later rejoin Takarazuka as one of its most productive and renowned playwright-directors (Ōzasa 1986:109).

In 1937, three years after the Revue's official females-only fan club was established, male fans wrote to the administration urging the creation of an official fan club for boys and men. One young aficionado pointed to a sexual division of labor in rationalizing the need for an all-male club:

> Males excel in theory (*riron*) and females excel in criticism (*hihyōgan*).
> Ideally, male and female fans should collaborate and meld their
> talents; males could analyze in greater depth the more general
> theater reviews produced by females. . . . Of course, each person
> has an individual opinion about [all-female] revues; but, neverthe-
> less, there are two basic, underlying viewpoints: male and female. . . .
> The existence of the all-female Takarazuka Friendship Club provides
> female fans the opportunity to exchange ideas and information,

which helps to sharpen their critical faculties. At present, males lack a similar organization, and because it is difficult to find other males with whom to attend and discuss performances, our critical abilities remain undeveloped. However, it may be that our naïveté occasions a certain idealism. If we male fans had [an official] club of our own, we would become more perceptive viewers, which, ultimately, is to the benefit of the Takarazuka Revue. I am not proposing a fan club that exists solely to procure choice seats for its members; rather, the all-male fan club I have in mind will foster the formation of genuine, high-quality fans.

(Igi 1937:32)

The author of this letter perceives fan clubs as structures that catalyze the transformation of "personal reaction into social interaction, spectatorial culture into participatory culture" (Jenkins 1991:175). Recall also that Riko Umehara founded Silk Hat in part to expand her social network. Henry Jenkins's observations about *Star Trek* fans today apply equally to and capture succinctly the intellectual and social agenda of Takarazuka fandom:

One becomes a "fan" not by being a regular viewer of a particular program but by translating that viewing into some kind of cultural activity, by sharing feelings and thoughts about the program content with friends, by joining a "community" of other fans who share common interests. For fans, consumption naturally sparks production, reading generates writing, until the terms seem logically inseparable.

(1991:175)

For the most part, the Takarazuka management did not and has not acted positively on requests by male devotees for their own official fan club, although in 1951 membership in the Takarazuka Friendship Club became available to boys and men (Hashimoto 1984:107, 111; Matoya 1937:230, 233). (The club's ratio of female to male members has not been made public.) Nevertheless, it is an ill-kept secret that from its inception the Revue has relied on the largesse of powerful male sponsors and has given the nod to the formation of private all-male fan clubs.

Although the young man quoted earlier arguing for an all-male fan club remarks on the difficulty of finding like-minded men with whom to "talk Takarazuka," thus implying the impossibility of forming an unofficial fan club, there was in existence at the time of his letter a private fan club consisting (still) mostly of male students from elite private universities such as Keio and Aoyama (Matoya 1937:230). The club in question is the Tokyo Takarazuka Club (Tōkyō Takarazukakai), founded in 1927, five years before the Tokyo Takarazuka theater was built. Among its illustrious founding members were Asano Sōichirō, president of the Tōyōkisen railroad company; *rakugo* artist Yanagiya Kingorō; and actor and theater critic Furukawa Roppa, to name but a few men (228). By 1928 the club boasted 3,000 members. The few females registered were involved in editing and publishing the group's monthly newsletter (231). Its first chair was Aoyagi Yūbi, who rose from supervising ushers at the new Tokyo Takarazuka theater to teaching classes on morality and ethics at the Takarazuka Music Academy. At the time the Tokyo Takarazuka Club was founded, Aoyagi was a regular writer for *Opera* and *Kabu* (*Song and Dance*), two prominent theater arts journals. Later, he became the editor of *Tōhō*, a magazine published by the Tokyo Takarazuka theater, and wrote several books on the Takarazuka Revue. Aoyagi has been described as the epitome of a *peragoro* (Matoya 1937:231), a term used to refer to fanatical male fans of popular operas and revues (Ōzasa 1986:82–84, 88; see also Seidensticker 1983:271).

Edward Seidensticker recounts the two theories as to the origin of the word *peragoro*:

> Everyone agrees that the first two syllables are the last two of "opera." As for the last two, some say that they derive from "gigolo," others that they are from *gorotsuki*, an old word for "thug" or "vagrant." The latter signification, whether or not it was there from the start, came to predominate. The *peragoro* were the disorderly elements that hung around the park. They went to the theaters night after night, provided unpaid claques for favorite singers, and formed gangs, whose rivalries were not limited to vehement support for singers.... Their lady friends ... were sometimes called *peragorina*, though this expression had by no means the currency of *peragoro*.
>
> (1983:271)

Ōzasa suggests that the neologism combines "opera" and "gigolo" to mean "opera fan." He also describes *peragoro* as mostly young men from affluent families who would monopolize theater seats and throw love letters onto the stage, often while shouting out the names of their favorite stars (Ōzasa 1986:83).

A 1937 article about the Tokyo Takarazuka Club provides a rare and detailed glimpse of the formal activities of this and probably most Takarazuka fan clubs at the time; in fact, it complements my earlier description of generic fan club activities today. Membership in this club cost sixty sen per half year and included receipt of the newsletter, *Takarazukakai* (*Takarazuka Club*). Monthly meetings were held to which the directors of the current show were invited to speak. Members also arranged tea parties for Takarazuka Music Academy instructors and Revue managers who were visiting Tokyo; the inside connections thus forged enabled them to purchase the best seats in the Tokyo theater (Matoya 1937:230–31).

Apparently, some Academy and Revue personnel used these social events as occasions to sell inside information about the Takarasiennes to the tabloids (Matoya 1937:231–32). Because the Takarazuka management forbade students and actors from giving unsupervised interviews to the mainstream press—and to "*shōjo* magazines" in particular—the public was thirsty for more colorful fare about the off-stage lives of Takarasiennes (234). Revue personnel who trafficked in gossip did so at the risk of losing their jobs, and theater critics whose stories were insufficiently adulatory were, and are, denied permission for further interviews and from access to dress rehearsals ("Gendai no ōoku" 1979:23–24). In contrast, the Shōchiku Revue seems to have displayed a much more liberal attitude toward both the mass media and fan clubs, and, unlike its rival, it encouraged from the start the formation of clubs for individual stars and the publication of fan magazines focused on individual performers.

The private Love Takarazuka Club (Aihōkai), founded in 1955, is another an all-male club, most of whose eighty members are men of letters, businessmen, and politicians; among the last group is Member of Parliament Sakurauchi Yoshio, who chairs the club ("Gendai no ōoku" 1979:21; Sugawara 1981:55). Apart from high social status and visibility, what these men have in common is a history of devotion to the Takarazuka Revue that stretches over several decades. The club distributes *Aihō* (*Love Takarazuka*), its private weekly fan magazine, and sponsors an annual awards ceremony for outstanding Takarasiennes at which the following awards are presented: the Violet Prize (*sumireshō*), to a *musumeyaku* who has completed her third year on stage; the Cherry Blossom Prize (*sakurashō*), to the best dancer; and the Wild Chrysanthemum Prize (*nogikushō*), to the best supporting actor ("Gendai no ōoku" 1979:22; Sugawara 1981:55).[16]

Several of the other all-male fan clubs made up of influential businessmen include the Kansai-based Club to Support and Encourage the Takarazuka Revue (Takarazuka kageki o kōenshi, shōreisuru kai; founded in 1960, 140 members), among whose members was the late electronics tycoon, Matsushita Kōnnosuke; a Kantō-based club with a virtually identical name (founded in 1974, 130 members), whose members include a couple of railroad company presidents; and the imperialist-sounding Club to Support the Overseas Advance of Takarazuka (Takarazuka kageki kaigai shinshutsu kōenkai), a very private and little-publicized fan club organized to underwrite the Revue's foreign tours, chaired by Saji Keizō, a former president of Suntory ("Gendai no ōoku" 1979:22; Sugawara 1981:56).[17] Other powerful male fans of Takarazuka include the late Prime Minister Satō Eisaku and the president of the Almond chain of coffee shops, Takihara Kenji ("Gendai no ōoku" 1979:23). It would be very instructive to utilize Takarazuka fan clubs as a framework within which to trace and analyze political and financial networks and alliances in Japan and abroad.[18] These all-male groups offer a cogent example of how the operations of fandom also have an impact on the "real" world of policy making and the capitalist market. Kobayashi's motives to establish the Takarazuka Revue must also be considered in this light, and such an analysis would supply the subject of another book.

SISTER

Fan clubs and fan magazines constitute particular forms of consumption, and for many Takarazuka fans, club activities—including the writing of letters, theater criticism, and the staging of plays—are the center of fan communities.[19] Whether or not that community is primary or alternative depends on the specific fan and group. For the dozen or so women who belong to "Sister," the fan club is a primary community in the sense that it is the central and self-determined referent in the everyday lives of its members.

In the spring of 1991, I arranged to meet the head of Sister, nineteen-year-old "Hosono Yuki," having learned of the all-female club from a Takarazuka fan.[20] After exchanging letters and telephone calls, I traveled from Tokyo by bullet train to a major city in western Japan to meet Yuki at a French-style café at ten o'clock in the morning. She proved to be a short but sturdy young woman with black, shoulder-length hair, dressed in a navy-blue sweater, denim miniskirt, and white sneakers. After winding up our two-hour conversation, we walked about a mile to the district office building, meeting up with several other members on the way. The district office also serves as a community center, and the club had rented an arts-and-crafts room for the afternoon. Following a pep talk by Yuki, they set about making intricate props for the upcoming performance of their original play about a Mafia "godmother." Yuki anticipated an audience of up to two hundred: mostly family, friends, neighbors, and other Takarazuka fans. Several hours later, we relocated to the Sister "clubhouse," a messy, concrete-floored storeroom, where we sat on squares of cardboard, snacked on junk food, and chatted about a wide range of topics. Yuki also gave a short stage makeup demonstration for one of the club's new members, reminding her charges that *musumeyaku* used a pink foundation, and *otokoyaku* brownish-pink. Several hours later I returned to Tokyo on the last bullet train.

The charismatic Yuki, a *musumeyaku* by choice, clearly relishes her leadership role in Sister. In contrast to the Revue, where actors are assigned their professional genders, fans choose their preferred gender(ed) role. Yuki sets the club's social agenda and production schedule, and she uses the detailed knowledge about Takarazuka that she possesses to demonstrate and exert her authority. Her mother is also a Takarazuka fan, as is often the case—recall the 1935 roundtable discussion among mothers and daughters recounted earlier—and approves of Sister so long as the club does not consume any of the household's finances. With respect to expenses, Yuki expressed her astonishment at the rather large sum of 500,000 yen spent by "Amaryllis," another Takarazuka fan club in the same city, on their productions. I asked Yuki if the Sister crew ever attended Amaryllis's performances, and she replied that they did indeed and that they made a point of snickering throughout the show!

At our café meeting, Yuki had suggested that although the *musumeyaku*'s role was to enhance the charm of the *otokoyaku*, the same relationship did not pertain offstage. Judging from comments made by members of Sister and other Takarazuka fans, I understood her to mean that whereas women would and should support females who assumed masculinity onstage, they would not or should not necessarily bolster actual males offstage in the same way.

During our clubhouse sojourn there had been a lot of joking about how *"otokoyaku* are actually male," and the normative axiom, opposites attract, was invoked to rationalize the attraction between two individuals of the same sex but different genders. According to Yuki, there were six *otokoyaku* and three *musumeyaku* present that day; that was fairly plain to see, given the obviousness of the sartorial and other markers for each (which were the same as those used to demarcate gender in the Takarazuka Revue). The stage names (*geimei*) used by the members when referring to one another were similarly gendered. "Keni," one of the *otokoyaku* present, was a junior in college studying Japanese classical literature, with an emphasis on the Edo-period playwrights and novelists Chikamatsu and Saikaku, mainly because references to their texts appeared in many Takarazuka plays. When one of the new members—an *otokoyaku*—insinuated that there had been a sexual relationship between those who had acted in an earlier revue, Keni responded, "Listening to you, you'd think we were all homosexual (*dōseiai*)! Don't say such weird things!!" Nonetheless, Yuki herself dropped several hints about Keni's own affairs with women— perhaps for my benefit as an interested foreigner and safe confidant (in the sense that I was neither a local resident nor known to their friends and family, nor likely to become so known).

In consolidating my impressions and ideas after several years of interacting with Takarazuka fans, I realized that Takarazuka fan club activities, and particularly the rehearsal and production of revues, provide women with an opportunity to manipulate the received relationship between sex and gender and to experiment with different (i.e., unconventional) gendered subject positions. Moreover, they are able to do this in the safe and sanctioned context of the fan club without self-consciously having to claim, practice, or live any one of those positions in their everyday lives. Historically in Japan and elsewhere, sexual practices have not presumed a specific sexual orientation or identity, although today, some lesbian and gay activists and homophobic critics alike tend to fuse the two. Most but not all fans, in my experience, tend to elide the relationship between sexual practice and identity. Same-sex sexual practices can be hinted at or even acknowledged, but most of the female fans with whom I have either corresponded or interacted, or about whom I have read, do not also claim, publicly at least, a lesbian identity or sexual orientation in their everyday lives. The *practice* may involve same-sex relations (in the broadest sense, which ranges from spiritual to physical connectedness), and the *style* may be "butch-femme," but the *identity* is as a Takarazuka fan and not necessarily as a "lesbian," much less a "lesbian feminist." Fans are certainly aware of the term, the identity, and the political significance of "lesbian," but some of those who do have female sexual partners do not always wish to claim membership in that category (at least openly).

Some Japanese feminists and lesbian feminists today follow the historical precedent of Hiratsuka Raichō in speaking disparagingly of the Takarazuka Revue as a martially informed patriarchal institution bent on promoting and idealizing heterosexism. True enough. Nevertheless, as I noted earlier, despite their outwardly nonfeminist politics and performances, the Revue's actors have inspired both a spirit of resistance to normative gender roles and expectations and also a distinct and significant sexual subcultural style, if not voice, among fans who would not necessarily identify themselves as politically conscious, much less politically active. When necessary to their respective agendas, Takarazuka fans and detractors alike have separated not only the actors from the management but also the actor from whatever other symbolic meanings she may supply.

In a sense, fan clubs and the all-female revue itself seem to extend and expand the *shōjo* period, even separating that period from the normative female life cycle altogether. To borrow a term from film theory, these organizations function as a "space-off," or an interstitial space where new or unconventional configurations of everyday life achieve materiality and practical importance and where they may or may not affect the status quo (de Lauretis 1987:26). This space can be as limited or as encompassing as the various social actors wish.

Keeping in mind the space-off, we can more easily understand the broader significance of an earlier scenario. In the spring of 1929, the author of a newspaper series on Takarazuka called "Abnormal Sensations" (*hentaiteki kankaku*) expressed his alarm that *otokoyaku* would begin to feel natural doing "male" gender. Their private lives, he fretted, would soon "become an extension of the stage" ("Hentaiteki kankaku" [4] 1929). The critic was certainly aware that the public vocation of acting reversed the usual association of females with the private domain. Recognizing that boundaries of the interstitial space of the revue theater could expand, he feared they could incorporate everyday life. However, inasmuch as many Takarasiennes had applied to the Music Academy because they were avid fans and wanted to be closer to their idols, or because they wanted to do "male" and in some cases "female" gender, the stage can also be understood as an extension of their private lives. The same can be said of fan clubs. As I elaborate in the next chapter, whatever the direction of incorporation, the space-off represents, depending on one's perspective, either a liberating or a problematic change of context wherein the received alignments of sex and gender become skewed.

5

Writing Fans

To Tsuba Rumiko-*san* [a player of men's roles]: With each
new day [my] dedicated enthusiasm for you grows. . . . You
are truly a gentle older sister. I would love to meet you and
bask in your tenderness (*amaetai*). Why is this so? I can't say.
Don't get upset and lose your temper. I just have to tell you
that you're my one and only older sister. That's impossible,
but in my fun-filled fantasies you're my only, gentle, older
sister.

When I'm lonely, I open my locket; your picture is on one
side, mine on the other. The two of us together in my locket!
Why does that make me so happy?

Meanwhile, I'm waiting with pleasure for a chance to
meet you. Please take care of yourself, my dearest older
sister. Okay?

From Wamata Kurenai[1]

"Daisuki na onēsama" 1938

FAN LETTERS AND MAGAZINES

In April 1990, partway through an eight-month field trip to Japan, I
placed a message in *Takarazuka Fan* (*Takarazuka Fuan*), a fanzine published by the semiofficial fan club of the same name. I identified myself as a scholar from California doing research on all-female revues
who was interested in learning from fans directly what could not be
found in the many books on Takarazuka.[2] Within a month I received
seventeen responses from fans who said that they were female, ranging in age from fifteen to forty. Some wrote on distinctive stationery:
pink with a floral motif; white and doilylike; white bordered with cute
cartoon animals and bearing the header "Right Moment"; and pur-
ple with cartoon figures imploring, "Please save my earth." Virtually
all the fans provided me with personal information, including age,
astrological sign, and blood type.[3] Most were eager to talk about their
favorite actors and shows, expressing a desire to assist me in whatever way they could; several wanted to get to know me better and
even to meet in person.

I have translated here one letter that stood out among the others in going beyond the usual litany of favorite actors and revues and putting into perspective my growing awareness about the fortresslike character of the Revue. It was written, on a word processor, by a middle-aged music teacher.

> How do you do?
> I read [your letter in] *Takarazuka Fan*. I don't think that I can respond to your request because I've only recently become a Takarazuka fan. However, it's my sense that not even my friends and acquaintances who do know a lot will talk about the Takarazuka you can't read about in books. Moreover, to be frank, it would be impossible for them to talk freely. If someone really familiar with Takarazuka [i.e., someone who works there] talked openly about things, they'd be fired. Among my acquaintances are directors of Takarazuka fan clubs, former Academy teachers, and others in the know, but all of them are tight-lipped and say only good things about the Revue. What exactly do you mean by "things that aren't discussed in books on Takarazuka"? There have been lots of books published on Takarazuka over its history, but none of them contain any private information. That's because it would be terrible if the Revue sued the authors for slander. I think that your objective approach to Takarazuka is good and interesting; perhaps I can be of some assistance? Please let me know. . . . Please forgive me for having written such a glum letter. I'd be happy to talk about various things with you though. . . . It would be very nice to become friends.

A couple of weeks later, this same fan telephoned to warn me about the censorship tactics of the Revue administration (see chapter 1). Eventually, I learned quite a lot about the murkier side of Takarazuka politics, including the sexual partners of certain actors and the abuses of the patronage system, from the fans and former members of the Revue I met with over the course of my fieldwork. Out of respect for Takarazuka fans and actors, I have opted not to repeat in detail all of what I learned from those conversations. With several pseudonymous and diluted exceptions, I have limited my comments on these matters to accounts published in newspapers and magazines (and thus part of the public domain).

As I have noted, it seems that until around 1935, books and articles on the Revue addressed topics and issues that today would not be approved by the administration or by many fan magazines not under the direct purview of the Revue. There have been a few exceptions, but for the most part, fans are not particularly interested—or so they say—in learning about the Revue's backstage politics, or in publicizing sensational exposés of an actor's private life. Nor are they invested in "outing" themselves. Fans who do write love letters to their favorite actors or admit to an erotic attachment to Takarasiennes either use pseudonyms, as in the epigraph above and the letter to Daichi Mao quoted in chapter 2, or insist on anonymity, as in the case of the fan quoted in Ingrid Sischy's *New Yorker* article (cited in chapter 1).

In small-scale fan clubs such as Sister, the "space-off" is represented by actual theater performances and club socializing; in other, much larger and more impersonal fan clubs, it more often takes the form of fan magazines and fan letters, together with the imaginary but contingent worlds they conjure up. The writing of fan and love letters to revue stars was perceived by critics of the early Revue as a way in which *shōjo* fans expressed their delinquency or perversion; the two "pathologies" were often equated. One of the first books published on the lifestyle of the Takarasiennes included a chapter on fan letters; the author dismissed love letters from female fans as examples of "abnormal psychology" (Kawahara 1921:113). Since the introduction of the English terms "fan" and "love letter" in the early 1900s, fan letters have figured as a newsworthy subject in their own right (Haruno 1936; Hattori K. and Uehara 1925:628; Yoshizawa N. and Ishiwata 1979:662).

An anonymous (and apparently female) critic writing in 1939, in the journal *Eiga to Rebyū* (*Movies and Revues*), mused at length about fan letters and coined the expression "to fan" (*fuan suru*) to characterize the kind of adulation that fans provided. Not only, she declares, is the fan letter a definitive sign of fandom, but "to be fanned" (*fuan sareru*) is the mark of a major star. Through their epistles, fans attempt to bridge the distance between an actor's stage character and her or his everyday life. In fact, many fans hope to use their very bodies as one such bridge, and in their letters they often ask to become a star's personal servant. But the most common request is for an autograph, followed by a date for tea. However, the critic reminds fans, it is one thing to feel alone with a particular actor while seated in a darkened auditorium, and quite another to actually have a face-to-face encounter with that person. Fans are cautioned to exercise common sense and to realize that actors in character on the screen or stage have transcended the bounds of reality; therefore, it is absurd to treat them as ordinary folk. Fans may have the power to persuade actors either to pursue or to reject certain career options—for example, the choice of a particular role—but should not interfere in the everyday life of their idols (A.Z. Joshi 1939:46–47).

The same critic also notes, with a certain resignation, that the gradual dismantling of the star system in response to wartime exigencies has reduced the number of big-name stars and, concomitantly, the number of fan letters: "fans need famous stars for whom they can fan," and likewise, stars need to "be fanned" (46). She reports that a new tactic of the Takarazuka administration, which had just recently forbidden students from responding to fan mail on their own, was to have a supervisor answer the Takarasiennes' mail, ostensibly to "protect the young women from depraved fans" (*furyō fuan*). And finally, she worries about the likelihood of Japanese stars adopting the mechanical autograph signer used by American actors, a change that will further erode the vicarious intimacy between actors and their fans (47).

The star system, which pushed select actors into the limelight, had been suppressed at the height of World War II; after it was resurrected in the 1950s, the number and content of fan letters received by screen and stage stars became a frequent subject of newspaper feature stories. Apparently, the actors in all-female revues were sent the most fan mail, which they were once again able to read and answer themselves. The several Takarasiennes interviewed noted that in their experience there were two basic types of fan letters, which often overlapped: those that focused on the actors and those that were overtly self-centered. Both types typically contained critiques of stage performances, commentaries on an actor's body, and requests for advice about how to deal with the trauma of an arranged marriage ("Fuan hyakutai" 1953). Some fan letters were overtly sexual in content. A Japanese movie actress and a female dancer reported that they had received envelopes containing condoms, sperm, and body hair ("Shisshin shisō na fuan retā" 1969:30–31). Suicide-notes-*cum*-love-letters constitute another type of fan letter that I shall discuss below.

A magazine article published in 1959 on the danger posed by zealous fans pointed out the following general contents of fan letters: critiques of performances, requests to receive letters or to become pen pals, proposals to become a star's "sister" or "brother," entreaties for advice, and donations of money. Fans also played a game in which they wrote identical letters to two different actors. The writer then became a fan of the actor who responded first ("Arashi o fukitobashita" 1959:71). However bothersome, the article continued, actors need fans, and the presence of loyal fans counterbalanced the unstable world of show business. Moreover, fan support was essential to the longevity of an actor's career since actors without fans (i.e., without a reliable audience) were dropped by production companies. Takarazuka also followed this pattern, with the exception of the early 1940s when the state's military-imperial agenda for the theater displaced the Revue's fan-driven star system.

In recent years, the text-making activities of fans have attracted the attention of scholars of popular culture. John Fiske, for example, writes:

> Fandom has been characterized as poised between popular culture and aesthetic discrimination. Fans [of *Star Trek*] are frequently not content to produce their own readings from the texts of the culture industry, but turn these readings into full-blown fan texts which in many cases they will circulate among themselves through a distribution network that is almost as well organized as that of the industry.
>
> (1991:111)

Not all Takarazuka fans are equally motivated or organized, but the Revue has engendered numerous private fan magazines, often in conjunction with fan clubs. I have already mentioned *Silk Hat*, the magazine published by the Takarazuka fan club of the same name (see chapter 4). Waseda University's *Bouquet of Dreams* is another, and it provides the following typical example of the often free-form criticism exercised by Revue fans. As the passage suggests, they do not limit their subject to particular revues but cover the managerial style and philosophy of the Revue as well. And clearly, the essay is directed toward both the Takarazuka administration and sympathetic fans.

> The public relations posters for Takarazuka need to be redone. It's too bad that the posters show Takarasiennes in heavy stage makeup as this only reinforces the impression ordinary people have of the revue actors as totally weird, and turns them off. A warmer, more positive response could be cultivated if the actors appeared—in character, to the extent possible—in a more natural (*nachuraru*) guise. Then there's the business about how hard it is to get tickets—and lately, it's been really hard to get tickets. How tickets are sold needs

to reconsidered. It's really a shame if only we fans get to see all those splendid Takarazuka revues. If the audience can be broadened, then the cloistered mood of Takarazuka will be opened bit by bit. I'd really like to see a more open and liberated mood!

I really wish that videotapes of Takarazuka revues were available for purchase. It's so disappointing how televised revues are either cut in crucial parts or not shown in their entirety. This is hardly a new request since so many people have written letters to *Kageki* on the subject. I'm so upset that I can't keep quiet about it! I really want to see all the great performances of the past [on video].[4] Thank you for your attention! Next, how about inaugurating a "Takarazuka script prize" open to the general public? You could divide the submitted scripts into drama and show categories, and select a winner from each. The winning scripts would then be staged within the year. I think that it would be really interesting to have a wide array of scripts to chose from. There could also be prizes awarded to musical scores and costumes. Wouldn't it be a good idea to try soliciting lots of different things?[5]

("Hontō ni iitai hōdai" 1991:64)

Similarly, the inaugural issue of *Silk Hat* included a feature story on the variety of ways (some plausible, some not) to procure tickets from official fan clubs and connections to ticket scalpers. Eight of the fanzine's thirty-three pages were devoted to reviews of Takarazuka stage productions. The inaugural issue also included a self-administered questionnaire on the "'Zuka fan disease" (*Zuka fuan byō*), a throwback to—and ironic twist on—the 1930s discourse of fan pathology. Briefly, this consisted of nineteen yes-no questions on aspects of the Revue and their performances, including the following:

1. You like violets.

2. You are polite and courteous. . . .

4. You like Takarazuka Familyland better than Disneyland. . . .

7. When you see someone with brown [i.e., peroxided] hair you automatically take a picture. . . .

10. When you walk around without makeup, you love to wear sunglasses. . . .

15. You've developed muscle spasms from dialing the phone too many times in search for tickets. . . .

16. Your friends refer to each other by their nicknames, and if someone doesn't have one, you assign one on the spot.

(Umehara 1991:14)

A person answering "yes" to three or fewer questions was labeled a "normal (*seijō*) person—a terribly lonely person. You should become infected by someone who carries the germs for fan pathology" (15). Fans answering sixteen to nineteen questions in the affirmative were deemed "incurable. You have a terminal disease, but you won't die, so enjoy as many Takarazuka shows as you can." In a section titled "Gossip Network" ("*Uwasa* Network"), *Silk Hat* readers were treated to the latest "clean" gossip wending its way through the fan grapevine.

Official and unofficial fan magazines engage quite unabashedly in information and knowledge brokering through meaty feature stories on individual stars, and also through regular columns detailing such specific data as what the stars like and dislike in the way of food, colors, flowers, movies, Takarazuka plays to date, and so forth ad infinitum. For example, on the occasion of the eightieth anniversary of Takarazuka's founding, *Kageki*, an official fanzine, ran a feature called the "Eightieth Anniversary Questionnaire" in which the top stars of each troupe were asked to answer ten questions:

1. What is special to you about this anniversary?
2. Which Takarazuka play do you like so much you'd like to see it revived?
3. What do you think you will excel in at the eightieth anniversary sports meet?
4. Think up a hook to attract to Takarazuka people who have never seen a revue.
5. Describe Takarazuka twenty years from now.
6. What do you think the world will be like eighty years from now?
7. Imagine yourself at eighty years of age.
8. What would you do if you had an eighty-day vacation?
9. If you found eighty yen, how would you use it?
10. What sorts of associations does the number eighty raise?
    ("Shuku hachijū-nen kinen ankēto" 1994:130–36)

Seemingly trivial and gratuitous, such question-and-answer features generate a theoretically limitless range of highly specific information about the Revue that whets and feeds the appetites of the fans who produce and consume it. The same sort of data is often recirculated among members of fan clubs and at club-sponsored tea parties to which Takarasiennes are invited. Information brokering is part of

fans' everyday lives and helps create a demand for even more esoteric knowledge about Revue actors, which in turn motivates the ongoing formation of private fan clubs, publication of magazines, and
collection of assorted Revue memorabilia.

Fan magazines, whether official or unofficial, historically have offered instruction on fan letter etiquette and on the proper relationship
that should be maintained between fans and their idols (Mizuki
1936). The two examples provided below alert us to the mutually constitutive relation between the economic interests of all-female revues
and their fears and desires, which determine their strategies of claiming an audience.

"Primer for Shōchiku Revue Fans," the title of a special report in
the official fanzine of the Shōchiku Revue, was published in the fall
of 1949 during the Allied Occupation of Japan, a time when the all-
female revues were attempting to reestablish their commercial via-
bility in the war-ravaged country. The article reads as a "how-to" lesson for neophyte fans:

1. First of all, you need to settle on a favorite star or stars. Since there
   is no limit on how many favorites you can have, the likelihood
   of fickleness and infidelity is great on your part. Nevertheless, the
   most ideal scenario is for you to develop a passionate desire for
   a cross-dressed star. The hallmark of an all-female revue fan is to
   form a companionship with a chic, beautiful youth (*seinen*) and
   to have her emotions (*kanjōsen*) powerfully stimulated (*bōsō saseru*)
   by "him."
   However, this lover (*koibito*) is *our* lover (*watakushitachi no aijin*)
   and not your *personal* lover (*watakushi no koibito*). You must not
   be disappointed when you realize how many rivals you have.
   Whereas *koi* (eros) is limited to two persons, *ai* (agape) is a much
   broader type of love.

2. You must not indulge in gallantry, or shout out a star's name in a
   shrill voice. You must also refrain from following her everywhere
   like a shadow.

3. You must become completely familiar with not only Shōchiku but
   also your favorite star. You must know what and how much she
   eats every day; whether or not she prefers *tokoroten* (agar) to rice,
   what time she leaves her home in the morning, what train line she
   takes to the theater, what brand of French face cream she favors,
   etc. In other words, you need to become a walking encyclopedia
   (*monoshiri hakase*). Finally, you must attend each play at least four
   times.

   ("Shōchiku kageki fuan kokoroechō" 1949)

Several years later, in 1955, a similar article published in the quasi-private *Takarazuka Fan* focused specifically on the twin topics of first love and same-sex love:

> Everyone has had the experience of first love (*hatsukoi*). In females, this occurs between the ages of fifteen and eighteen. What follows is an account of first love, not between actual males and females (*hontō no danjo*), that is, Adam and Eve, but between Eve and Eve. What we will discuss is somewhat different from S (*esu*).[6] There are many pessimists and introverts among females and this is the root cause of a tendency toward S. This phenomenon will not disappear with coeducation. Of course, compared to the past, the number of Ss may appear to be fewer today, but the tendency existed well before coeducation and one cannot presume that mixed-sex classrooms have brought about a decrease in the number of Ss.
>
> One seventeen-year-old student thought about making [sexual] love (*koi o shiyō to omoimashita*). She got together with a boy, but didn't have the courage to follow through. Disappointed, she became lost in her thoughts. On her way home from school one day, she passed by a souvenir shop and became enraptured with a photograph of a Takarazuka *otokoyaku*. Here was her ideal man, epitomized perfectly by the actor.
>
> She thought about how if she actually got together with a male, she would become trapped in a feudal household system, and if she got together with a female student, the relationship might not work out. If a young woman chooses same-sex love, and if she happens to be infatuated with an *otokoyaku*, then her female partner should be dressed "as if" she were actually male but more handsome and more refined. And because both partners are female, this being a case of same-sex love, their fathers won't scold them.
>
> So the young woman saved her money and began attending Takarazuka. She bought a gift for the star, and started to get excited. But she was only one among countless fans, all of whom wanted to meet the player of men's roles. Although the young woman was able to present her gift, the star uttered not a word, and the experience frustrated the fan. Our advice to those who are seeking a love match is, approach your selected partner with an open and pure heart. Don't calculate your moves, for love is not a matter of mathematics.
> ("Takarazuka fuan ni kansuru jūnisō" 1955)

Both of these postwar examples of advice to fans are quite frank about the importance and centrality of sexual desire in young women's lives and the erotic appeal of the all-female revue. The authors draw a fine, almost invisible line between encouraging sexual

Figure 23. "Marriage Fantasy" and "Dating in March." *Above*, a Shōchiku Revue couple as ideal postwar newlyweds in 1950; the feature article also included photographs of another couple in a Japanese-style wedding ceremony. *Opposite*, the 1990 Takarazuka "golden combination" of *otokoyaku* Ichiro Maki and *musumeyaku* Murasaki Tomo out on a "date." From "Kekkon fuantajii" (1950:[4]) and *Takarazuka Gurafu* (1990).

desire, which occupies the affective core of the actor-fan relationship, and actually condoning same-sex practices. The "special friendships" between fans and stars keep the Revue solvent and are promoted—but only to up to a point. They are in this sense not unlike the "buddy system" characteristic of military outfits in which homoerotic elements are exploited but never directly encouraged to manifest as sexual practices (see chapter 3). Following the postwar period and the burgeoning variety of entertainment media, the Revue's administration (as did Shōchiku's) has assiduously cultivated and nurtured female fans, even to the point of titillating their "S" sensibility, as with photo spreads in fanzines on heterogender couples (figure 23). It seems that the exotic and ambivalently erotic allure of the Revue is manipulated strategically by the management on the condition that the Takarasiennes remain objects of fans' desires without any reciprocating sexual agency of their own.

ICHIRO ♥ TOMOKO

Dating in March

一路真輝

WRITING *SHŌJO*

In the 1920s and 1930s, fan letters were criticized as symptomatic of the pathological excessiveness of the revue theater and its hangers-on. Over the past ten years, the very script in which fan letters are written has been singled out by certain critics to demonstrate the "cultural delinquency" of *shōjo*. In 1986, Yamane Kazuma, a nonfiction writer and social commentator, published a scathing critique of what he calls "abnormal *shōjo* script" (*hentai shōjo moji*), a derogatory reference to the faddish manner in which female—and male, pace Yamane's emphasis—junior high school and high school students have altered the Japanese script. Basically, following the precedent set in the 1970s by new advertising fonts and female comic book artists, young people—Yamane claims *shōjo* in particular—began rounding, flattening, and idiosyncratically stylizing Chinese and Japanese characters (figure 24). Yamane regards this development as a serious breach of calligraphic protocol, dramatically claiming that "abnormal *shōjo* script breaks the rules of Japanese letters and is a pathological phenomenon that signals the destruction of the Japanese [written] language" (1986:35, 222).

Yamane, among others, is attentive to the effects of different forms of writing on bodies and minds. The allegedly deviant character of *shōjo* is diagnosed through an aesthetic-ethical analysis of the script they employ, which is disparaged as a form of "unrestrained and lascivious" writing (cf. Jed 1989:65–66). Although adolescent boys also use an "abnormal" script, the suspect lettering is associated exclusively with *shōjo*, who, as we know, have been identified since the early 1900s as an anomalous and therefore potentially dangerous category of female. The *shōnen*, or male counterpart of the *shōjo*, has not been linked unconditionally to deviance and delinquency; like the *mobo*, or Modern Boy of the 1920s, he has generated comparatively little critical interest. There is no equivalent "abnormal *shōnen* script."

Pop ethnographer Ōtsuka Eiji draws a direct connection between the sartorial style of the Modern Girl and the typographical style of *shōjo* today. Whereas Western-style fashions were modeled publicly in the 1920s and 1930s by the boulevard-cruising *moga*, today girls and young women who wish to be seen utilize an "abnormal *shōjo* script" (Ōtsuka 1989:60). The *shōjo* who is accused of writing in an un-

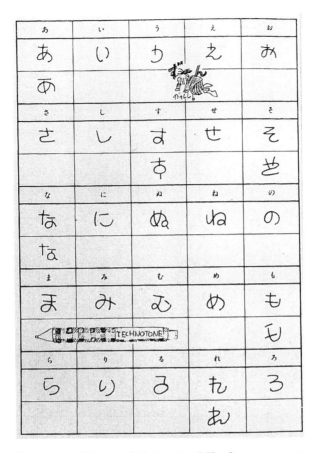

Figure 24. "Abnormal *shōjo* script." The five narrowest
rows present the Japanese cursive syllabary (*hiragana*)
in its "normal" typographic form. Below each standard
model syllable is its "abnormal" variant, sometimes
two. (The figure represents only a portion of the
complete syllabary.) From Yamane (1986: inside cover).

orthodox script is but a contemporary version of the same old trope:
females represent social disorder. In this case, that disorder is marked
by a breach of "tradition" as a result of the general decline of calligraphic skills linked to the virtually universal use of ballpoint pens
(not brushes) and, more recently, to a growing reliance on word pro-
cessors. In the eyes of Yamane and others of his patriarchal ilk, *shōjo*
are dangerous because they alter preestablished grammatical and

calligraphic codes. Theirs is a subversive style or aesthetics, a self-conscious appropriation of "bad" writing.

In her analysis of the ideology of early Florentine humanism, focusing on "the reading and writing practices which reproduce the rape of Lucretia as a literary *topos*" (Jed 1989:4), Stephanie Jed helps illuminate the political significance of *shōjo* script:

> In the field of the history of writing, contemplation of the material formation of letters leads to a whole different range of aesthetic criteria. In this context, the beautiful representation of an idea is no longer the object of aesthetic experience; rather, the formation of letters, the thickness or thinness of the pen stroke, the ways in which letters are slanted or straight, connected or unconnected, their size, their peculiarities, etc. become signs of a moment in the history and diffusion of different kinds of writing, historical signs which produce aesthetic feelings.
>
> (69)

Jed also notes that different graphic habits "attract the inscription of different kinds of stories." In modern Japan, the "graphic habits" of *shōjo* include the writing of poems, diaries, letters, fanzines, and comic books in a script that has drawn attention to the material formation of Japanese letters (or syllables and ideographs). What Yamane and other social critics have found unacceptable about *shōjo* script is the subversive aesthetic it produces as it eschews a traditional aesthetic. (I here follow Jed [1989:69] in using the term "aesthetic" in its etymological sense as having to do with sense perception.) In this connection, Ōtsuka—rightly, in my view—suggests that the "abnormal" in "abnormal *shōjo* script" should actually read "antipatriarchal" (1989:66).[7]

The relationship between *shōjo* script and the revue theater is especially evident in the production of fan letters and fan magazines, as well as in the staging of plays. Even the shift in 1930 from traditional whiteface to modern stage makeup can be interpreted as marking a change in the relationship between writing and aesthetics. Whiteface is a theatrical equivalent of the colonial policy of assimilation discussed in chapter 3. It involves an erasure, or a whiting out, of an actor's facial features and the substitution of inscribed signs of ideal masculinity or femininity.[8] Greasepaint, on the other hand, is makeup that accentuates a Revue actor's inherited features, which determine her secondary gender assignment in the first place. With the introduction of colored makeup, the actor's body became more central to the aesthetics of her performance of gender—and much more problematic, as we have seen, when Takarasiennes and their fans began to script a subtext to the Revue's official text.

This fan-scripted subtext is also illustrated by *The Rose of Versailles*, the comic book that formed the basis for Takarazuka's blockbuster revue discussed in chapter 2. The refinement of conventions to represent speech and interior monologues (and thoughts) in comic books parallels the emergence of *shōjo* script. Capsulated speech—that portion of speech enclosed in a bubble—represents the audible, dialogical voice, or the dominant text of the comic book. Unencapsulated "speech," a stylistic device that apparently emerged in the mid-1960s, represents the silent, monological voice, or the subtext. According to Ōtsuka, monologues are printed in a non-Gothic font and, more recently, in the squat and rounded fonts that directly informed the initial creation of "abnormal or antipatriarchal *shōjo* script." He points out that the use of *shōjo* script in comic books expands the subjectivity (*shutaisei*) of the monologue (*monorogu*) portion of a caption (Ōtsuka 1989:62–64).[9]

Many of the various types of fan texts reviewed in this chapter are written by hand, some in the so-called *shōjo* script. Just as the content of love letters from fans to their revue idols was regarded in the 1920s and 1930s as examples of deviant sexual desire, so the calligraphic form of fan letters is chastised today by some critics as the equivalent of cultural pornography. Whereas official fanzines are all typeset, private fanzines are either handwritten or a mixture of print and pen. These latter texts might productively be regarded as monologues, or exercises in self-subjectivity and self-representation: voices from the space-off, from the margins and interstices of the dominant discourse of gender. They can be understood as interior monologues made public and visible. Through the form of their words and the look of their texts, revue fans and *shōjo* in general have expanded those margins and interstices into an active, aestheticized space of their own.

SUICIDE AND FANDOM

One other type of fan text that remains to be considered is the suicide note. In the 1930s especially, suicide and attempted suicide were particularly especially compelling expressions of pathological fandom and of a response to compulsory heterosexuality. In addition to reports on the attempted suicides of well-known revue performers, the daily press regularly ran stories on the suicides and attempted suicides of revue fans. Not a few fans threw themselves in front of a Hankyū train.

Attempted double suicides among revue actors and their fans were popularly perceived as manifestations of the social disorder fostered by the theater, but for many women, these attempts were acts of resistance against the marriage system and the ideology of Good Wife, Wise Mother (cf. Hirozawa 1987). As psychologist Yasuda Tokutarō mused in 1935, "Why are there so many lesbian double suicides reported in the society column of the daily newspaper? One can only infer that females these days are monopolizing homosexuality" (1935:150). Unlike the majority of his contemporaries, however, Yasuda was unusual in both acknowledging Japanese lesbian practices and casting them in a favorable light. In his view, lesbianism represented female and ultimately cultural emancipation; sexual egalitarianism would ensure that neither sex was reduced to servile status (152; see also Roden 1990:54). Yasuda's interest in the "widespread phenomenon of same-sex love among females" was provoked by press coverage of the attempted double suicide between a revue fan and her stage idol (1935:146). This case is worth detailing here for at least two reasons. It drew its inspiration from and profoundly affected the all-female revue theater, and it provoked different types of writing about *shōjo* fans and revues, such as the satirical verses below.[10]

> Her love for a woman
> Was greater than her parent's love for her;
> And her older sister was cold-hearted.
> She blushed and her heart danced when first they met.
> But because they are two women together,
> The fan's life is short.
>
> Dashing from east to west,
> Theirs was a passionate love
> In a baneful world
> Only to succumb to nihilism.
> When will it fade, the anger in her heart?
> For lesbians, the answer is suicide.

Because they are not man and woman,
The fan's grief is deep.
("Modan otona tōsei manga yose" 1935)

These verses were submitted by an amateur songwriter to the humor column of the *Asahi Shinbun*, a nationally distributed daily newspaper. That day, February 17, 1935, the column was devoted to spoofing an attempted lesbian double suicide that had taken place about two and a half weeks earlier. The feminine partner was Saijō Eriko, a twenty-three-year-old leading player of women's roles in the Shōchiku Revue, and the masculine partner was Masuda Yasumare, a twenty-seven-year-old affluent and zealous fan of the star. (Yasumare was a masculine name she gave herself; her parents had named her Fumiko.)

As in the case of the Nara-Mizutani affair in 1929, the media focused mostly on Masuda, whose masculine appearance was perceived as a marker not only of aggression but also of deviance. Saijō, on the other hand, was treated more leniently for the likely reason that her feminine appearance did not make her appear different enough to be perceived as a heretic. Masuda belonged to the urban upper class whose female constituents were expected to epitomize the Good Wife, Wise Mother ideal.

The circumstances of the couple's attempted love suicide were publicized by Saijō, who published an autobiographical account two months after the event in a leading woman's magazine, the *Fujin Kōron*. She recalls how she first met Masuda backstage after a show in May 1934 at an Osaka theater: Saijō was stepping out of her bath wrapped in a towel, when Masuda approached and struck up a short conversation. The cross-dressed fan's physical beauty—especially her straight, white teeth, her round "Lloyd" spectacles, and her "Eton crop" (a short hairstyle)—impressed the actress, and the visits became a daily affair (figures 25 and 26). Come autumn, after a half year of constant contact at different venues in eastern and western Japan, Saijō reports that Masuda's letters to her grew intensely passionate; the handsome fan would write such things as "I can't bear to be apart from you for even a moment." "Although these letters could be interpreted as expressions of lesbian love," the actress explains, "I viewed them as the confessions of a sincere fan" (Saijō 1935:170). Saijō's admission of the fuzzy boundary between fandom and lesbian desire played into the dominant perception of female fans of the all-female revue as

Figure 25.   Saijō Eriko of the Shōchiku Revue. *Left*, Saijō depicted at
home writing her confessional essay for *Fujin Kōron; right*, onstage.
From Saijō (1935:169, 172).

Figure 26.   Masuda Yasumare. *Left*, Masuda with her "Lloyd"
spectacles; *right*, without them. From Tani (1935:251) and Nakano
(1935:162).

pathological and socially problematic. "Fan" was often used as a euphemism for lesbian (or for a girl or woman with lesbian proclivities); by the same token, as noted earlier, fandom was identified as a serious illness marked by an inability to distinguish between sexual fantasies (themselves problematic phenomena in women) and actual lesbian practices ("Hogosha wa kokoro seyo" 1935; "Kore mo jidaisō ka" 1935).

Saijō describes herself as a gullible actress, as highly impressionable and thus "naturally inclined" to become absorbed into Masuda's charismatic aura. She waxes nostalgic about the couple's walks, hand in hand, along the bay: "for those who didn't know who they were, they probably looked just like [heterosexual] lovers." The couple traveled widely in the Kansai area, and New Year's Day 1935 found them together in bed in a Kyoto hotel. Saijō claims that at that point she had wearied of the intensity of their relationship and wanted to return to Tokyo where she had a photo shoot scheduled for the first week of January. But whenever she mentioned the word "return home" (*kaeru*), Masuda became deathly pale and stern, and Saijō would lose her courage to insist (Saijō 1935:171–72).

To make a long story short, the two women eventually decided to commit double suicide in a Tokyo hotel, an act that, like their joint travels, was followed closely by the press corps, who had been alerted by Masuda's mother. In fact, a woozy Saijō was even interviewed in the lobby by a reporter after she had swallowed an overdose of sleeping pills. The reporter followed her to her room, found Masuda in a near coma, and called for medical help (Nakano 1935). Both women survived, and months later their double suicide attempt was still the subject of dozens of feature stories in newspapers and magazines.

Saijō included Masuda's suicide note/love letter/fan letter in her account in *Fujin Kōron*:

> Eriko.
> Even though it seems as though we've known each other forever, ours was a very short-lived relationship. But you more than anyone have left a deep and everlasting impression on my heart. What this means not even I know for sure. What I do know is that I loved you (*suki deshita*) unconditionally. Now as I approach the end of my life, I can say that I never thought that I would become so profoundly indebted to you. In any case, thank you; thank you very very much. I

don't know how I can thank you enough. No, it's not merely thanks; I will die indebted (*osewa*) to you and that is a happy thought. My incorrigibly selfish ways have caused you much grief. Please forgive me. Once I had made the decision to die, I cried and cried thinking of all that we've shared and how much I would miss you. And I realized how sad it was to die alone. To be perfectly honest, I wanted you to die with me. But I am aware of your circumstances, and you always assumed a rational stance against my emotional one. So, I'll go alone after all. Good-bye Eriko.

Yasumare
January 28, evening

(Saijō 1935:178)

The letter was likely edited by Saijō or someone else to exonerate the revue actor from any complicity in the suicide attempt by making her out to be the victim of Masuda's willful passion. Perhaps this was a strategy designed to minimize the incident's damage to her acting career. In any case, Saijō left Shōchiku to pursue a career in film and disappeared from that revue's fanzines, where before she had been featured regularly.

Like revues, double suicide attempts were often dramaturgic affairs representing the inversion of private and public, involving players of men's and women's (i.e., differently gendered) roles, theatricalized travels, press coverage and critical reviews, and scripts in the form of suicide notes and love letters. The Masuda-Saijō double suicide attempt, together with other even more vivid accounts, suggests an apparently ironic correspondence between the resolve to commit suicide and the resolve to challenge on some level a family-state system in which girls and women were rendered docile and subservient (see Robertson forthcoming). Historically in Japan, suicide or attempted suicide was recognized and to a certain extent valorized as an empowering act that illuminated the purity and sincerity of one's position and intentions. A suicide note corroborated these virtues by documenting one's motives. In other words, in Japan suicide was a culturally intelligible act. The Modern Girls who attempted suicide understood that it was an act that turned a private condition into a public matter. Obviously, an attempted or unsuccessful suicide accrues more direct political capital as the women live to tell in greater complexity about the circumstances informing their resolve to die, to act on their resolve, and to encourage action on the sometimes radical vision articulated in their suicide notes. Saijō, for example, claims in her autobiographical account that she was able to exert significant influence on the Masuda family lawyer, requesting that Yasumare be allowed to form a branch household (*bunke*) and live independently (1935:178).[11]

Like fan letters and other writings, suicide notes and stories by Japanese female couples about their attempts at suicide collectively constituted another voice—explicitly controversial, defensive, or both—in heated public debates about the interrelationship of sexuality, gender ideology, cultural identity, and national image. Moreover, like the acts and attempted acts of suicide itself, these texts, including those that doubled as love letters, were both a private exploration and a public proclamation: "public" because by writing letters one attempted to make one's views known to the correspondent, whether a lover, parent, sibling, or anonymous reader. Suicide notes in this sense were an extension of, as opposed to a substitution for, lesbian practices. Finally, largely on account of the cultural intelligibility of suicide in Japan, stories of attempted suicide can also be interpreted as an effective way to get controversial ideas into print under auspices that were perceived in a more sympathetic, less threatening, light.

FAN EROTICS

The motives and effects of both fandom and fan writing, from lesbianism to suicide, have been the focus of countless analyses since the earliest years of the Revue. I would like to return to the subject of male fans at this juncture and suggest that an erotic aesthetic—as opposed to, but in some cases in addition to, an identity politics—informs the attachment of male fans (and female fans also, as we have seen) to the Takarazuka Revue. When male fans *are* acknowledged, it is generally assumed that they are "naturally" attracted to the *musumeyaku* (cf. Haruno 1936:247), although this is not necessarily true. Leading *otokoyaku* Gō Chigusa (retired 1971), who referred to herself as *boku*, a masculine self-referent, and claimed to "look like a man," thus expressed surprise to receive letters from male fans ("Puraibēto intabyū" 1966:42). One contemporary *peragoro*, or zealous male fan, a well-known professor of English literature at the University of Tokyo, apparently was feverishly devoted to *otokoyaku* Mitsuki Jun (retired 1983) "because she closely resembled the French film actor, Alain Delon." He likened the handsome *otokoyaku* to "a car with a purring engine" (quoted in "Gendai no ōoku" 1979:23).

Indeed, the player of men's roles provides some men with an opportunity to experience (an unacknowledged) homoerotic desire within the parameters of a nominal and symbolic heterosexuality. Even the attraction of male fans to the *musumeyaku* is not necessarily for the naive and simple reason that males are "naturally" drawn to women; the players of women's roles are equally attractive to transvestites among the male fans as models for cross-dressing (figure 27), just as the *otokoyaku* are emulated by the "new dandies." And, as the example of the university professor suggests, the *otokoyaku* are recipients of the displaced erotic desire some male fans have for male movie stars.

A 1975 book on Takarazuka fans includes the story of Yazaki Hatahita, a middle-aged man, who took after his father and became a fan of Takarazuka *otokoyaku*, declaring that "females dressed as men are incredibly sexy." This was an admission absent from most accounts of the sensuous appeal of the players of men's roles. The Kabuki *onnagata*, however, makes him uncomfortable and defensive. Yazaki continues: "*Otokoyaku* can't quite pass as men. When females wear trousers their rear ends are a dead giveaway. When I see [an *otokoyaku*'s] bottom, I realize that 'he' is a 'she.' That's mind-blowing! In fact, I find it thrilling to try to uncover the female in the man. Maybe I'm horny or something, but then horniness is a defining characteristic of males!" (quoted in Suzuki T. 1975 [1974]:95).

Universal essentialist and social constructionist views of gender are evident in Yazaki's view of both himself, *as a male*, and the Takarazuka *otokoyaku*. He acknowledges that females can perform as men (a constructionist argument); nevertheless, as a male, his horniness (an essentialist argument) motivates him to scrutinize the shape of their bottoms, which can be associated only with female bodies (an essentialist argument). Yazaki is typical of many if not most people in mixing essentialist and constructionist views of sex and gender.

It is worth recounting here a similar story from 1935 featuring a female fan who identifies herself as a man. The fan is cruising Ginza for Takarazuka actors. Someone passes by in a man's suit who the fan believes is a "crossed-dressed beauty" (*dansō no reijin*). She gives pursuit only to realize that the person is an actual male. "I thought that that person was a 'cross-dressed beauty' but I've found a real male. Males these days are so flabby (*kunyakunya*) that it's easy to mistake them for females!" (quoted in Nishikawa 1935:64–65). The focus on

宝塚グラフ 1969 12

Figure 27. A *musumeyaku*. Yashiro Mari of the Moon Troupe in a glamorous Western guise. From *Takarazuka Gurafu* (1969).

the buttocks as a distinct indicator of sex makes it strikingly similar to Yazaki's account. The story also alludes to the alleged feminization of males as a consequence of the masculinization of females, as discussed in chapter 2.

Several related points come to mind. First, Yazaki seems to suspend his a priori knowledge of the fact that Takarazuka *otokoyaku*, by definition, are female in order to pursue his sport of uncovering the female in the man. Second, he attributes his prurient interest in this pursuit to his maleness; and third, he essentializes buttocks and not genitalia as a defining attribute of sex (as defined in the introduction). For Yazaki, the absence of a penis follows from the shape of the performer's buttocks. He deduces that an *otokoyaku* is female because he has noticed that the performer has a "female" bottom; but since he already knows that the *otokoyaku* is female, and since he also already "knows" that female bottoms are different from male bottoms—presumably his own in this case—he confirms, via this circular reasoning, the essential femaleness of the *otokoyaku*.

As scholars of sex-gender systems have shown, buttocks per se— like eyebrows, hairstyles, shoulders, and facial shape—are salient sex and gender markers only insofar as they are part of conventionalized knowledge (i.e., "common sense") about gender; they are socially constructed signs of sex, learned as part of the process of socialization. Yazaki effectively confirms the commonsense understanding of the dichotomous construction of sex and gender. Finally, he compares the *otokoyaku* to himself in assessing her "maleness," or lack thereof, and not to the *musumeyaku*, whose femininity is staged in order to make the player of men's roles appear more masculine in contrast. By the same token, Yazaki's own masculinity is overdetermined, which makes the *otokoyaku* appear less masculine in contrast. It is significant that the Kabuki *onnagata* makes him uncomfortable, or so he claims in print: for Yazaki to turn his prurient gaze onto the *onnagata* in an effort to recover the male from within the woman would be tantamount to self-consciously participating in this homoerotic exercise, since he knows that the *onnagata* is, after all, a male. It would seem that his libidinous desires and sexual identity are not confluent.

Yazaki alludes to the erotic dimension of the Revue when, remembering his youth, he recalls how the "sheer sexiness of a female dressed as a man caused my heart to pound" (quoted in Suzuki T. 1975 [1974]:94–95). Perhaps for this male fan, the erotic distinction between the *onnagata* and the *otokoyaku* is a case of males desiring not males—as that would be a literal homosexualization of desire, contrary to common sense (as opposed to historical practices)—but rather females who are themselves desired as men: *otokoyaku*, for example (Kaite 1987:165). As the history of Revue criticism suggests, players of men's roles are bewitching to some males provided they remain onstage; offstage, they represent and threaten social disorder. However, it is also true that many males are attracted to the spectacle of male-as-Woman, as in the case of transvestite soldier shows, the Kabuki *onnagata*, the cross-dressed transvestite performer, or the nightclub "hostess" today—the last two identified by such categorical names as She-Male (*shii mēru*), Sister Boy (*shisutā bōi*), Mr. Lady (*misutā redei*), and New Half (*nyū hāfu*).

NEW HALF

"New Half" refers to the representation, in ordinary and pornographic comic books and cartoons alike, of fantastical, exotic, intersexed, androgynous bodies, most typically portrayed in the form of a figure with breasts and a penis (figure 28). Another term for the New Half phenomenon is *nijikon* (double complex): living males and fictive men (in comic books, for example) who cross-dress in the much fetishized style of Lolitas, or sexually precocious, cute teenage girls. For this reason such persons and "male" images are also called *rorikon*, an abbreviation of *rorita konpurekusu*, Lolita Complex. New Half comic books and their readers are linked to male fans of the Takarazuka Revue by way of a homoerotic aesthetic that alerts us to the convoluted constructions of (Japanese) male sexuality, a complex subject that I can only touch on in this chapter.

When applied to human beings, New Half identifies male cross-dressers who may or may not identify themselves as homosexual, a category of sexuality (like "heterosexual") whose semantic limits are constantly exceeded by actual sexual practices. The prefix "new" distinguishes the term from Half (*hāfu*), a word used, somewhat pejoratively, to indicate a person of ethnically mixed parentage—"half and half"—one parent an ethnic Japanese and the other, usually, non-Asian. As exoticized hybrids, the Takarasiennes represent a link between the Half and the New Half not because they are of mixed ethnicity—apparently very few actors are—but because they engage in cross-ethnicking as well as cross-dressing.

Figure 28.   She-Male. "I know it
must be a shock, but I'm a She-Male.
Oh no! It's stood up!" From Watanabe Tsuneo (1990:87).

The Elizabeth Club is one of hundreds of New Half clubs advertised in magazines aimed at gay males, such as *Barazoku* (*Rose Tribe*),
Adon (*Adonis*), and *Samson*. The club offers its male members an opportunity to cross-dress—to perform androgyny—and maintains a
rental wardrobe of about 200 dresses and kimonos to facilitate their
fantasies. Six beauticians are on call; of some 600 members, half are
married. All the members apparently identify themselves as homosexual and enjoy cross-dressing as a stress-releasing hobby. Once
cross-dressed inside the club, the males take on a feminine name and,
accordingly, speak in a high, somewhat nasal, feminine voice. One
member claims that assuming a feminine persona allows him to write
songs about emotional subjects that elude him at other times. Not surprisingly, he hopes to be reborn as a female in his next life. The club
provides him with an opportunity to occupy another gendered subject position, just as private fan clubs enable Takarazuka devotees to
perform the gender(ed) role of their choice. It seems that once again

the male body has become a visible site and surface for gender experiments. The performance artist and Takarazuka fan Morimura Yasumasa, for example, has capitalized on this trend. In his latest work, he "masters" the technologies of gender by posing not as ordinary females, but as famous European, American, and Japanese actresses with distinctive personas (Morimura 1996a, 1996b).

Ample breasts distinguish the New Halfs from the otherwise flat-chested "beautiful boy" (*bishōnen*) comic book characters whose genitals are represented ambiguously ("Dansei no naka no 'chōshōjo' tachi" 1986:36). Not only are ostensibly male readers excited by images of sexually mature yet adolescent New Half characters, but, according to sexologist Watanabe Tsuneo, they also identify with those very images. Watanabe, who does not consider female readers, suggests that the New Half characters, and, by extension, cross-dressed males, provide "ordinary" males—as opposed to Kabuki *onnagata*—with an opportunity "to possess a woman completely"; more specifically (in an apparent reference to Jung), to recover their "lost feminine aspect" (1990:87–88; "Dansei no naka no 'chōshōjo' tachi" 1986). In a related but different vein, feminist sociologist Ueno Chizuko suggests that the intersexed New Half is a metaphor for males who do not want to become adults (1990 [1989]:131–32)—"adult" here apparently defined as an unambiguously heterosexual male. According to Ueno's altogether normative view of sexuality, males attracted to the New Half characters want to engage in sexual activities but do not want to assume the other responsibilities associated with social adulthood in Japan.

Pornographic New Half comics most often feature androgynous figures masturbating or as party to manual and oral sex scenes, as opposed to "straight" sex scenes. A New Half's orgasm—the visible "money shot"—is "his," but the vocal effects—the standardized "ah, ah, ahs"—are "hers." If, as Watanabe suggests, male readers identify with the intersexed New Half, then this suggests a suturing of the subject-object split that characterizes the usual understanding of the pornographic image: that is, the construction of the female's sex as other, as the object of a masculine gaze (cf. Kuhn 1985:40). New Half pornography is quite different, for it conjoins femininity and "male" genitalia. The same yoking describes the Kabuki *onnagata*, while the Takarazuka *otokoyaku* represents the combination of masculinity and "female" genitalia (i.e., the female man). In short, both the comic book and flesh-and-blood New Halfs, like the Kabuki and Takarazuka actors, embody an unconventional realignment of sex and gender, signifying a body that doubles as its other (Kaite 1987:158). The spectator or reader can have his or her scopophilia, or desire for pleasurable looking, both ways. Spectatorship and identification are collapsed. Watanabe further suggests that the erotic allure of the male woman and female man translates into a self-love directed toward the other within (cf. Watanabe T. 1990; see also chapter 3). Similarly, Takarazuka actors performed in wartime revues as various colonized Asian subjects who sang of their "love" for Japan, while at the same time Japanese colonial administrators pursued an assimilation policy aimed at Japanizing other Asians and cultivating a "love" for Japan.

The conflict between the commonsensical notion that "opposites attract" and an awareness of the arbitrary alignment of sex and gender creates a tension that can erupt as erotic desire. (I am interested not in analyzing the psychological dimensions of this condition but rather in examining its social expressions and ramifications, for example, as assimilation policy.) Clearly, the commonsense construction of sexuality, premised on opposition and otherness, can be experienced and contained in one body. Thus, the horniness that Yazaki, the Takarazuka fan, feels in scrutinizing the *otokoyaku* by way of his own self-perceived masculinity suggests an element of "self-directed eroticism" (*jikoshikijō*), to borrow Watanabe Tsuneo's expression (borrowed in turn from Magnus Hirschfeld) (1990:85). For this male fan, the boundary-blurring Revue occasions a form of sexual self-sufficiency whereby one body, his, is able to accomplish the erotic work of two. Similarly, since Takarasiennes are forbidden to have love interests during their tenure in the Revue, some critics have noted with sarcasm that they are obliged to make love to their mirrored selves, thus ensuring their sexual self-sufficiency (Tō 1972:11). And thus fans perceive the player of men's roles, whether the revue *otokoyaku* or the dandies at Club New Marilyn, as a female body that accommodates both genders without being constrained by either one. The compelling charm and appeal of the Revue's players of male roles, the New Half comics, Miss Dandies, and androgynous celebrities such as Gao (discussed below), inheres in the assimilationist logic of "body double": namely, that the "other" is best knowable as the "self" the other way around.

ANYTHING GAOS?

These fluid negotiations of the relationship of sex, gender, and sexuality recall the positively valenced views of androgyny put forth by Akiyama Satoko, Asano Michiko, Carolyn Heilbrun, and Kurahashi Yukiko. As elaborated in chapter 2, Akiyama, for example, valorizes a Jungian construction of androgyny in debunking the notion of "sexual perversion" (*seitōsaku*). She argues that the sexual choices available to females and males are as varied as the combinations of feminine and masculine tendencies they embody (Akiyama 1990; see also Ifukube 1932). Asano suggests, problematically in my view, that the "traditional Japanese harmony of masculine and feminine qualities" was disrupted by Japan's modernization in the late nineteenth century;[12] but she also observes, accurately in this case, a recent fascination in Japanese popular culture with androgyny and cross-dressing (1989:201–2).

Actually, there is more than just a fascination today with crossdressing; androgyny is big business. New Half comic books and animations,[13] transvestite clubs for males, Miss Dandy clubs for females, clothing fashions, cross-dressed celebrities, and of course the perennially popular Takarazuka Revue, enjoying an all-time high number of applicants to the Academy, are all part of the powerful and metaphoric—if ambivalent—salience of androgyny.

There is also Gao, a Japanese version of the gender-bending Canadian popular singer k. d. lang. The Japanese pop icon was discovered —or rather, invented—in 1993. Her public relations campaign capitalizes on and commodifies the image of the androgyne (figure 29). The calculated and exotic ambiguity of her image is also evident in a publicity statement in English aimed at Japanese consumers. It calls attention to the slippery sexual politics at play in many areas of show business past and present: "How does Gao spend her one-day-of-theyear? That voice, that presence, that style—A man? Or is it a woman? How old is she? What's her true sexuality? A million possibilities surface, but if we look at her, none seem to fit. She's unlike anyone else. She's Gao!" ("Gao" 1993:32).

Despite the use of "she," the statement questions Gao's sex, gender, and sexuality, and it clues us in to the commodification and manipulation today of gender ambiguity and ambivalence; the space of the dominant is being enlarged to encompass the very margins that

Figure 29.   Gao. A Japanese version of singer k. d. lang. From Gao (1993:32).

define the center. Gao, like Mine Saori's ode to androgyny in chapter 2, is the creation not of some radical queer underground but of a powerful corporation (in this case, Victor Entertainment). The idol singer thus is situated in the mainstream discourse of gender in Japan today. Recall that Takarazuka too is a component of the giant Hankyū Group of companies. The marketing of Gao and the Takarasiennes alerts us to the operations of the "libidinal economy" of the capitalist market and corporate world, which, like imperialist regimes, is quick to incorporate alternative or marginal trends into the commonsensical mainstream, thereby minimizing the possibility of social disruption. As wartime assimilation policy illustrates, the difference posed by the potentially disorderly other can be appropriated and neutralized, although the possibility always remains that such difference may reassert itself at some point, in which case it may be purged altogether. Ambiguity and ambivalence have gathered significant cachet in Japanese cultural history: Gao and other Japanese androgynes and their fans signify, allegorically, a national culture that is an ever-contemporizing, self-consciously hybrid formation.

Epilogue

If you haven't savoured "Takarazuka," you don't know Japan.

Takarazuka 1989:[4–5]
(public relations brochure)

STRATEGIC AMBIVALENCE

In 1969, the Japanese playwright Tō Jūrō shocked audiences with *Shōjo Mask* (*Shōjo kamen*), his surrealistic play about the Takarazuka Revue. It opened at Waseda University, home of a large, coed Takarazuka fan club. Whereas the popular image of the Revue was of a glitzy spectacle with erotic tinges, Tō portrayed Takarazuka as a nefarious remnant of Japanese imperialism; actors and fans alike were cast as pathological and pathetic.

KASUGANO: The Asakusa operas have disappeared and only Takarazuka remains. "Our Takarazuka" alone still squeezes out the tears of virgins from all over Japan. Kai [a *shōjo*],[1] listen to what I have to say—it's for your benefit. The bathwater that you've plunged your feet into consists of the tears of crazed virgins collected over the past fifty-five years—it's a tear bath. [Stick your finger in and] taste it; see, it's a little sour, isn't it?

KAI: (Tastes the water on her finger.) Yes.

KASUGANO: You know, my (*atashi*) tears are mixed into that water too; rather, my (*boku*)[2] tears. . . . I sobbed along with the fans. . . . When I soaked my body, I (*atashi*) was theirs, and they were mine.

Tō 1972:19

Kasugano is a character who represents Takarazuka's veteran classic *otokoyaku*, Kasugano Yachiyo (see figure 9). Kasugano, who has remained unmarried, consequently is allowed to perform on the revue stage, usually in special numbers that frame her talent in Japanese-style dance. She appears in Tō's play as the owner of a basement coffee shop called Nikutai, a word meaning both "human flesh" and "carnality." The café is posed as a homologue of both the Revue and a hospital in Manchuria, where, apparently, the real Kasugano was hospitalized with pneumonia in 1941. In the play, she claims to have been befriended there by Amakasu Tadahiko, the police captain who organized the murder in 1923 of the leading anarchist Ōsugi Sakae and his wife, Itō Noe, an editor of the feminist journal *Bluestocking*. Kai has been brought to the coffee shop by her grandmother, a lifetime fan of the actor, to see Kasugano. Neither Kasugano nor her employee, a sadistic man, has ventured outside the café since the end of World War II, and they are as clueless about modern-day Japan as they are awash in nostalgia for the days of empire. Tō's satire effectively deconstructs the official story of the Takarazuka Revue.

In *Shōjo Mask*, set in the "miracle sixties," the once avant-garde Revue is depicted as a musty but dangerous anachronism—dangerous because of the willful nostalgia it conjures for the dreamworlds of yesterday without addressing the exigencies of present-day Japan. As cultural critique, *Shōjo Mask* operates on many levels. It attacks the dystopian aspects of postwar popular culture and the deliberate amnesia both enabling and induced by it, represented by the dotty Kasugano. It mercilessly satirizes the Takarazuka Revue itself, with its feudalistic administration and allegedly sexually frustrated cast of aged *shōjo*; and it caustically denounces Japanese imperialist aggression in which the Revue was complicit, if only opportunistically.

Shōjo Mask attests to the continuing salience of Takarazuka as a site of and for social commentary and criticism. Of course, the Revue's self-referential exoticism and public image as a dreamland effectively places it outside Japanese history. Consequently, Japan's imperial past has not been revisited in its productions since the "emergency situation" reviews of the wartime period. One exception was the performance in 1953 of *The Tomb of the Red Star Lily* (*Himeyuri no haka*), a tragic story about a volunteer brigade of Japanese schoolgirls who perished in the Battle of Okinawa. The playwright, Kikuta Kazuo, who was inactive during the height of the war with the United States, acknowledged that this was an atypical Takarazuka revue, but he replied to his critics that he wished to produce an antiwar drama to help kindle the spirit of constitutional democracy in postwar Japan (Kikuta 1982). Of course, just as the Revue exploited the wartime need for emergency-minded entertainment, so it seized the opportunity to amplify the antiwar sentiments spreading through the public immediately after the war: the new social climate called for a new corporate strategy. However, *The Tomb of the Red Star Lily* focused not on

Japanese imperialism but on the intrepid spirit of the vanquished girls—it was an antiwar play that drew the line at criticizing Japanese warmongers. Generally speaking, the postwar Revue administration decided early on to stage only revues that recalled a safely distant Japanese past or conjured up fantastic visions of exotic lands across the ocean.

Unlike Tō's satirical play, which was appreciated by a small intelligentsia, Takarazuka continues to attract enormous audiences throughout Japan and abroad. It remains a lucrative asset of the Hankyū Group and contributes to the ongoing definition of Japanese (popular) culture. The Revue claims to sell dreams; the fans claim that Takarazuka is a bouquet of dreams; the Takarasiennes claim that they protect their fans' dreams. However, those fans who consider themselves sympathetic critics, like Umehara Riko of Silk Hat, single out the Revue administration as Takarazuka's own worst enemy, warning that if its members do not begin to improve the quality and relevance of scripts and introduce challenging dramatic material, then the actors will not be sufficiently motivated to perform to their potential and even the most loyal fans will begin to lose interest in their beloved theater (Umehara 1994:170–71).

The mid-1970s marked a period when Japanese began to reassess the costs of the unquestioned pace of postwar reindustrialization and economic growth, which peaked in the decade between the Tokyo Olympics of 1964 and the *Rose of Versailles* in 1974. "Japanese tradition" was revalorized in spirit if not in actual form (Robertson 1994 [1991], 1997b; see also Ivy 1995). The Revue adopted a two-pronged strategy to ensure its popularity and financial solvency: it proclaimed itself one of Japan's "traditional" theaters, and it unabashedly undertook to capitalize on the erotic appeal of the Takarasiennes to (especially) female fans, who from the postwar period onward constituted the vast majority of the Revue audience.

The first prong is summed up in the Revue's public relations brochure for foreigners:

> Foreigners visiting Japan often comment on how difficult it is to understand the Japanese. There is no code, no secret key. Japanese culture is simply too vast and too varied to be fully comprehended. Nonetheless, rare glimpses are possible, and occasional insights are sometimes painlessly attainable. "Takarazuka" is one of these. It affords both Japanese and foreigners an instant history of an incredi-

bly complex artistic heritage, a window to view Japanese life, dance, music, culture and, what is perhaps most interesting of all, a play-back of how the Japanese see and interpret the West.

"Takarazuka" is Japan. It is a race through history, a course in theatre and a cultural experience all wrapped up in sparkling sequins and gorgeous costumes. . . . [E]very visitor is urged to come to "Takarazuka" because nowhere else is there so much to learn and see and enjoy about Japan.

(Takarazuka 1989:[4–5])

But, as we have seen, the "race through history" offered by Takarazuka is ahistorical: its version of what Kobayashi announced to be a "pure, righteous, and beautiful" national cultural genealogy is a montage of invented and revised traditions. Takarazuka's Japan is unsullied and uncompromised by the ugly realities and uncomfortable memories of wartime atrocities.

The second prong is evident in the open experimentation with an-drogynous *otokoyaku* in the late 1960s and 1970s, foreshadowing Os-car in *The Rose of Versailles* (1974) and culminating in the 1985 revue *Androgyny*. The Revue's interest in selling erotic dreams is also no-ticeable in fan magazines and photograph albums of players of men's and women's roles portrayed in words and pictures offstage but in character, such as Mine Saori's ambivalent musings (in the epigraph of chapter 2), as well as in the special features in official fanzines ti-tled "Twosome," "Talk of Two," and "Dating in March." In these fea-tures, Takarazuka stage couples, or "golden combinations," assume poses that idealize "butch-femme" and heterosexual couples simul-taneously (see figure 23). The Revue has not been alone in toying with the boundaries of sexual transgression. In the mid- to late 1970s Pink Lady, a female duo that dominated the pop music charts, and the equally popular Beauty Pair, a female pro-wrestling duo that also sang, were often featured in girls' and women's magazines posed as golden combinations, and even as newlyweds. Women find another contemporary venue of negotiable sexuality and erotic titillation in the Miss Dandy clubs.

The Revue continues to manipulate the long problematic erotic al-lure of Takarasiennes by anticipating the appetite of fans for physical beauty. In 1958 an annual newcomers' performance (*shinjin kōen*) was inaugurated to give recent Academy graduates an opportunity to dis-play their new skills on stage, as well as to provide fans with an opportunity to track the careers of newcomers and to develop affectionate loyalties to them. Many fans admit to poring over newcomers' performance programs, singling out for attention those actors whose looks appeal to them—a ritual known inelegantly as "eating face" (*menkui*). The Revue also revitalized the close actor-fan relations that had been suspended during the wartime years, including annual sports festivals and regular parties. These functions serve to cultivate affective ties among Takarasiennes and their fans, and they help nurture enthusiastic, faithful, and dependable revue spectators.

As the Takarazuka audiences have become more self-selected in the recreational media–saturated environment of postwar Japan, they have become more critical spectators. Sooner or later the Revue administration will probably have to act on fans' warnings that the erotic allure of the Revue, however thrilling, can no longer substitute for high-quality dramatic productions that separate the talented professionals among the "students" from the rank amateurs. Loyal Takarazuka fans build their personal lives, desires, and communities around the Revue, and they are increasingly less content to settle for recycled oldies and formulaic new material.

In a way, the eighty-year-old Takarazuka Revue has completed a developmental cycle. From the perspective of national popular culture, the revue theater was a founding "text" of modernism in early-twentieth-century Japan, the so-called revue age. With its fast-paced juxtaposition of fragmentary episodes, the montage-like revue allowed for a "blossoming of allegories—providing multiple jumping-off points in the present from which to imagine a better future" (Lavin 1992:53). It represented a new synthesis of Japanese and non-Japanese cultural artifacts and institutions, not imposed from without but produced by the deliberate selection and repositioning (both official and unofficial) of forms and symbols. As conceptualized by Kobayashi and revue age pundits, the Takarazuka Revue was a whole new, national phenomenon of popular culture: a unique, wholesomely exotic hybrid institution representative of a New Japan. And like the New Japan, it was a mixture of various cultural forms from which it was sometimes differentiated.

This aspect of the modern Revue's ambiguity and ambivalence was less problematic than its identification with the Modern Girl and the New Woman. Critics often referred sarcastically to the players of men's roles—and all Modern Girls and New Women were perceived as players of men's roles to some extent—as *modan*, using the ideographs for "cut hair" instead of the syllabary ordinarily used to transliterate "modern" (Inoue 1989:[4]). Whereas the montage-like structure of the Revue was exploited by the state in its efforts to enact a vision of Greater East Asian culture, the fans of the Revue, pathologized collectively as Janus-faced *shōjo*, embodied the more troublesome aspects of the strategic ambivalence of New Japan. Unlike the peoples in the Revue's pan-Asian fantasies, whose discomforting cultural differences were aestheticized and eroticized on stage, the offstage conduct of girls and women lumped together in the category of *shōjo* continually perplexed educators, politicians, social critics, psychologists, and Revue administrators alike who could not fathom their motives and desires. And, as evident in the utterly sexist debate about "abnormal script," the *shōjo* remains both titillating and threatening, and therefore in need of surveillance and control. One mode of control, as discussed previously, involves her assimilation by the (pornographic) New Half.

Since the postwar period Takarazuka, the only remaining revue theater from the revue age, has positioned itself as an integral part of Japanese tradition: a quick précis of the "artistic heritage" of modern Japan. In a sense, the Revue's public relations brochure is right: Takarazuka does offer many insights into the workings and meanings of Japanese social and cultural formations and practices—but not in the anachronistic and chimerical way that the Revue insists upon. Takarazuka *is* Japan, more truly than the administration realizes.

Modernity, as the experience of modernization and its impact on contemporary life, is not the acme of a "Western" teleology but exists under different signs—"Japanese," for example—at different times (Bhabha 1991:207; see also King 1995). Although it is still modern in the sense of occupying an important place in contemporary Japanese popular culture, Takarazuka can no longer claim, as it could in the 1920s and 1930s, a monopoly on conveying technology, speed, exotica, and consumerism. The Revue and the Takarazuka Music Academy may, however, retain a limited monopoly today on the system of values that helped fan the libidinal economy of imperialism. If the Revue's present repertoire of recycled and formulaic productions is arguably more limited than before in the types of allegories it allows to flower, the one dominant allegory that continues to flourish—and to bud new allegories—is that of hybridity and the ambivalent dreams it engenders.

Andreas Huyssen's oft-cited thesis of "mass culture as woman," as "modernism's other," does not, in my view, quite capture the texture of the sexual politics at play in Japanese national popular culture (Huyssen 1986). True, the *shōjo* and all-female Revue remain sites for displaced fears and personal and political anxieties provoked by the new social crossings and conflicts associated with modernism and its accomplice, modernization. But they suggest instead that "modernism's other" is a mirror image of itself, an enantiomorph: that is, the same thing the other way around. The *otokoyaku* yesterday, the New Half today: symbols of modernism under different signs at different times, both retain an underlying gender dichotomy even as they present a singular if ambiguous appearance. In other words, the New Half is a corporeal koan: a body that doubles as its other. Contrary to Huyssen then, popular (or mass) culture is not "woman" but androgyne. Adrienne Rich has argued that the androgyne creates an illusion of symmetry and equality (1976:76–77) and in this way conceals the asymmetry of power that is the cause of its existence in theory and practice (Bauman 1991:14). Similarly, for eighty years now the hybrid Takarasiennes have exemplified how ambiguity and ambivalence can be used strategically in multiple, intersecting discourses, from the sexual to the colonial, both to contain difference and to reveal the artifice of containment. What Kobayashi knew, the imperial state sensed, and critics of the all-female revue seemed to have missed is that ambivalence *is* all about order, whether a New World Order or social order at home.

It poses little challenge to sketch out the gist of a Takarazuka Revue called "Twenty-First-Century Modern." O la la! Cultured Parisians dressed for the opera would file along the "silver bridge" reeling off a breathless litany of all the desirable hi-tech equipment made in Japan for export. Then, following a cancan by actors costumed as camcorders, the star *otokoyaku*, resplendent in a glittery white tuxedo, would croon a haunting melody that traced Tokyo's emergence as a world city. But a far less fun and more pressing challenge at century's end is to understand better the contradictory politics—sexual, colonial, and other—that ambiguity and ambivalence enable and disable. Can there be peace and freedom with ambivalence? Can there be peace and freedom without it? These are questions in search of a theater.

Notes

INTRODUCTION

1. Although I was introduced to Takarazuka during my childhood I had no specific memory of the Revue.

2. Kobayashi served as minister of commerce and industry from July 1940 to April 1941, and as minister of state from October 1945 to March 1946, before assuming the presidency of the Postwar Rehabilitation Agency. However, because of his government role during the war, the Occupation forces removed him from public office and for several years prevented him from engaging directly in his businesses, including the Revue.

Kobayashi began his successful career with the Mitsui Bank; his résumé includes the presidencies of the Tokyo Electric Light and Japan Light Metal companies, and directorships of the Korean Electric Power and North China Electric companies, in addition to the Imperial Theater and Mitsubishi department store. He also founded the Tōhō Motion Picture Company in 1932, which grew into one of the largest movie theater chains in Japan. The indefatigable Kobayashi was often characterized as the "Japanese Ziegfeld," an analogy drawn on the Takarazuka stage thirty years after his death in the 1986 *Revue Symphony* (*Rebyū kōkyōgaku*), a "true story of Florenz Ziegfeld" (*Rebyū kōkyōgaku* 1986:50).

3. Theater historian Ōzasa Yoshio suggests that Kobayashi also may have been inspired by an all-girl chorus organized by the Shirokiya Department Store in Tokyo in 1912 (Ōzasa 1986:25).

4. *Kageki* is often translated as either "opera" or "revue," although the latter is most common in reference to Takarazuka.

5. The theater was originally designed to seat 4,000 and continued to be advertised as having that seating capacity even after the number of seats had been reduced.

6. The Academy was first called the Takarazuka Musical Theater Academy (Takarazuka ongaku kageki gakkō) and renamed in 1939 the Takarazuka Music and Dance Academy (Takarazuka ongaku buyō gakkō). Its present name (Takarazuka ongaku gakkō) dates to 1946.

7. See Shōchiku Kagekidan 1978 for the official history of that revue.

8. The first Japanese talkie, *Madam and Wife* (*Madamu to nyōbo*), was produced by Shōchiku in 1931.

9. Although a woman, the legendary dancer Okuni from Izumo, is credited with having initiated Kabuki at the start of the seventeenth century,

women have been banned from that stage since 1629. Apparently, the newly installed Shogunate was disturbed by the general disorder, including unlicensed prostitution, following the performances; patrons regularly fought with each other for access to their favorite dancers. Replacing the women with boys did not solve the problem, for the male patrons were equally attracted to their own sex. Eventually, the prohibition of females, and later boys, prompted the emergence of the *onnagata*, adult males who specialize in "female" gender (see Shively 1970). Despite the shogunal decrees, women continued to perform in private, parlor theaters, often in tea houses that doubled as brothels.

10. The Shinpa theater movement arose around the 1890s in Osaka through the efforts of amateurs who, with some knowledge of the Euro-American theater world, staged "Western" dramas in colloquial Japanese. *Shinpa* continues to be used to describe plays with a contemporary setting.

11. A Takarazuka "matrilineage" has been developing gradually over the past decade. There is one case of a three-generation line of actors, and in sixty-seven cases daughters have followed in their mother's footsteps. Seventy-five pairs of sisters have performed together, including four sets of twins, and in twelve cases three sisters have shared the stage (Hashimoto 1994:196–97).

12. The number of Revue actors increased from initially 20 to about 350 by 1931 (Hashimoto 1984:118–120). For over the past two decades, the Takarazuka Music Academy has accepted an average of 40 new students each year.

13. I am grateful to Dr. Michael Cooper in Tokyo for updating me on Revue affairs.

14. *Nimaime*, literally "second sheet," is one type of *otokoyaku*. The term derives from the Edo-period practice of listing on Kabuki programs the name of the romantic lead after that of the lead actor.

15. The violet is the official Revue flower.

16. This regimen resembles that of Stanislavski System–based acting schools and theaters in the United States, such as the American Laboratory Theatre and the Goodman School. At the Goodman School, the first-year students are responsible for doing the "dirty work": washing the floors and windows, cleaning the toilets, dusting the furniture, etc. In the 1960s the Goodman School posted a 50 percent attrition rate (Schechner 1964:203; Willis 1964:113).

17. The main theatrical task of the *musumeyaku* is strikingly similar to what Aristotle claimed was the only function of women: to provide the limits of the male subject, which helps him complete his outline—to highlight their differences from him, which serves to emphasize his qualities (Case 1988:17).

18. Most references to the term in the Takarazuka fan literature are made in the *katakana* syllabary, which is usually used to denote loanwords or to give a Japanese word special emphasis, as in this case. The Chinese characters mean "affectation." *Kiza* is an important component of the charisma of a player of men's roles; if her *kiza* is deemed insufficient, then she is reassigned to women's roles (Tanabe and Sasaki 1983:135).

19. I refer to "the state" in the singular, as a thing-in-itself, for the sake of

convenience. I follow Corrigan and Sayer (1985:2–3) in regarding "the state" not simply as an "organ of coercion" or a "bureaucratic lineage," but as a repertoire of agencies (sites, technologies, institutions, ministries) that collectively, albeit not without internal contradictions, shape and reproduce the dominant ideology, or status quo.

20. A joke I heard from a number of Takarazuka fans is based on the Revue's reputation for cost-cutting. Hankyū, they say, is really short for *hanbun kyūryō* (half salary).

21. See Robertson (1984, 1991a) for a discussion of gender ideology in the Edo period.

22. The *jo* in *josei* may also be read as *onna*, and *dan* as *otoko*. Other suffixes commonly used to denote gender include -*ppoi* (as in *otokoppoi*, or "boyish/mannish"); -*mitai* (*otoko mitai*, or "look like a boy/man"); -*teki* (*danseiteki*, or "manlike"); and *no yō* (*otoko no yō*, "in the manner of a boy/man").

23. Some of these assumptions about cultural specificity, which become virtually indistinguishable from cultural relativity, are part of the so-called Western self-critique—"so-called," because critical reappraisals of anthropology and the colonial encounter nevertheless retain an asymmetrical relationship between "the West" and "the third world." Although neither the West nor the third world exists as an internally coherent entity, there is a tendency to treat both as singular formations defined in terms of their experience of colonialism and imperialism, where the West is the supreme change agent and the third world the irreversibly changed reactant (Ahmad 1986). Moreover, this formula ignores the histories of multiple non-Euro-American colonizers and imperialist regimes, including Japan.

Few would disagree with the observation that the world (whether first or third) was *never not* transcultural. Cultural encounters and their effects are the sine qua non of human life, whether that life is lived by a New Guinea hill tribe or an urbanized population in Japan. Of course, one must never forget that there have been imbalances, often large, associated with "the crossing of cultural borders: conquest, colonialism, imperialism, tourism, or scholarly interest all involve choice and require power, even if only buying power." Neither can one forget, as Latin American anthropologists have reminded us, that transcultural encounters, while not strictly dialectical, and however uneven or unequal in power or degree, are "shifting processes": they do not constitute unidirectional teleologies. All parties to and involved in the encounter are affected and modified by it, albeit with different consequences (D. Taylor 1991:63).

24. *Ome* is a neologism that combines *osu* (male) and *mesu* (female), terms reserved for plants and animals and applied pejoratively to humans.

CHAPTER 1.
AMBIVALENCE AND POPULAR CULTURE

1. Passionate but supposedly platonic friendships among girls and women were referred to as "S" or "Class S," with the "S" standing for sister, sex, "es-

cape," Schöne, and *shōjo* (girl) or all five combined. (See chapters 2, 4 and 5 for a discussion of Class S and *shōjo*.) This article sensationalized a perceived shift in same-sex attraction from an innocuous passion to a more problematic "butch-femme"-type of attachment.

2. Silverberg suggests that "Gonda's awareness of Weimar social policy, linked with his Marxist focus on the practices of the proletariat, prevented him from taking a critical stance toward the intrusion of the state into the realm of cultural policy" (1992:46).

3. By the 1930s, the population of 65 million purchased 10 million copies of daily newspapers, and there were 11,118 registered magazines and journals. There was nearly 100 percent literacy in Japan at this time, and print culture was available to all classes of consumers (Silverberg 1993:123–24).

4. *Shō* is also used to denote "illegitimate," an association I draw on in referring to pedigree.

5. Kurihara advances an argument for the triply inflected structure of this new mass formation of the postwar period. (Marilyn Ivy's brief summary of his argument [1995:195] is actually more lucid than Kurihara's own somewhat convoluted and redundant scheme, which he compares to Freud's id, ego, and superego.) The first inflection in an ascending order pertains to "autonomous actions" (*jiritsu kōi*), which he equates with style (*sutairu*); the second to "value" (*kachi*), which he equates with "genre" (*janru*); and the third to function (*kinō*), or "mode" (*mōdo*). For example, work (*shigoto*) is occupation (*shokugyō*) is production (*sangyō*), while preservation or conservation (*hozen*) is defense (*bōei*) is military (*guntai*) (Kurihara 1980:63). Kurihara aims to show similarly triply inflected structures of different everyday activities, such as "looking," which proceeds from comics, letters, and graffiti; to a second order involving movies, newspapers, weekly magazines, and popular novels; and then to a third order of television, efficiency reports, and prison surveillance.

As I worked through Kurihara's thesis, it occurred to me that his implicit intention is to theorize how everyday activities are appropriated by a managerial or entrepreneurial class and processed as rule-bound, bureaucratic, institutional functions; this is a "pessimistic" notion of popular/mass culture —"the culture industry"—similar to that of Adorno and Horkheimer (1972), as Ivy also notes.

6. In socialist thought, the phrase "the masses"—also "mass movements," "mass meetings," etc.—is used to invoke a revolutionary tradition: a united people acting to change their condition. Conservatives, on the other hand, tend to invoke "the masses" disparagingly, as an unstable, amorphous, aggregate of people: a mob.

7. My use of "distinction" here is only nominally similar to that of Pierre Bourdieu (1984 [1979]), as he focuses primarily on class-based tastes.

8. I am grateful to my graduate student Dan Bass for bringing Paul Lukas and *Beer Frame* to my attention.

9. Whereas some feminists are disturbed by the overdetermined quality of the stereotypical feminine model replicated in drag performances, others

have noted the subversive potential of drag in drawing attention to the hyperbolic construction of that model (see the articles in Meyer 1994a).

10. I have more to say about fans and sexuality in chapters 4 and 5, where I also examine the desires of male fans, and simply hint at the neglected subtexts here.

11. The directors of *Dream Girls* (distributed by Women Make Movies) are Kim Longinotto and Jano Williams.

12. Ian Buruma's *Behind the Mask* (1985 [1984]) is an example of an ungrounded and unnuanced approach to analyzing and understanding Takarazuka and other popular cultural institutions. Neither understanding the difference between sex and gender nor having perused any sources on the Revue in any language, Buruma claims that Takarazuka actors represent a "third sex" and fulfill the escapist yearnings of "modern young girls" (112–35). While offering readers images of a Japan to which not enough serious scholars have turned their attention, Buruma's book, filled with sweeping and flippant claims about "the Japanese," amounts to cultural critique from the hip.

Two Anglophone works of fiction in which the Takarazuka Revue plays a central role should also be mentioned: James Michener's *Sayonara* (1954 [1953]) and James Melville's *Go Gently Gaijin* (1986). The former, later made into a movie starring Marlon Brando, is a story that inverts the plot of Puccini's *Madame Butterfly*: whereas Lieutenant Pinkerton deserts his Japanese mistress Cio-cio-san for his (white) American wife, Major Gruver forsakes his (white) American fiancée for Hana-ogi—a Takarazuka *otokoyaku*. The latter is a murder mystery involving a Takarazuka star and a "scrawny" American Ph.D. candidate studying "sex role reversal among Japanese women" and using the Revue as a frame of reference. Not a few friends have asked me if I had been interviewed by Melville! I am grateful to Dr. Laurel Kendall for sending me a copy of this book.

13. This fan (who is discussed again in chapter 5) saw a message I had placed in a fan magazine requesting information about Takarazuka that was not included in the usual public relations books about the Revue. Her telephone call came after we had exchanged letters about my request for unofficial data. I did not sense that she was calling on behalf on the Takarazuka administration; she was just reporting on their position and tactics. We talked for over an hour on various aspects of the Revue, from the sexuality of the actors to the quality of recent productions.

14. Material was available at other libraries and archives, with the notable exception of scripts and fan magazines.

15. I am grateful to Dr. Yohko Tsuji for sending me this article.

16. I presented my first paper on the gender politics informing the Revue at the annual meeting of the Association for Asian Studies in 1987 (Robertson 1987). Another article on Takarazuka was published in 1990 by Lorie Brau, then a Ph.D. candidate in Berlin's own Department of Performance Studies at New York University.

17. Academic politics and rivalries also exploit sexist prejudices. Work on

sexualities has been and is too often dismissed with flippant comments, such as "Oh, so-and-so just studies lesbians/gays in Japan," as if constructions of gender and sexuality were totally unrelated to ideology and discourses of citizenship, social policy (such as eugenics and family planning), medicine, political policy, economics, religion, aesthetics, human development, and so on.

18. Some recent Anglophone exceptions are Schalow 1990 and Leupp 1995, works dealing with male-to-male sexual relations in the Edo period.

19. Among the major English works dealing with Japanese suicide are Benedict 1974 (1946); De Vos 1973; T. Lebra 1976; Pinguet 1993 (1984); and Seward 1968. Japanese works in which homosexual double suicide figures quite prominently include Komine and Minami 1985; Ōhara Kaoru 1965, 1973; Tadai and Katō 1974; and Yamana 1931.

20. Recent works addressing lesbian practices include the "lesbian special issues" of *Bessatsu Takarajima* (1987) and *Imago* (1994); Furukawa 1994; Roden 1990; Yoshitake 1986; and of course my own publications. Privately circulated newsletters (e.g., printed by women's/feminist/lesbian groups), some of which are also distributed at feminist book stores, such as Crayon House in Harajuku, Tokyo, provide another source of information about Japanese female sexualities.

CHAPTER 2. STAGING ANDROGYNY

1. Other Japanese sites include female swordplay dramas (*onna kengeki*); the New Theater (Shingeki), active since the turn of this century, which includes cross-dressed actors; cross-dressing clubs, which I discuss in chapter 5; and an eclectic assortment of television shows that focus on gender-bending, such as the current *Mr. Lady Song Grand Prix* featuring males performing as women.

2. Yasui (1953) notes that a vernacular expression for androgyny is *otoko-onna*, literally "male-female," although the social scientific, literary, and scientific literatures tend to use only *ryōsei* and *chūsei* when referring to androgyny.

3. Much of the Euro-American literature on androgyny deals with non-ethnographic theoretical issues and/or film and literary characters (e.g., Bell-Metereau 1985; Bergstrom 1991; Butler 1990; Heilbrun 1982 [1964]; Pacteau 1986; Stimpson 1989 [1974]), or with intersexed and transsexed bodies (e.g., Foucault 1980 [1978]; Millot 1990 [1983]). This insightful literature has given me ideas for making visible the construction and uses of androgyny in Japan as a "surface politics of the body."

4. Jung proposed that all people were androgynous; that is, that everyone, whether female or male, has both a feminine side and a masculine side. "Anima" was his term for the feminine archetype in males, and "animus" for the masculine archetype in females. The sexist essentialism of Jung's proposal is evident in his description of these terms. Anima included irrationality, spirituality, emotionalism, and animus rationality, courage, strong convictions (Hyde and Rosenberg 1980 [1976]:19).

5. For information on cross-dressing before the Edo period, see Takeda 1994.

6. Perhaps early *onnagata* were recruited from among the itinerant *rōnin*, or masterless samurai, who staged cross-dressed performances as a means of livelihood (Tomioka 1938:99).

7. Information about Take is summarized from Robertson 1991a.

8. Asano (1989) notes that there are several sutras for the purposes of facilitating the *henjo nanshi* process, and that certain unorthodox sects—such as the Fujikō (late sixteenth century), Nyoraikyō (late eighteenth century), and Ōmotokyō (early twentieth century)—incorporated the concepts of androgyny qua "cross-dressing" into their doctrines and ritual practices (see also Hardacre 1990).

9. *Otoko ga onna ni nari yaku o enjiru* and *onna de aru otoko ga yaku o enjiru*, respectively.

10. *Onnagata wa nichijōteki ni onna de aru koto.* Such an *onnagata* is more specifically referred to as *ma no onnagata*, or "true" *onnagata*, in contradistinction to some present-day Kabuki actors who perform women's roles in addition to a plethora of men's roles.

11. The primer was written by Kaibara Ekken, a leading representative of the "practical school" of Confucianism and a self-appointed critic of females. Ekken proclaimed that while necessary for the reproduction of male heirs, female genitalia promoted dull-wittedness, laziness, lasciviousness, a hot temper, and a tremendous capacity to bear grudges. He was not alone in suggesting that a female-sexed body was contrary to and even precluded the achievement of "female" gender (see Robertson 1991a).

12. Roden does acknowledge in passing that it was the New Woman and not her male counterpart who "triggered" the debates about the relationship of sex, gender, and sexuality, although his essay as a whole suggests that unconventional males and females received equal criticism in the media (1990:43).

13. Most of the pundits bemoaning the "masculinization" of females focused their critiques on urban, middle- and upper-class girls and women, singling out unconventional sartorial style and public behavior. The employment of unprecedented numbers of lower-class girls and women in factories apparently did not trouble them. According to a poll taken in 1881, there were 14,228 factories in Japan, over half spinning mills. Sixty percent of factory workers were female, many of whom were children. Of a total of 793,885 factory workers, 476,497 were female, over 10 percent of whom were under fourteen years of age. Eighty percent, or 48,821 of a total of 61,013 children employed, were girls. Only in Japan, the reporter claimed, was the number of female factory laborers greater than that of males (Tsumura 1914a, 1914b).

14. For more information in English on the "woman problem," see Nolte and Hastings 1991; Sievers 1983; and Silverberg 1991.

15. Ever since the Revue's establishment there have been loud noises from various corners encouraging the addition of males to ensure the existence of a truly "national" revue theater. Protests from actors and fans have been so

vociferous that those integrationist impulses have all but been abandoned in the postwar period. The rationale for maintaining an all-female revue corresponds to the argument for retaining the *onnagata* in Kabuki despite the presence of capable female actors.

16. One variant is "daddy gal" (*oyaji gyaru*).

17. Tomioka refers to such women as examples of "acquired" (*kotenteki*) cross-dressing, noting that these "working women are not mentally disturbed, but rather passing as men in order to earn a livelihood" (1938:103). It is clear from his article, and especially the section on "inherent" (*sententeki*) cross-dressing, that he uses "cross-dressing" to mean androgyny. Generally speaking, his "inherent" androgyny corresponds to *ryōsei*, and his "acquired" category to *chūsei*.

18. The *Shin Nippō*, a daily newspaper, carried an article on a leading Takarasienne under the headline, "Still a *shōjo* at 36!" ("Sanjū-rokusai demo shōjo" 1940). Takarasiennes by definition were unmarried, but the reporter here was drawing attention to the disturbing lack of correspondence between chronological age and *shōjo* identity.

19. Kobayashi's interest in girls' and women's education followed the precedent set by Mori Arinori (1847–89), the leading architect of modern education. As a spokesman for the Meiji state, Mori proclaimed that "the foundations of national prosperity rest upon education; the foundations of education upon women's education" and insisted that the household was the "ultimate school" (Nolte 1983:5).

20. The Meiji government ruled in 1872 that primary education, while sex-segregated, was compulsory for girls and boys alike, although home economics constituted the bulk of education for girls. Public and private secondary schools for girls and young women, called "higher schools," were established countrywide in the early 1900s; by 1907, 40,273 female students were enrolled in 133 higher schools (Pflugfelder 1989:7). For a comparative perspective, see Martha Vicinus's work on English boarding school friendships (1989).

21. See p. 219, n. 24. An 1818 reference to *ome* refers not to a same-sex, different-gender couple but to an androgyne, in this case a female who passed as a man (Tomioka 1938:102).

22. Furukawa lists some of the other terms that were coined at this time in the course of translating foreign sexological literature, such as *dōsei kōsetsu* (same-sex intercourse), *dōseiteki shikijō* (same-sex lust), *dōseiteki jōkō* (same-sex intercourse), *dōseiyoku* (same-sex desire), *dōseikan seiyoku* (same-sex sexual desire), *dōsei ren'aishō* (same-sex love illness), and *dōsei sōshinshō* (same-sex love illness). Some sexologists deemed these terms (with the exception of the last two) less appropriate than *dōseiai* in reference to females as they alluded to physical love and carnal desire (Furukawa 1994:115).

23. The difficulty of diagnosis arises because the "male" partner was not intersexed, but had a "normal" female body.

24. *Shinkeishitsu* originated around the turn of the century as a category of sociosexual dis-ease, with special relevance to urban middle-class women (who represented about 30 percent of the female population at that time).

25. See also Yoshiwara 1935:187 for essentially the same argument.

26. A Japanese sexologist, in a 1934 newspaper interview, drew distinctions between what he called "pseudo-homosexuality" (*gisei dōseiai*) and "true homosexuality" (*shinsei dōseiai*), the former consisting of a "transitory love relationship" (*awai ren'ai kankei*) and the latter of "actual sexual practices" (*honkakuteki na seikoi*). According to his criteria, Class S relations would fall into the category of pseudo-homosexuality, "butch-femme" relations into that of true homosexuality (Hori Kentarō, cited in "Dansō hi ari" 1935).

27. The writer used "cross-dressing" where others used "androgyny" and tucked information about contemporary practices between long accounts of Edo-period cross-dressers, possibly as a way to avoid the wartime censors.

28. Yoshiya, an openly recognized lesbian, wrote articles and popular short stories on such topics as "same-sex love," the uselessness of husbands, and patriotism in leading magazines and journals. Her relationship with her life partner, Monma Chiyo, was referred to in the mass media as "homosexual husband and wife" (*dōseiai fūfu*) (Usumi 1935:43).

29. Yoshiya wrote at least two essays on Takarazuka and Kobayashi (Yoshiya 1950, 1963).

30. The use of *garçon* likely reflects the French influence on the development of the all-female revue and the role of the player of men's roles. It was also fashionable for young urbanites to incorporate French loanwords into their vocabulary.

31. Kawashima, born into the Chinese royal family but raised by her adopted family in Japan, began to wear men's clothes from the age of sixteen (Kamisaka 1984:87). She eventually was executed on charges of treason. Muramatsu's short story was serialized in a leading women's journal, *Fujin Kōron*.

32. Ashihara suspected Kobayashi of forging a fan's allegedly negative reaction to her nickname, *aniki* (Ashihara K. 1979:157).

33. In 1989 the play was revived for a two-year run to satisfy nostalgic "old fans" and attract new fans.

Oscar is also reminiscent of the "female son" in *The Changelings* (*Torikaebaya monogatari*) and *Parting at Dawn* (*Ariake no wakare*), stories written and circulated during the Heian period (794–1185). The persistence of the "changelings" theme in Japanese literary genres offers much grist for the anthropological mill with regard to the connection between gender attribution and kinship relations.

The practice of raising a female as a son brings to mind marriage ("female husbands"), succession ("female fathers," "female sons"), and assorted "gender-bending" practices among certain North American Indian, South Pacific island, west and east African, and South Asian peoples. It attests to the disjunction between sex and gender, along with the fluidity of gender in different cultures and societies (see, e.g., Amadiume 1987; Evans-Pritchard 1951: 104–23; Gough 1971; Kessler and McKenna 1985 [1978]; Meigs 1976; Nanda 1990; Porter Poole 1984; Roscoe 1991; A. Singer 1973; Whitehead 1984; Williams 1986).

34. The fan's signature, literally Star Violet, is obviously a pseudonym

composed from, possibly, the "star" in Star Troupe—and from the violet, the Revue's official flower.

CHAPTER 3. PERFORMING EMPIRE

1. The full title appearing in Anglophone newspapers at the time was *Made in Nippon; For World Market;* it was *Sekai no ichiba* (*World Market*) in Japanese. Four years earlier, in 1937, the rival all-female Shōchiku Revue had staged a musical titled *Made in Japan* (*Meido in Nippon*) at the International Theater (Kokusai Gekijō) in Tokyo. Doubtless the Takarazuka playwright was familiar with the Shōchiku production; directors and playwrights of the two revues often borrowed heavily from each other. The two versions of *Made in Japan* are similar in celebrating the international demand for Japanese manufactures, although the Shōchiku piece is limited largely to song-and-dance sequences with very little dialogue (*Rebyū: Meido in Nippon* 1937). An updated version of the play was staged by Takarazuka in 1962—during the "miracle sixties," when the Japanese economy was moving into high gear.

2. There is relatively little research on Japan that considers ways in which theater interacts with imperialism and colonialism. In the case of Japanese studies, the uses of film and radio as vehicles for the spiritual and physical mobilization of the Japanese and colonial peoples have been expertly documented and discussed (e.g., Dower 1993; Fukushima and Nornes 1991; Goodman 1991; Hauser 1991; Kasza 1988; Silverberg 1993). There is, however, a dearth of critical research on wartime theater, where staged performances operated as social metacommentaries on and motivators for such interconnected practices as nationalism, imperialism, racism, militarism, sexual politics, and gendered relations (cf. Bratton 1991; Pickering 1991:229). Similarly, theater-state relations are overlooked or ignored in the otherwise excellent scholarship on the Japanese colonial empire; among the most recent publications are Beasley 1987; Dower 1986; Duus, Myers, and Peattie 1989, 1996; Myers and Peattie 1984; Peattie 1988; and Shillony 1991 (1981). Rimer 1974 offers a complementary overview of the New Theater (Shingeki) movement through the career of the playwright Kishida Kunio.

3. The Co-Prosperity Sphere, formalized in 1940, was an integral part of Prime Minister Konoe Fumimaro's idea of a "New Order" in which the Japanese would lead a Pan-Asian effort toward Asian self-sufficiency and stability, anticommunism, and resistance to Western imperialism. The projected area of the sphere covered Japan, China, and Manchukuo; the former Dutch, French, and British colonies in Southeast Asia; and the Philippines. Japan had already occupied Manchuria, Taiwan, and Korea since, roughly, the turn of this century. Some ideologues included Australia and New Zealand in the projected area (Hunter 1984:42, 143–44; see J. Lebra 1975).

4. See also Takagi H. 1993 on the wartime assimilation of the Ainu, an "aboriginal" people in northern Japan.

5. As a general concept, assimilation was not uniquely Japanese and was

most articulately expressed in French colonial theory, with which Japanese ideologues were familiar. But Japanese assimilationist theory differed significantly in practice from its French counterpart, in which assimilation was defined as "that system which tends to efface all differences between the colonies and the motherland and which views the colonies simply as a prolongation of the mother country beyond the seas" (S. H. Roberts 1929:67, quoted in Peattie 1984b:96). See also Peattie 1984b for a discussion of competing versions of Japanese assimilationist theory.

6. See the discussion in Young 1995:23–26.

7. Miura, a pioneering actress, performed the role of Madame Butterfly at the London Opera House in 1915. In her career she sought success in Europe as well as in Japan.

8. Archer was a theater scholar and critic active in the early twentieth century. His book *Masks or Faces? A Study in the Psychology of Acting* (1888) was consulted by many Japanese directors.

9. Similarly, the "patriotic extravaganzas" staged in English music halls at the turn of this century invariably presented the British colonies as "willingly subservient," masking palpable tensions between the colonizers and the colonized (Summerfield 1986:29).

I am not claiming that cross-ethnicking is unique to the Takarazuka Revue. Cross-ethnicking is a standard practice in many theaters; so standard, in fact, that with few exceptions, it is taken for granted. The protests several years ago by Asian Americans against the casting of a white actor in the role of Kim, a Vietnamese woman, in Alain Boublil and Claude-Michel Schonberg's *Miss Saigon* demonstrates that cross-ethnicking is not always unproblematic. At the same time, all sorts of boundary crossings constitute theatrical performance and can, if properly highlighted, reveal much about the constructedness of gender and ethnicity in ways that can both reinforce and destabilize the status quo.

10. As Stefan Tanaka notes in *Japan's Orient*, by the twentieth century, *tōyō* (east seas) signified the opposite of "the Occident" in both a geopolitical sense and an ideological sense (1993:4). He argues that the contested discourse of *tōyō*/the Orient helped occasion a new sense of national and cultural identity in Japan even as it revealed the ambiguity of Japan's place in Asia and the world (11–12).

11. As Stefan Tanaka observes, "Whereas Romantic [European] historians looked to the Orient for their origins, Japanese historians found them in *tōyō* [the Orient]" (1993:14).

12. In *Male Fantasies*, Klaus Theweleit explores the desires and anxieties of fascist soldiers and writers of the Freikorps in an effort to describe the political culture out of which Nazism developed. This eclectic, encyclopedic book aims, in part, at understanding the pleasurable play of male cross-dressing in wartime or in military contexts in general. Several accounts and photographs of transvestite performance are provided, and Theweleit suggests that "what the soldier males seem to find enjoyable is the *representation* of sex-role inversion" (1989 [1978]:330, 327–35; italics in original). More re-

cently, articles have appeared on the gender-bending homoerotic rituals codified and performed at military academies in the United States (Adams 1993; Faludi 1994). See Maruki Sato 1930 on homosexual practices among Japanese soldiers.

13. See Kurasawa 1991 for a consideration of the effects of and resistance to Japanese colonial propaganda in Java.

14. Japan's first feature-length cartoon, *Momotarō's Sea Eagle* (*Momotarō no umiwashi*, 1943), which I was able to see in Tokyo in the fall of 1995, also capitalized on this well-known folktale. In the film, Momotarō's conquest of Onigashima symbolized the 1941 attack on Pearl Harbor; the liberated inhabitants of the island, Asian peoples under the "benevolent rule" of the Japanese.

15. The Japanese were interested in the Federal Theater Project (1935–39) largely because it involved the direct intervention of the federal government in theatrical production at the same time it employed, and thereby contained, activists from the indigenous workers' theaters (McConachie and Friedman 1985a:10). Japanese reformers viewed the project as a "cultural movement" (*bunka undō*) from which they could learn much about local-level mobilizing along with strategies of targeting and controlling working-class audiences (Nakagawa 1941). The Axis Alliance of 1940 occasioned a flurry of interest in strategies to organize leisure in fascist Italy and Nazi Germany, which represented other versions of the fusion of politics and national culture (Niizeki 1940:37).

16. Although the 1927 revue was widely referred to as *Mon pari*, the "official" Japanese title was *Waga pari yo*, literally *My/Our Paris. Mon pari* was the title of all subsequent revivals.

17. An eclectic Pan-Asianism is evident here as well, in that both the original and later versions of *Mon Paris* confuse India and Sri Lanka as well as the cities of Colombo and Kandy.

18. *From Manchuria to North China* deals with the China Incident, more popularly referred as the Marco Polo Bridge Incident, of July 1937. The "incident" in question refers to the clash of Chinese and Japanese troops at a bridge near Beijing, which led to a full-scale war lasting until 1945. Earlier, in 1931, a group of Japanese soldiers based in Manchuria plotted to blow up a section of the South Manchurian railway line, an act subsequently known as the Manchurian Incident. The soldiers then blamed Chinese troops as a pretext for occupying the city of Mukden and, eventually, several Manchurian provinces (Hunter 1984:120–22).

19. Industry figures show about 6 million train passengers in 1920, increasing to 10 million in 1927 and to over 12 million in 1928, and reaching to nearly 18 million passengers by 1936 (Takaoka H. 1993:12).

20. "Train dance" is also known in Japanese by the neologism *rain dansu* (line dance).

21. The *gingyō* consists of a narrow platform that arcs around the orchestra pit from either side of the stage proper, and its intimate reach is augmented by wing extensions of the stage, which dominates the auditorium. It was first employed in the revue *Rose Paris* (*Rōsu pari*, 1931) by the leading Takarazuka

playwright Shirai Tetsuzō, who claims to have been inspired by a similar structure used in Parisian revues (e.g., the Casino de Paris and Folies-Bergère) (Shirai 1967:121–22). However, although the structure itself may be related to a Parisian model, Shirai equates the function of the "bridge" with the Kabuki theater's *hanamichi* (flower way), or passageway through the auditorium (121). Most of the time in Kabuki, the passageway or bridge is used as a kind of private stage, where an actor can both improvise and focus exclusively on texturing a leading character without interference.

22. Takarazuka was one of several symbolic "bridges" linking imperialist fantasies and colonial realities. The Tokyo Peace Exposition of 1922 included the recreation of colonial holdings linked to "Japan" by a Peace Bridge (Silverberg 1993:127).

23. Japanese theater critics were aware of such innovations in Italy and elsewhere. By 1936, these troupes had a million spectators throughout Italy. The actual effectiveness of the cars is another matter (see de Grazia 1981:162–63).

24. "Induction" has many layers of meaning and signification beyond its standard definition as the process of inferring a generalized conclusion from the particular instances that are relevant here. It also refers to an initial experience, or an initiation or beginning; to an act of bringing something on; and to the sum of processes by which morphological differentiation is brought about.

25. The allegorist pulls one element out of the totality of the life context and isolates it. "Allegory is therefore essentially fragment . . . . The allegorist joins the isolated fragments of reality and thereby creates meaning. This is posited meaning; it does not derive from the original context of the fragments" (Peter Bürger, as translated in Buck-Morss 1991 [1989]:225).

26. New China, or *shinkō shina*, refers to parts of China under Japanese control. *Shina*, in use since the eighteenth century as a name for European-dominated China, is regarded as a pejorative term for China.

27. This transcription is the anglicized version of the Japanese syllabic rendition of the Mongolian expression as it appeared in the script.

28. Nochlin here subscribes to the notion of an unconscious underclass, a characterization with which I disagree although the gist of her acute observations on pageants are accurate. See also Tsubouchi 1921.

29. Many articles on this subject were published in *Kokumin Engeki* (1941–43), some of which are cited in this chapter.

30. Whereas *kokumin engeki* can be translated literally as "citizens' theater," "state theater" is a more accurate description of the movement, which was sanctioned by the military state as a means of claiming the people through the interpellative power of dramaturgy.

31. In this 1922 article, Iizuka refers to "the people" by the socialist term *minshū*. Nevertheless, his ideas about the theater as central to Japanese culture are essentially the same here as in his later works, which deal explicitly with the Citizens' Theater Movement and the category of *kokumin*, or "citizen."

32. Under the Meiji Civil Code, the patriarchal household was the small-

est legal unit of society. In the postwar constitution of 1947, that smallest unit is the individual person.

33. This bureau was established in December 1940 with offices in Tokyo's Imperial Theater, and it created in turn the Japanese Federation of Mobile Theaters in June 1941 to centralize and regulate the activities of traveling theater groups (Toita 1956 [1950]:251). The two journals were the short-lived *Nippon Engeki* (*Japanese Theater*) and *Engekikai* (*Theater World*).

34. As Reynolds notes, only the flimsiest of evidence supports the "blood relatives" theory: "Thailand's Therevada [*sic*] and Japan's Mahayana Buddhism offered little more basis for accord than Italian Catholicism and British Protestantism" (1991:94).

35. The Japanization of vocabulary was widespread: although baseball already was referred to as *yakyū*, *sēfu* (safe) was changed to *yoshi*, "*auto* (out) to *dame*, etc.; and cigarette brands were changed from Goruden Batto (Golden Bat) to Kinshi, Chierii (Cherry) to Sakura, and so on. Entertainers, athletes, and celebrities with foreign names were required to alter them to their Japanese equivalent; the singer Dick Mine, for example, became Mine Kōichi (Hashimoto 1993:54).

36. Plays grouped under these categories included, respectively, *Bathed in Glory* (*Hikari o abite*, 1943); *Victory Pledge* (*Kachinuku chikai*, 1944); *Legends of Virtuous Japanese Women* (*Nippon meifu den*, 1941); *Cheerful Neighborhood Associations* (*Tanoshiki tonarigumi*, 1941); and *Made in Japan* (Hagiwara 1954:240–43).

37. Kobayashi traveled to Batavia (Jakarta) in the fall of 1940 to secure Indonesia's place in the sphere by seeking, unsuccessfully, to obtain mineral oil and other concessions from the Dutch (Beasley 1987:228–29; Hall 1981 [1955]:858–59; Mook 1944:42–65).

38. The author was Phra Sarasas, a bureaucrat and proponent of Thai-Japanese entente who resided in Japan between 1939 and 1945. His novel, a "fable of political morals" (Batson 1996:156) written in "flowery English" (N. Matsumoto 1942) and first published in London in 1940, is *Whom the Gods Deny* (*Unmei no kawa*, or "river of fate," in Japanese).

39. *Misapur*, the name used in Sarasas's book, is likely a wordplay on Mirzapur in North India, which is how I rendered the name from the Japanese in Robertson 1995. Matsumoto 1943d used the odd transliteration "Musapool" in his review of the play.

40. It is striking how *Return to the East* also anticipates the path of the militant nationalist Subhas Chandra Bose, from India to Southeast Asia via Germany and Japan. In 1943 he proclaimed a provisional government of *Azad Hind* (Free India) and led the Japanese-supported Indian National Army, recruited before his arrival, in anticipation of his invasion of British India. Bose's activities were followed closely in Japanese domestic and colonial newspapers.

41. A scathing review of this play appeared in *Engei Gahō* (*Theater Graphic*), an important theater arts journal whose publication eventually was suspended by the state. The author describes the revue as simplistic, conceptually weak, vapid, and inappropriate for the Takarazuka stage. He also asserts

that none of the Takarazuka playwrights or directors have been able to work creatively within wartime parameters (Mogami 1941).

42. This revue was produced by the Propaganda Section of the Imperial Rule Assistance Association (Taisei yokusankai).

43. As Zygmunt Bauman has observed, "Power turns out its enemies by denying them what it strives to secure for itself; and the enemy exists only of and through that denial. Through disgorging the enemy, power wishes to purify itself of ambivalence, to turn ambiguity into a neat division, polysemy into an opposition" (1991:174).

44. New Woman (*atarashii onna*) was a category of female created in the 1910s and used in reference to women whose ideas and style contradicted the Good Wife, Wise Mother model of femininity codified in the patriarchal Meiji Civil Code. To critics such as Kobayashi, the label "New Woman" referred to "an indulgent and irresponsible young Japanese woman, who used her overdeveloped sexuality to undermine the family and to manipulate others for her own selfish ends" (Sievers 1983:175–76).

45. As Silverberg (1991) also notes, the Modern Girl was an ambiguous symbol of modernity; however, unlike the Takarazuka actor, she was not regarded as harboring a Japanese spirit. In my view, the Westernized Modern Girl served as a foil against which Japanese males, who had been encouraged by the state to modernize (Westernize) themselves, could reclaim their core Japanese identity. The character of Naomi in Tanizaki Jun'ichirō's *A Fool's Love* (*Chijin no ai*, 1924–25), translated into English under the title *Naomi* (1985), was one such foil (see Silverberg 1991:244–47, 244 n. 18).

46. Similarly, Homi Bhabha has observed that it is "in relation to the place of the Other that colonial desire is articulated" (1990:187).

CHAPTER 4. FAN PATHOLOGY

1. *The Waltz Princess* (*Warutsu no joō*) was staged by Takarazuka in September 1935.

2. Several informative books and articles on fans and the conditions of fandom have been published (in English) in the past decade, in part extending into popular culture the literary critical interest in reader response and reception theory, and in part acknowledging the critical agency of persons outside a professional corps of interpreters and commentators (see, for example, Fiske 1989; Jenkins 1992a, 1992b; Lewis 1992; Pribram 1988a; Radway 1984; H. Taylor 1989). They reflect and help constitute the increasing visibility of cultural studies, an emergent interdisciplinary set of theories and practices within the humanities and social sciences aimed at interrogating sociocultural constructions of power, domination, and "common sense," all of which coincide in the discourse of fandom.

It is my general perception, however, that much of the current Anglophone research on fans and fandom, and on popular culture in general, is too narrow, being either of a presentist bent or of a restricted historical focus. My two chapters on fans proceed from the commonplace that present practices have histories, and historical practices have present significance. Some research (e.g., Jenkins 1992b) also does not seem to fully acknowledge the wider public debate within which fandom is attributed with powers of great social and political significance, which I emphasize in this chapter and the next.

3. The irony of Matsumoto's using the Western, and by definition well-behaved, audience as a rhetorical foil was underscored decades later in the context of the Citizens' Theater Movement, as we saw in the previous chapter.

The need to discipline audiences is a newsworthy subject in the United States today. In May 1993, the *Ann Arbor News* published an article from the Cox News Service with the headline "Manners Important at Performances." A summary of the "basic rules of etiquette" passed along by "those who regularly attend concerts, plays, lectures and even games or graduations," the article was perhaps aimed at the thousands in the area who attend the many spring and summer performing arts festivals in Ann Arbor ("Manners Important at Performances" 1993:D4).

4. One prominent fan and fan club director (who shall remain anonymous) ventured the opinion that *musumeyaku* were more likely to become lesbians since their role was to devote themselves to and identify with the charismatic *otokoyaku!*

5. We had learned about Kikoshi and other Japanese lesbian bars in a special issue of a journal of popular culture, *Bessatsu Takarajima* (1987), on "women who love women."

6. The reference to hiking here alludes to the focus in the Japanese eugenics movement on the physical development of girls and women, and by association, on the improvement of their capability to bear children (Robertson 1997a).

7. The reference to widows is especially significant, as these women often faced humiliation and ostracism in their communities as victims of malicious gossip about their allegedly formidable sexual appetites (see Tsurumi 1979:260).

8. In 1993 the entertainment guide *Pia* issued a detailed survey volume on Takarazuka. Relying on a questionnaire answered by twenty-seven Revue spectators, the editors divided fans into two types: *jōnetsuaikei* (passionate love–type) and *boseiaikei* (motherly love–type) (*Fushigi no kuni Takarazuka* 1993:103–4). It is not clear to me how the published responses justify this division, and since the editors do not clarify their methodology, my hunch is that the two types actually preceded the questionnaire and were derived from the two types of love discussed in chapter 2, agape and eros.

Zeke Berlin also conducted a fan survey of sorts. He defined "fans" as those girls and women "who waited at the stage entrance and in front of the rehearsal hall," and "audience" as all other spectators (Berlin 1988:181). Apart from its arbitrary and inaccurate premises, Berlin's survey reveals an a priori assumption about what a Takarazuka fan *must* be like—namely, a teenage girl; this assumption precludes from his consideration both male fans and other categories of fan. Whereas *Pia* at least recognized differences among fans, Berlin's survey employed a singular typology.

9. For example, the cute "Hello Kitty" writing paraphernalia exported to the United States and elsewhere.

10. One could even argue that in Japan historically, the letter has been the preferred mode of communicating "difficult" thoughts, whether they be about love or suicide.

11. A mass meeting for *Kageki* subscribers (*Kageki* shiyū taikai) held at Takarazuka in 1921 was the earliest official fan club–like organization. The inaugural issue of the fan magazine had been published earlier that same year. This meeting was likely spurred by the informal fan club–like factions that had gelled around the two leading Takarasiennes of that time, Kumoi Namiko and Shinohara Asaji (Hashimoto 1984:118; Ōhara Kaori 1992 [1991]:284).

12. The first two membership options cost 7,500 yen annually to join, and the last 2,600 yen (as of 1995, when the exchange rate was about 100 yen to the U.S. dollar). The club maintains offices in Takarazuka, Tokyo, and Nagoya.

13. The "living newspaper" was a dramaturgic form in which current events were "editorialized" through dramatic metaphors and visual effects. In the United States, its provocative use was associated with the American Federal Theater Project of the 1930s. The boundary between actor and audience was blurred by the practice of planting actors in the audience to ask questions during the play or to challenge the ongoing action. Housing, health care, public utilities, labor organizing, and consumer unions were among the issues and subjects dramatized, and the plays "usually concluded that working people could (and should) solve the problems either by taking action themselves or by demanding that their elected representatives act for them" (O'Connor 1985:179–80). As a movement, the living newspaper was initiated in 1923 by students from the Institute of Journalism in Moscow who formed the company Blue Blouse. Their typical program consisted of headlines, news items, editorials, cartoons, and official decrees, the intention being to make current events and themes "penetrate the masses more deeply" (Stourac and McCreery 1986:3, 30).

I am using the term "living newspaper" loosely with respect to the Takarazuka Revue's wartime practice of staging plays whose themes and subjects corresponded with those addressed in the print media. The Revue's directors effectively harnessed the operatic power of these themes and subjects in an effort to accommodate the directives of the state.

14. Abe Nobuyuki (1875–1953) was a general who served as prime minister from 1939 to 1940.

15. *Senjafuda* are "votive papers" inscribed with the star's symbol and the fan's name, age, and address. This is one example of many in Japan in which the religious practice of pilgrims leaving votive papers pasted to the walls of the temples and shrines along their route has been secularized. In the context of Takarazuka fan clubs, *senjafuda* serve as a type of graffiti marking public buildings.

16. The all-female counterpart to the Aihōkai is the Ryokuhōkai, discussed earlier.

17. There are also clubs for Hankyū employees.

18. It is my hunch that these clubs function much in the manner of academic cliques (*gakubatsu*) (see Nakane 1972 [1970]:128–29).

19. Parallels can be drawn with the reading groups noted by Janice Radway in her study of romance novels, although distinctions must be drawn between official and private fan clubs: "Most [reading groups] seem to be informal networks of neighbors or co-workers who exchange romances and information about these books on a regular basis.... [T]he California-based 'Friends of the English Regency' ... publishes a review newsletter and holds an annual Regency 'Assemblee' at which it confers a 'Georgette' award on favorite Regency romances" (1984:248 n. 1).

Jenkins's book *Textual Poachers* (1992) focuses in large part on the fan communities formed around the television show *Star Trek*.

20. The names of this and another fan club noted in this section are fictitious, and I have used pseudonyms and disguised locations to respect the privacy and protect the identities of the club members.

CHAPTER 5. WRITING FANS

1. The signature on this published fan letter is clearly a pseudonym; its literal meaning is "Me Again, Scarlet." Scarlet (*kurenai*) is a metaphor for the all-female revue as memorialized by Kawabata Yasunari in his serialized novel, *Scarlet Gang of Asakusa* (*Asakusa kurenaidan*, 1929–35) (see also Seidensticker 1990). This letter appeared in a fanzine published by the Shōchiku Revue.

2. I was an assistant professor of anthropology at the University of California, San Diego, at that time.

3. Blood type, or *ketsuekigata*, forms the basis of a system of character analysis in Japan, by which each of the four blood types is associated with particular behavioral traits.

4. Only in the past several years has the Revue begun to produce videotapes of stage performances for commercial purposes.

5. Here, the essayist is criticizing the tendency of Takarazuka directors to recycle popular revues, such as *The Rose of Versailles, Gone with the Wind*, and *Me and My Girl*, with the express purpose of recruiting new fans through tried and tested material. This tactic has prompted, as in this case, the complaint among older fans that the Revue is getting stale and that its future hinges on new and timely scenarios.

6. On S, a slang word for homosexual relations between females, see chapter 2.

7. But would his taking into account the boys and men who use "abnormal" script alter Ōtsuka's suggestion? After all, men are also repressed by patriarchy, and some more than others. Just as critics cannot conceive of, much

less explain, the presence of married female fans of Takarazuka, so they cannot conceive of the use by males of the so-called *shōjo* script.

8. Roland Barthes's essay "The Written Face" in his imaginary ethnography about Japan, *Empire of Signs*, provides a lucid account of the effect of whiteface that focuses on the Kabuki *onnagata* as a signifier of femininity (1982 [1970]:88–94).

9. It is worth pointing out in this connection that the Revue has devised ways of symbolizing uncapsulated or monological speech in plays based on comic books. *The Golden Wings*, for example, discussed in the introduction, was based on *Where the Wind Blows* (*Kaze no yukue*), the comic book novel by Kasuya Noriko. To recreate theatrically Clarice's thoughts or uncapsulated speech, the stage was blackened and, as an illuminated mirror ball splattered the audience with colored dots of light, a voice was heard over the loudspeakers revealing her innermost feelings.

10. See my article on sexuality and suicide for a more elaborate treatment of this and other cases (Robertson forthcoming).

11. This was an unprecedented arrangement in that almost invariably heads of branch households are (real male) sons. Japanese household succession strategies have been innovative and flexible, as in the case of the practice of adopting a son-in-law as a son (*muko yōshi*), but not so flexible as to regard daughters or females in general acceptable in this position except as a temporary measure.

12. Asano subscribes to a notion of Japan as an internally harmonious, pristine culture until disturbed by external forces, a view that I disagree with and critique in chapter 1.

13. There are countless comic books and animated films that feature androgynous, cross-dressed, or intersexed characters. *Sailor Moon*, which also appears on American television dubbed in English, seems to be a current favorite of Japanese and American critical theorists.

EPILOGUE

1. As noted in chapter 2, *kai* (shellfish) is a symbol of an euphemism for "female" and also "lesbian."

2. *Boku* refers to a masculine/male self; *atashi* is gender neutral.

Bibliography

JAPANESE SOURCES

Adeyū NDT "hanseiki" (Adieu N[ichigeki] D[ancing] T[eam]'s "half century"). 1977. *Asahi Shinbun*, April 9.

Akiyama Satoko. 1990. Ryōseiguyūsei to seitōsaku (Androgyny and sexual perversion). *Imago* 2:57–61.

Anna Jun. 1979. "Berubara" de taitoku shita iroke no enshutsu (The erotic performance mastered in *The Rose of Versaille*). *Fujin Kōron* 8:196–201.

Aochi Shin. 1954. Takarazuka kageki tai Shōchiku kageki (The Takarazuka Revue versus the Shōchiku Revue). *Fujin Kōron* 2:230–39.

Aoki Ryōichi. 1942. Engekiteki kankyaku bunseki (Analysis of theater audiences). *Gendai Engeki* 5(8):90–93.

Aoki Tōichi. 1934. Otoko ni naru onnanoko (Girls who become boys). *Kageki Shōjo* 2(4):42.

Aoyagi Yūbi. 1924. *Peraguro sōshi* (A [male] opera fan's story). Takarazuka: Takarazuka Shōjokagekidan Shuppansha.

———. 1930. Seito-san no chūisubeki koto (Matters that students should be attentive to). *Kageki* 124:6–8.

Arashi o fukitobashita fuan no jōnetsu (The passion of fans who have braved the storm). 1959. *Josei Jishin*, October 21, pp. 69–71.

Arasoi wa koko ni mo (The battle is also here). 1943. *Takarazuka Kagegidan Kyakuhonshū* 26(8):18–25.

Asagawa Kiyo. 1921. Joyū to onnayakusha (Actresses and female performers). *Josei Nihonjin* 4:112.

Asano Michiko. 1989. Minshū shūkyō ni okeru ryōseiguyūkan (The idea and image of androgyny in folk religion). In *Shiriizu: Josei to bukkyō* (Series: Women and Buddhism). Vol. 2, *Sukui to oshie* (Salvation and teachings), ed. Nishiguchi Junko and Ōsumi Kazuo, 200–229. Tokyo: Heibonsha.

Ashihara Eiryō. 1936. Gendai rebyū tokuhon (A modern revue primer). *Tākii* 28:6–7.

Ashihara Kuniko. 1979. *Waga seishun no Takarazuka* (The Takarazuka of our youth). Tokyo: Zenbonsha.

Asu no shōjo kageki (Tomorrow's *shōjo* revue). 1940. *Ōsaka Mainichi and Tōkyō Nichinichi Shinbun*, January 13.

A.Z. Joshi. 1939. Fuan retā sanpo (An excursion into fan letters). *Eiga to Rebyū* 1:46–47.

Bessatsu Takarajima. 1987. [Special issue] Onna o aisuru onnatachi no mono-gatari (A tale of women who love women). No. 64.

Daisuki na onēsama (My beloved older sister). 1938. *Shōjo Kageki* 7:12.

Dan Michiko. 1935. Shōjo kageki no joyū ni naritagaru shōjo e (To girls who want to become actresses in *shōjo* revues). *Fujin Kōron* 4:280–85.

Dansei no naka no "chōshōjo" tachi (The ultra-*shōjo* within males). 1986. *Shōjoza* 2 (Spring):36.

Dansō hi ari. Fushizen na dōseiai no taishō ni nariyasui (There is adversity in cross-dressing as a man. [Cross-dressed females] easily become the object of unnatural homosexual love). 1935. *Ōsaka Mainichi Shinbun,* January 31.

Dansō no reijin shōmetsu (The disappearance of cross-dressed women). 1939. *Ōsaka Nichinichi Shinbun,* August 20.

Dansō wa shūaku no kiwami (Cross-dressed females are the acme of offensiveness). 1939. *Asahi Shinbun,* Osaka ed., May 15.

Dō, oiroke aru kashira (Well, is there any erotic charm?). 1977. *Asahi Shinbun,* evening ed., December 21.

"Dōseiai" to ieba okoru (If you say "same-sex love" [she] gets angry). 1929. *Tōkyō Nichinichi Shinbun,* November 29.

Endō Shingo. 1943. Nanpō no engeki kōsaku (An inquiry into theater of the Southern Regions). *Engei Gahō* 37(2):1.

Engei gahō. 1942. [Photograph of Hanayagi Shōtaro]. No. 7:n.p.

Enshutsuka ni kiku (Ask the director). 1968. *Takarazuka Gurafu* 9:66–67.

Fuan hyakutai (Various types of fans). 1953. *Asahi Shinbun,* Osaka ed., January 18.

Fujikawa Yū. 1919a. Seiyoku no kagaku (The science of sexual desire). *Tōa no Hikari* 1:70–73.

———. 1919b. Seiyoku no kagaku. Shōzen (The science of sexual desire, continued). *Tōa no Hikari* 3:51–53.

———. 1923. Seiyoku no mondai (The problem of sexual desire). *Chūō Kōron* 7:51–62.

Fujin muki no shinshiki densha o tsukuru (Designing a new-style train for female [passengers]). 1923. *Ōsaka Shinbun,* February 10.

Fujioka Toshiko. 1937. Yūjō, hihan, musumeyaku (Friendship, criticism, players of the woman's role). *Takarazuka Shōjokageki Kyakuhonshū* 10:49–50.

Fukumoto Masaji. 1942. Kōba to bunkakōsei no mondai (The problem of factories and cultural welfare). *Gendai Engeki* 5(5):51–53.

Fukushima Shirō, ed. 1984 (1935). *Fujinkai sanjūgonen* (Thirty-five years of women's world). Tokyo: Fuji Shuppansha.

Fukutomi Mamoru. 1985. "*Rashisa*" *no shakaigaku* (The sociology of "gender"). Kōdansha gendai shinsho 797. Tokyo: Kōdansha.

Furuya Toyoko. 1922. Dōseiai no joshi kyōikujō ni okeru shin'igi (The new significance of homosexuality in the context of girls' and women's education). *Fujin Kōron* 7(8):24–29.

Furuya Tsunatake. 1932. *Shōjo no tame no seikatsuron* (Lifestyle guide for girls). Tokyo: Ōmidō.

Fushigi no kuni no Takarazuka (The strange country of Takarazuka). 1993. Tokyo: Pia.

Futaba Jūjirō. 1939. Senjika rebyū hyōbanki (Popularity ratings of wartime revues). *Kaizō* 3:165–70.

Fuwa Suketoshi. 1941. Engekihō shimon dai'ichigo tōshin'an (Draft report of questions related to the theater law). *Engei Gahō* 35(1):2–3.

Gao. 1993. *Queen's Pal* 4:26–33.

Gendai no ōoku: Takarazuka sutā o torimaku seizaikai toppu jinmyaku (The inner castle of today: Key businessmen and politicians who patronize Takarazuka stars). 1979. *Asahi Geinō*, July 26, pp. 20–28.

Gonda Yasunosuke. 1941. *Kokumin goraku no mondai* (The problem of citizens' entertainment). Tokyo: Kurita Shoten.

Gunji Masakatsu. 1988. Kabuki to nō no henshin, henge (Metamorphosis and apparitions in Kabuki and Nō). *Shizen to Bunka* 19:4–9.

Habatake ōgon no tsubasa yo (Wings of gold). 1985. *Takarazuka kageki, Yuki-gumi kōen* (Takarazuka Revue, Snow Troupe's performance). Takarazuka: Takarazuka Kagekidan.

Hachida Motoo. 1940 (1937). *Enshutsuron* (Treatise on directing). Tokyo: Takada Shoin.

Hagiwara Hiroyoshi. 1954. *Takarazuka kageki 4onenshi* (Forty-year history of the Takarazuka Revue). Takarazuka: Takarazuka Kagekidan Shuppanbu.

Hanafusa Shirō. 1930. Petchi, ruiza, sono hoka ("Petchi," "ruiza," and others). *Hanzai Kagaku* 12:75–79.

Hanayagi Shōtarō. 1939. Onnagata o kataru (On *onnagata*). *Asahi Shinbun*, April 21.

Hankyū. 1987. No. 6.

Hara Kie. 1987. *Fujin Kōron* (*Women's Central Review*). In *Fujin zasshi kara mita 1930 nendai* (The 1930s as observed in women's magazines), ed. Watashitachi no Rekishi o Tsuzuru Kai, 16–46. Tokyo: Dōjidaisha.

Haruna Yuri. 1979. *Haruna Yuri no sekai* (Haruna Yuri's world). Tokyo: Futami Shobō.

Haruno Kasumi. 1936. Rebyū fuan no kyōki sata (Report on the fanaticism of revue fans). *Hanashi* 6:241–47.

Hasegawa Tokiame. 1914. Onnagata wa nokorimasumai (*Onnagata* should not remain). *Engei Gahō* 10:96–98.

Hasegawa Yoshio. 1931. *Onnagata no kenkyū* (Research on *onnagata*). Tokyo: Ritsumeikan Shuppanbu.

———. 1941. Atarashiki hata jōen ni tsuite (On the performance of *New Flag*). *Takarazuka Kagekidan Kyakuhonshū* 24(11):11–14.

Hashimoto Masao. 1984. *Takarazuka kageki no 7onen* (Seventy-year history of the Takarazuka Review). Takarazuka: Takarazuka Kagekidan.

———. 1988. *Sa se Takarazuka/Ça C'est Takarazuka*. Tōkyō: Yomiuri Shinbunsha.

———. 1993. *Sumire no hana wa arashi o koete* (The violet transcends [the] storm). Tokyo: Yomiuri Shinbunsha.

———. 1994. *Yume o kaite, hanayaka ni: Takarazuka kageki 8onenshi* (Write the dreams beautifully: Eighty-year history of the Takarazuka Revue. Takarazuka: Takarazuka Kagekidan.

Hata Toyokichi. 1948. *Takarazuka to Nichigeki* (Takarazuka and Nichigeki). Tokyo: Itō Shobō.

Hattori Kakō and Uehara Michirō. 1925. *Atarashii kotoba no jibiki* (Dictionary of new words). Tokyo: Jitsugyō no Nihonsha.

Hattori Yukio. 1975. *Hengeron: Kabuki no seishinshi* (Treatise on metamorphosis: A psychological history of Kabuki). Tokyo: Heibonsha.

Hayashi Misao. 1926. Danjo to shiyū (Man and woman, male and female). *Nihon Hyōron* 3:319–25.

Hentaiteki kankaku (4): Otokoyaku ni natta toki no kageki joyū (Abnormal sensations [4]: When revue actresses become players of men's roles). 1929. *Shin Nippō*, March 16.

Higashi e kaeru (Return to the East). 1942. *Takarazuka Kageki Kyakuhonshū* 25(3):41–68.

Hijikata Tadami. 1944. Kankyaku ni tsuite (On audiences). *Engekikai* 2(7):8.

Hirabayashi Tazuko. 1935. Takarazuka onna fuan retsuden (Profiles of female fans of Takarazuka). *Kageki* 10:73–75.

Hirai Fusato. 1933. *Takarazuka monogatari* (Tale of Takarazuka). Tokyo: Shōjo Gahō.

Hiroo Mōyaku. 1936. Gendai engekisaku haiyūron (Treatise on actors for the production of modern plays). *Chūō Kōron* 3:140–51.

Hirozawa Yumi. 1987. Iseiai chōsei to iu fuashizumu (The fascism of compulsory heterosexuality). *Shinchihei* 6 (150):67–73.

Hogosha wa kokoro seyo—byōteki na fuan buri (Guardians, be on the alert for the signs of pathological fandom). 1935. *Asahi Shinbun*, January 31.

Hontō ni iitai hōdai (Speaking my mind). 1991. *Yume no Hanataba* 20:64–65.

Horikiri Naoto. 1988. Onna wa dokyō, shōjo wa aikyō (Women are brave, *shōjo* are winsome). In *Shōjoron* (Treatise on *shōjo*), ed. Honda Masuko, 107–28. Tokyo: Seiyu.

Hoshi Sumire. 1987. Ano onna (hito) e no rabu reta (A love letter to that woman [person]). *Bessatsu Takarajima* 64:55.

Hosokawa Shūhei. 1992. Nanyō (South Seas). Seiyō ongaku no nihonka/taishūka (The Japanization and popularization of Western music) 43. *Music Magazine* 10:144–49.

Hyūga Akiko. 1971. Sei no henshin ganbō (The desire for sexual metamorphosis). *Dentō to Gendai* 2(6):26–37.

Ichikawa Hiroshi. 1985. *"Mi" no kōzō: Shintairon o koete* (The structure of the "body": Surpassing physiology). Tokyo: Aonisha.

Ichikawa Ken. 1972. *Nihon shomin no kyōikushi* (A history of the education of commoners in Japan). Tokyo: Tamagawa Daigaku Shuppanbu.

if . . . . 1977. *Takarazuka Gurafu* 7:60–61.

Ifukube Takaki. 1932. Dōseiai e no ikkōsatsu (Thoughts about homosexuality). *Hanzai Kagaku* 1:290–93.

Igi Ryōshi. 1937. Dansei fuan no kai e (Toward a male fan club). *Takarazuka Shōjokageki Kyakuhonshū* 12:32.

Iizuka Tomoichirō. 1922. Gekijō kaihō no hitotsu keishiki to shite no shit-sunaigeki (Indoor theater, one form of a liberated theater). *Fujinkai* 10:20–25.

———. 1930. *Engeki to hanzai* (Theater and crime). Kindai hanzai kagaku zen-shū (Collection of works on modern criminology) 15. Tokyo: Bukyōsha.

———. 1936. *Engeki kenkyū no hōhō* (Theater research methodology). Tokyo: Okakura Shobō.

———. 1941. *Kokumin engeki to nōson engeki* (Citizens' theater and farm-village theater). Tokyo: Shimizu Shobō.

Ikita koishita onna no 100nen (One hundred years of women who have lived and loved). 1988. Tokyo: Kyōdō Tsūshinsha.

Imago. 1991. Tokushū: Rezubian (Special issue: Lesbian) 2(8).

Imao Tetsuya. 1982. *Henshin no shisō* (The idea of metamorphosis). Tokyo: Hō-sei Daigaku.

Inoue Shōichi. 1989. Gyaru to gāru no Shōwashi (The history of gals and girls in the Shōwa period). In *Geppō (Modan gāru no yūwaku)* (Monthly bulletin [The seductive allure of the Modern Girl]). No. 12, pp. [1–6]. Tokyo: Hei-bonsha.

Ishii shakkin'ō mo patoron no hitori ([Mr.] Ishii, the loan shark king, is one patron). 1925. *Ōsakato Shinbun*, July 20.

Iwahori Yasumitsu. 1972. *Isai Kobayashi Ichizō no shōhō* (The remarkable Ko-bayashi Ichizō's business strategy). Tokyo: Hyōgensha.

Izawa Miki. 1931. Dōseiaikō (A study of homosexual love). *Hanzai Kagaku* 9:224–28.

Janpu oriento! (Jump Orient!). 1994. *Takarazuka kageki, Hoshi-gumi kōen* (Takarazuka Revue, Star Troupe's performance). Takarazuka: Takarazuka Kagekidan.

Jidai ni kakaru hashi: San'nin musume no merodorama hōdan (A bridge across time: The melodramatic stories of three young women). 1962. *Kageki* 444:38–44.

Jishuku wa seitō dake (Only the students must exercise self-discipline). 1940. *Yomiuri Shinbun*, August 29.

Joseitachi no Taiheiyō sensō (Women and the Pacific War). 1994. *Bessatsu rekishi tokuhon* (History reader), no. 34. Tokyo: Shinjinbutsu Ōraisha.

Joseito no matsuro wa jōdama de bā no yō (Dancing at bars is the fate of fe-male students). 1925. *Ōsakato Shinbun*, July 22.

Kabeshima Tadao, Hida Yoshifumi, and Yonekawa Akihiko, eds. 1984. *Meiji Taishō shingo zokugo jiten* (Dictionary of new words and colloquialisms in the Meiji and Taishō periods). Tokyo: Tōkyōdō Shuppan.

Kakko yosa batsugun no kiza wa nimaime ([Takarazuka] otokoyaku have good form and outstanding style). 1969. *Takarazuka Gurafu* 12:38–40.

Kamisaka Fuyoko. 1984. *Dansō no reijin: Kawashima Yoshiko den* (The cross-dressed beauty: The biography of Kawashima Yoshiko). Tokyo: Bungei Shunjū.

Kamura Kikuo. 1984. *Itoshi no Takarazuka e* (To beloved Takarazuka). Kobe: Kōbe Shinbun Shuppan Sentā.

Karakuri no ōi shōjokagekidan (Too many contrived girls' revues). 1925. *Ōsakato Shinbun*, July 15, 17, 18.

Kawahara, Yomogi. 1921. *Takarazuka kageki shōjo no seikatsu* (The life of *shōjo* in the Takarazuka Revue). Osaka: Ikubunkan.

Kawazoe Noboru. 1980. Nihon bunmei to taishū bunka (Japanese enlightenment and mass culture). *Jurisuto* 20:6–12.

Kaze to tomo ni hige ka (Gone with the mustache?). 1977. *Asahi Shinbun*, evening ed., April 23.

Kekkon fuantajii (Marriage fantasy). 1950. *Opera Fuan* 16:[1–5].

Kikuta Kazuo. 1982. Himeuri no higeki (The tragedy of Red Star Lily). In *Aishite koishite namidashite: Takarazuka to Kikuda Kazuo* (Love and tears: Kikuda Kazuo and the Takarazuka Revue), ed. Hashimoto Masao, 18–19. Takarazuka: Takarazuka Kagekidan.

Kindan no Takarazuka e jūsan'nin no seinen (To Takarazuka, where males are forbidden, go thirteen youths). 1940. *Miyako Shinbun*, November 2.

Kitamura Nobuya. 1943. Engeki no gendaiteki shomondai (Recent problems facing the theater). *Kokumin Engeki* 3(7):38–50.

Kobayashi Ichizō. 1934. Taishū geijutsu no jin'ei (The mass performing arts camp). *Chūō Kōron* 1:268–73.

———. 1935a. "Dansō no reijin" to wa? (What is the "cross-dressed beauty"?). *Kageki* 4:10–12.

———. 1935b. Goraku yo katei e kaere (Entertainment should return to the household). *Ōsaka Mainichi Shinbun*, January 8.

———. 1948. Omoitsuki (Idea). *Kageki* 271:29.

———. 1961a. Shibai zange (Confessions on theater). In *Kobayashi Ichizō zenshū* (The collected works of Kobayashi Ichizō), 2:207–439. (Originally published in 1942.) Tokyo: Daiyamondosha.

———. 1961b. Takarazuka manpitsu (Takarazuka jottings). In *Kobayashi Ichizō zenshū*, 2:443–575. (Originally published in 1955.) Tokyo: Daiyamondosha.

———. 1962. Watakushi no ikikata (My way of life). In *Kobayashi Ichizō zenshū*, 3:3–244. (Originally published in 1942.) Tokyo: Daiyamondosha.

Kodomo no suki na henshin dorama (The morphing dramas that children like). 1968. *Asahi Shinbun*, Osaka ed., January 13.

Kōjien. 1978. 2d enl. ed. Tokyo: Iwanami Shoten.

Kokumin no hansū jogai (Half the citizens are excluded). 1935. *Fujo Shinbun*, January 27.

Komashaku Kimi, ed. 1989. *Onna o yosōu* (Dressing women). Tokyo: Keiso Shobō.

Komatsu Sakae. 1942. Rebyū seisaku soshiki (2) (The method of producing revues [2]). *Gendai Engeki* 5(5):61–67.

Komine Shimoe and Minami Takao. 1985. *Dōseiai to dōsei shinjū no kenkyū* (Research on homosexuality and homosexual suicide). Tokyo: Komine Kenkyūjo.

Kore mo jidaisō ka (Is this too the shape of the times?). 1935. *Asahi Shinbun*, January 30.

Koyama Shizuko. 1982. Kindaiteki joseikan to shite no ryōsaikenbo shisō (The

Good Wife, Wise Mother as a modern idea about women). *Joseigaku Nenpō* 3:1–8.

———. 1986. Ryōsaikenboshugi no reimei (The dawn of Good Wife, Wise Motherism). *Joseigaku Nenpō* 7:11–20.

Kudō Nori. 1963. Uchira ni mo teinen ga irunyaroka (Do we too really need a retirement age?). *Shūkan Asahi*, February 8, pp. 22–26.

Kumano Norikazu. 1984. Takarazuka kageki to Kobayashi Ichizō (The Takarazuka Revue and Kobayashi Ichizō). *Takarazuka* 2:1–24.

Kure Hidemitsu. 1920. Dōsei no ai (Homosexual love). *Fujin Gahō* 10:24–27.

Kurihara Akira. 1980. Kanri shakaige no taishū bunka (Mass culture under a management society). *Jurisuto* 20:59–66.

Kuwatani Sadahaya. 1911. Senritsu subeki joseikan no tentō seiyoku (Shocking sexual inversions among females). *Shinkōron* 26(9):35–42.

Maeda Isamu. 1973. *Edogo daijiten* (Dictionary of Edo-period language). Tokyo: Kōdansha.

Maruki Sato. 1930. Aisuru senyū (War friends who love each other). *Hanzai Kagaku* 11:84–89.

Maruki Sunado. 1929. Modan kigo (Modern signs). *Kaizō* 6:29–32.

Maruo Chōken. 1932. Ojōsama wa danpatsu ga osuki (Young ladies like their hair short). *Nichinichi Shinbun*, April 24.

———. 1950. *Takarazuka sutā monogatari* (The tale of Takarazuka stars). Tokyo: Jitsugyō no Nihonsha.

———. 1981. *Kaisō Kobayashi Ichizō: Sugao no ningenzō* (Onward Kobayashi Ichizō: A sober image). Tokyo: Yamaneko Shobō.

Masatomi Ōyō. 1920. Danseibi to seiyoku honnō (Male beauty and sexual instinct). *Nihon Oyobi Nihonjin*, September 20, pp. 129–31.

Matoya Jūrō. 1937. Takarazuka shōjokageki kōenkai o ura kara miru (Examining Takarazuka Revue fan clubs from behind the scenes). *Hanashi* 6/7:228–35.

Matsui Shōyō. 1914. Onnagata demo joyū demo (Whether an *onnagata* or an actress). *Engei Gahō* 10:94–96.

Matsumoto Haruko. 1916. Shibai kenbutsu no fujin no kata e (To women who attend the theater). *Fujin Zasshi* 4:131–33.

Mimi to me to kuchi to (Ears, Eyes, and Mouths). 1941. *Takarazuka Kageki Kyakuhonshū* 24(3):26–43.

Mine izu main (Mine is mine). 1986. Takarazuka: Takarazuka Kagekidan.

Misato Kei. 1974. Sutā tankyū (Star research). *Takarazuka Gurafu* 7:68–69.

Mitsuda Kyōko. 1985. Kindaiteki boseikan no juyō to henkei (The reception and transformation of the modern concept of motherhood). In *Bosei o tou* (Questioning motherhood), ed. Wakita Haruko, 100–29. Tokyo: Jinbun Shoin.

Miyasako Chizu. 1986. Nakahara Atsukazu no hikari to kage (The light and shadow of Nakahara Atsukazu). *Shōjoza* 2:58–61.

Miyatake Tatsuo. 1942. Barii-shima no onna (Women of Bali). *Takarazuka Kageki Kyakuhonshū* 25(8):8–14.

Miyazaki Ichirō. 1942. Kokumin engeki ni tsuite engekijin ni taishū wa konomu (The Citizens' Theater gains popularity). *Gendai Engeki* 5(1):19–23.

Mizukawa Yōko. 1987. Tachi: Kono kodoku na ikimono (Butch: This lonely creature). *Bessatsu Takarajima* 64:18–23.

Mizuki Nobuo. 1936. Fuan echiketto daigaku 1 (Fan etiquette primer 1). *Tākii* 23:74–75.

Modan otona tōsei manga yose (A variety show of modern adult cartoons). 1935. *Asahi Shinbun*, Osaka ed., February 17.

Mogami Atsuyoshi. 1941. Itarazu Takarazuka kageki (The unaccomplished Takarazuka Revue). *Engei Gahō* 35(5):73.

Mon pari (Mon Paris). 1948. *Takarazuka Kageki Kyakuhonshū* (Nagoya Takarazuka theater). 5:10–16.

Monbusho goraku chōsa (Ministry of Education entertainment survey). 1932. *Asahi Shinbun*, December 2.

Mongōru (Mongol). 1941. *Takarazuka Kageki Kyakuhonshū* 24(10):60–77.

Morimura Yasumasa. 1996a. Chikaku no genshōgaku to shite no "Ō Takarazuka" (Oh Takarazuka: A local school of phenomenology). *Taiyō* 420:105.

Mukai Sōya. 1977. *Nihon minshū engekishi* (A history of Japanese popular theater). Tokyo: Nihon Hōsō Shuppan Kyōkai.

Murakami Nobuhiko. 1983. *Taishōki no shokugyō fujin* (Working women of the Taishō period). Tokyo: Dōmesu Shuppan.

Mure Isao. 1985. '85nen kōenhyō: *Tendā guriin, Andorojenii* (Roster of performances in 1985: *Tender Green, Androgyny*). *Takarazuka Gurafu* 462:38–39.

Nagisa Natsumi. 1937. Fuan tokuhon (Fan primer). *Shōjo Kageki* (Shōchiku) 5(2):90–95.

Naitō Meisetsu. 1914. Onnagata yōron (On the usefulness of *onnagata*). *Engei Gahō* 10:100–103.

Nakagawa Ryūichi. 1941. Amerika no renpō engeki undō (The American Federal Theater Project). *Gendai Engeki* 4(3):51–52.

Nakano Eitarō. 1935. Dansō no reijin to Saijō Eriko (The cross-dressed beauty and Saijō Eriko). *Fujin Kōron* 3:161–67.

Nihonkai. 1987. April 18.

Niizeki Ryōzō. 1940. *Nachizu Doitsu no engeki* (Theater in Nazi Germany). Tokyo: Kōbundō.

Nimaime zadankai (*Nimaime* roundtable). 1936. *Shōchiku Kageki* 4(1):48–49.

Nippon gekijōnai biyōin, fujinkaikan no tanjō (The inauguration of a beauty parlor and women's center in the Nippon Theater). 1937. *Shahō* (Tōhō) 12:5.

Nisemono Takarazuka kageki (Pseudo-Takarazuka revues). 1923. *Taiyō Nippō*, March 11.

Nishikawa Tatsumi. 1935. Misu Choppe (Miss Pshaw). *Tōhō* 22 (October):64–65.

Nishimura Hitoshi. 1916. Saita, saita. Sakura no hana ga saita. ([They've] bloomed, [they've] bloomed. Cherry blossoms have bloomed). *Fujin Zasshi* 4:85–89.

Nishiyama Eiko. 1984. Otoko demo onna demo nai kōto (A coat that is neither masculine nor feminine). *Asahi Shinbun*, December 3.

Nogami Toshio. 1920. Gendai seikatsu to danjo ryōsei no sekkin (The association of modern life and androgyny). *Kaizō* 2(4):185–204.

Noguchi Takehiko. 1980. Yomigaetta yomihon [*sic*]: Nihon no taishū shosetsu to sono bunka (Revived reader: Japan's popular novels and their culture). *Jurisuto* 20:24–29.

Ōhara Kaoru. 1992 (1991). Kankyakuron (Treatise on audiences). In *Takarazuka no yūwaku* (Takarazuka's allure), ed. Kawasaki Kenko and Watanabe Miwako, 182–92. Tokyo: Seikyūsha.

Ōhara Kenshirō. 1965. *Nihon no jisatsu: Kodoku to fuan no kaimei* (Suicide in Japan: An interpretation of loneliness and anxiety). Tokyo: Seishin Shobō.

———. 1973. *Shinjūkō: Ai to shi no byōri* (A treatise on double suicide: The pathology of love and death). Tokyo: Rogosu Sensho.

Okada Shichirō. 1938. Shōjo kageki no "kakushin" ("Renovation" of the *shojō* revue). *Tākii* 7(10):10–11.

Okamura Tsunematsu. 1942. Mo hitotsu no engeki undō: Shōgyō toshi engeki no shuppatsu (One more theater movement: The start of commercial theater). *Gendai Engeki* 5(1):16–17.

Okazaki Fumi. 1971. Miwaku so sutā, Kō Nishiki (A bewitching star, Kō Nishiki). *Takarazuka Gurafu* 287:48–51.

Ōki Shintarō. 1942. Kōba engeki no mondai (The problems of factory theater). *Gendai Engeki* 5(4):60–63.

Onna to kekkon suru uwasa (The rumor that [she's] to marry a female). 1929. *Taishō Nichinichi Shinbun*, November 30.

Onnagata kikin (*Onnagata* famine). 1939. *Asahi Shinbun*, January 31.

Osanai Kaoru. 1914. Onnagata ni tsuite (On *onnagata*). *Engei Gahō* 10:82–88.

Otoko ni mo sukāto jidai? (An age of males in skirts?). 1985. *Asahi Shinbun*, May 15.

Ōtsuka Eiji. 1989. *Shōjo minzokugaku* (Ethnography of *shōjo*). Tokyo: Kōbunsha.

Ōyama Isao. 1941. Kokumin engekiron josetsu (Preface to a treatise on Citizens' Theater). *Kokumin Engeki* 1(1):106–14.

———. 1943a. Kokumin engeki to Shingeki (Citizens' Theater and Shingeki). *Kokumin Engeki* 3(6):44–49.

———. 1943b. Kokumin engeki to Shinpageki (Citizens' Theater and Shinpa theater). *Kokumin Engeki* 3(4):50–55.

———. 1943c. *Kokumin engekiron* (Treatise on Citizens' Theater). Osaka: Shinshōdō.

Ozaki Hirotsugi. 1986. Sannin no joyū o chūshin ni (On three actresses). In *Meiji no joyūten* (Exhibition of Meiji actresses), 10–16. Hakubutsukan, Meiji-mura (Museum, Meiji Village). Nagoya: Nagoya Tetsudō.

Ōzasa Yoshio. 1985. *Nihon gendai engekishi* (History of modern Japanese theater). Vol. 1, *Meiji Taishō hen* (Meiji, Taishō volume). Tokyo: Hakusuisha.

———. 1986. *Nihon gendai engekishi*. Vol. 2, *Taishō Shōwashoki hen* (Taishō, early Shōwa volume). Tokyo: Hakusuisha.

———. 1990. *Nihon gendai engekishi*. Vol. 3, *Shōwa senzen hen* (Prewar Shōwa volume). Tokyo: Hakusuisha.

———. 1993. *Nihon gendai engekishi*. Vol. 4, *Shōwa senchū hen* (Wartime Shōwa volume). Tokyo: Hakusuisha.

Ōzumi Narumitsu. 1931. Hentai seiyoku (Abnormal sexual desire). *Hanzai Kagaku* 4:75–83.

Paparagi (Papalagi). 1993. *Takarazuka kageki, Hoshi-gumi kōen* (Takarazuka Revue, Star Troupe's performance). Takarazuka: Takarazuka Kagekidan.

People: Ōura Mizuki. 1986. *Takarazuka Gurafu* 7:48–49.

Puraibēto intabyū: Gō Chigusa (Private interview: Gō Chigusa). 1966. *Takarazuka Gurafu* 6:42.

Rebyū: Meido in Nippon (Revue: Made in Japan). 1937. *Shōchiku shōjokageki Kokusai gekijō kōen* (Shōchiku Revue's performance at the International Theater). Tokyo: Shōchiku Kabushikigaisha Jigyōbu.

Rebyū kōkyōgaku (Revue symphony). 1986. *Takarazuka kageki, Hoshi-gumi kōen* (Takarazuka Revue, Star Troupe's performance). Takarazuka: Takarazuka Kagekidan.

Rebyūgai senpū—gunsō buromaido kinshi (Whirlwind on revue avenue—photographs of [female actors in] military uniforms forbidden). 1939. *Asahi Shinbun*, February 3.

Saburi Yuzuru. 1942a. *Higashi e kaeru* o mite (Review of *Return to the East*). *Gendai Engeki* 5(4):70–72.

———. 1942b. Shōjo kageki tokuhon (4) (A girls' revue primer [4]). *Takarazuka Kageki Kyakuhonshū* 25(9):24–25.

Saijō Eriko. 1935. Dansō no reijin Masuda Fumiko no shi o erabu made (Up until Masuda Fumiko, the cross-dressed beauty chose death). *Fujin Kōron* 3:168–78.

Saitō Hikaru. 1993. "2onendai, Nihon, yūgaku" no ikkyokumen (One aspect of "the 1920s, Japan, eugenics"). *Gendai Shisō* 21(7):128–58.

Sakabe Kengi. 1924. *Fujin no shinri to futoku no kisō* (The foundation of women's psychology and morality). Tokyo: Hokubunkan.

Sakada Toshio. 1984. *Waga Kobayashi Ichizō* (Our Kobayashi Ichizō). Tokyo: Kawade Shobō.

Sakata Hidekazu. 1935. *Rebyū oriori* (Revue miscellany). Tokyo: Sara Shobō.

Sanjū-rokusai demo shōjo (Still a *shōjo* at 36!). 1940. *Shin Nippō*, April 2.

Sassō Hitora fuan (The gallant fan of Hitler). 1939. *Miyako Shinbun*, September 9.

Sawada Bushō. 1921. Onna ga shujutsu o ukete otoko ni natta hanashi (The story about the female who underwent an operation and became a male). *Fujin Kōron* 8:59–70.

Sekai no ichiba (World market). 1941. *Takarazuka Kageki Kyakuhonshū* 24(4): 71–86.

Sensei to kataru (Talking with [our] teacher). 1977. *Takarazuka Gurafu* 362: 36–38.

Sērā haishi: jogakusei no shinseifuku kimaru (Sailor outfits discontinued: New girls' school uniforms are decided). 1941. *Asahi Shinbun*, Osaka ed., January 11.

Serizawa Kōjirō. 1937. Shōjo rebyū to josei (Girls' revues and females). *Bungakkai* 3:201–4.

Shasetsu: Engeki bunka to engekihō (Editorial: Theater culture and the theater law). 1942. *Asahi Shinbun*, November 22.

Shida Aiko and Yuda Yoriko. 1987. *Shufu no Tomo* (*Housewife's Companion*). In

Fujin zasshi kara mita 1930 nendai (The 1930s as observed in women's magazines), ed. Watashitachi no Rekishi o Tsuzuru Kai, 48–121. Tokyo: Dōjidaisha.

Shima Osamu. 1984. *Za Takarazuka* (The Takarazuka). Tokyo: Tairiku Shobō.

Shin Nippō. 1936. July 17.

"Shinjū" no shibai kinshi (Suicide plays forbidden). 1939. *Asahi Shinbun*, Osaka evening ed., December 17.

Shirai Tetsuzō. 1947. *Mon pari* saijōen, enshutsu ni tsuite (On the revival of *Mon Paris* and directing). *Takarazuka Kageki Kyakuhonshū* 30(10):17.

———. 1967. *Takarazuka to watakushi* (Takarazuka and I). Tokyo: Nakabayashi Shuppan.

Shisshin shisō na fuan retā (Bewitching fan letters). 1969. *Heibon Panchi*, April 14, pp. 30–31.

Shōchiku kageki fuan kokoroe (Directions for fans of the Shōchiku Revue). 1949. *Shōchiku Kageki* 1 (November):[1].

Shōchiku Kagekidan. 1978. *Rebyū to tomo ni hanseiki: Shōchiku kagekidan 50nen no ayumi* (A half century with the revue: The fifty-year history of the Shōchiku Revue). Tōkyō: Kokusho Kankōkai.

Shōjo kageki o kataru—musume to haha no kai (Talking about the *shōjo* revue—a gathering of mothers and daughters). 1935. *Fujin Kōron* 4:288–97.

Shōjo no niji massatsu (The two characters of *shōjo* erased). 1940. *Kokumin Shinbun*, September 8.

Shuku hachijū-nen kinen ankēto (Felicitous eightieth anniversary questionnaire). 1994. *Kageki* 6:130–136

Sonoike Kinnaru. 1933. *Engeki no tsukurikata* (Theater production). Tokyo: Gakujutsu Gakuin Shuppanbu.

Sugahara Tsūzai. 1971. *Dōseiai* (Homosexuality). Tokyo: San'aku Tsuihō Kyōkai.

Sugawara Midori. 1981. *Takarazuka episōdo 350* (350 Takarazuka episodes). Tokyo: Rippū Shobo.

Sugita Masaki. 1929. Seihonnō ni hisomu sangyakusei (Sadomasochistic qualities latent within sexual instinct). *Kaizō* 4:70–80.

———. 1935. Shōjo kageki netsu no shindan (An analysis of the feverish interest in *shōjo* revues). *Fujin Kōron* 4:274–278.

Sumida Tadaichi. 1944. Kangeki no seisanka (Productivity and theatergoing). *Engekikai* 2(2):5–6.

Sutā to sutaffu (Stars and staff). 1968. *Takarazuka Gurafu* 9:61–64.

Suzuki Tazuko. 1975 (1974). *Zuka fuan no kagami: "Mon pari" kara "Berubara" made* (Mirror of [Takara]zuka fans: from *Mon Paris* to *The Rose of Versailles*). Tōkyō: Ushio Shuppansha.

Suzuki Zenji. 1983. Nihon no yūseigaku (Japanese eugenics). *Sankyō kagaku sensho* 14. Tokyo: Sankyō Shuppan.

Tachibana Kyō. 1890. Fūzoku hōtan (Forsaking custom). *Fūzoku Gahō* 14: 15–16.

Tadai Yoshinosuke and Katō Masa'aki. 1974. *Nihon no jisatsu o kangaeru* (A consideration of suicide in Japan). Tokyo: Igaku Shoin.

Tagō Torao. 1941. Shirōtogeki no shuppatsuten (The launch pad for amateur theater). *Kokumin Engeki* 1(1):144–46.

Takada Gi'ichirō. 1926 (1917). *Hōigaku* (Medical jurisprudence). Tokyo: Kasseidō.

Takada Tamotsu. 1934. Rebyū jidai kōsatsuki (An inquiry into the revue age). *Shinchō* 3:57–64.

Takagi Hiroshi. 1993. Fuashizumuki, Ainu minzoku no dōkaron (The assimilation of Ainu during the fascist period). In *Bunka to fuashizumu: Senjiki Nihon ni okeru bunka no kōbō* (Culture and fascism: Illuminating Japanese wartime culture), ed. Akazawa Shirō and Kitagawa Kenzō, 247–83. Tokyo: Nihon Keizai Hyōronsha.

Takagi Masashi. 1989. "Taishō demokurashii" ki ni okeru "yūseiron" no tenkai to kyōiku (The development and instruction of eugenics during the "Taishō Democracy"). *Nagoya Daigaku Kyōikugakubu Kiyō* 36:167–78.

———. 1991. 1920–1930 nendai ni okeru yūseigakuteki nōryokukan (The eugenic perception of intelligence in the period 1920–1930). *Nagoya Daigaku Kyōikugakubu Kiyō* 38:161–71.

———. 1993. Senzen Nihon ni okeru yūsei shisō no tenkai to nōryokukan, kyōikukan (The development of eugenic thought in prewar Japan and the perception of intelligence and education). *Nagoya Daigaku Kyōikugakubu Kiyō* 40:41–52.

Takagi Shimei. 1976. *Takarazuka no wakaruhon* (Guidebook to Takarazuka). Tokyo: Kōsaidō.

Takagi Shin'ichi. 1942. Kōba kokumin engeki juritsu e no teishin (Toward the establishment of Citizens' Theater in factories). *Gendai Engeki* 5(3):22–24.

Takagi Shirō. 1983. *Rebyū no ōsama: Shirai Tetsuzō to Takarazuka* (The king of revues: Shirai Tetsuzō and Takarazuka). Tokyo: Kawade Shobō.

Takahashi Kumitarō. 1930. Rebyū jidai (Revue age). *Kaizō* 6:117–22.

Takano M. 1987. Chōshōjo to fueminizumu no kyōhan kankei ni (The conspiratorial partnership between ultra-*shōjo* and feminism). *Kuriteiiku* 6:53–63.

Takaoka Hiroyuki. 1993. Kankō, kōsei, ryokō: Fuashizumuki no tsūrizumu (Sightseeing, welfare, and travel: Tourism during the fascist period). In *Bunka to fuashizumu: Senjiki Nihon ni okeru bunka no kōbō* (Culture and fascism: Illuminating Japanese wartime culture), ed. Akazawa Shirō and Kitagawa Kenzō, 9–52. Tokyo: Nihon Keizai Hyōronsha.

Takaoka Nobuyuki. 1943. *Kokumin engeki no tenbō* (A view of Citizens' Theater). Tokyo: Yoshi Bundō.

Takarazuka bijin hensenshi (4): Kurasu S kara butai no otokoyaku e no shibokōfun (Vicissitudes of Takarazuka beauties [4]: From Class S to feverish longing for players of men's roles). 1930. *Ōsaka Nichinichi Shinbun*, July 21.

Takarazuka bijin hensenshi (5): Josei ga horeru (Vicissitudes of Takarazuka beauties [5]: Females fall in love). 1930. *Ōsaka Nichinichi Shinbun*, July 26.

Takarazuka eiga no senku (Advances in Takarazuka films). 1938. *Takarazuka Daigekijō Kyakuhonshū* 209:20–25.

Takarazuka Fuan. 1954. [Cover photograph]. No. 93.

Takarazuka fuan ni kansuru jūnisō (Twelve meditations for Takarazuka fans). 1955. *Takarazuka Fuan* 97:7.

Takarazuka fuan ni tsugu (Announced to Takarazuka fans). 1940. *Ōsaka Nichinichi Shinbun*, August 19.

Takarazuka Goods Selection. 1996. Tokushu: Takarazuka (Special issue: Takarazuka). *Taiyō*, no. 420, pp. 94–95.

Takarazuka Gurafu. 1968. [Cover photograph]. No. 1.

———. 1969. [Cover photograph]. No. 12.

———. 1987. [Photograph]. No. 4, p. 2.

———. 1990. [Photograph]. No. 3, p. 17.

Takarazuka ihen (Takarazuka calamity). 1932. *Hōchi Shinbun*, July 26.

Takarazuka kageki ni seifuku chakuyō (Uniforms for the Takarazuka Revue). 1939. *Ōsaka Nichinichi Shinbun*, September 22.

Takarazuka kageki no dansei kashu (The Takarazuka Revue's male singers). 1940. *Asahi Shinbun*, Osaka ed., October 16.

Takarazuka Kagekidan. 1943. *Takarazuka nenkan* (Takarazuka yearbook). Ōsaka: Takarazuka Kagekidan.

Takarazuka manga (Takarazuka cartoons). 1935. *Tōhō* 22 (October):59–62.

Takarazuka ni dai 5 no kumi (A fifth troupe for Takarazuka). 1997. *Mainichi Shinbun*, August 26.

Takarazuka shōjokageki wa doko e yuku? (Whither the Takarazuka Girls' Revue?). 1940. *Kokumin Shinbun*, September 15.

The Takarazuka: *Takarazuka kageki 80shūnin kinen* (Takarazuka: The eightieth anniversary of the Takarazuka Revue). 1994. *Asahi Gurafu Bessatsu* (separate volume of *Asahi Graph*). Tokyo: Asahi Shinbunsha.

Takayanagi Kaneyoshi. 1965. *Edojō ōoku no seikatsu* (Life in the inner quarters of Edo Castle). Tokyo: Yūzankaku.

Takeda Sachiko. 1994. Dansō, josō: sono nihonteki tokushitsu to ifukusei (Cross-dressing as man, cross-dressing as woman: Special Japanese characteristics and sartorial regulations). In *Jendā no Nihonshi (jō)* (History of gender in Japan, vol. 1), ed. Wakita Haruko and Susan Hanley, 217–51. Tokyo: Tōkyō Daigaku Shuppankai.

Tamura Toshiko. 1913. Dōseiai no koi (Homosexual love). *Chūō Kōron* 1:165–68.

Tanabe Seiko and Sasaki Keiko. 1983. *Yume no kashi o tabete: Waga itoshi no Takarazuka* (Eat the dream candy: Our beloved Takarazuka). Tokyo: Kōdansha.

Tani Kazue. 1935. "Dansō no reijin" no jogakusei jidai o kataru (The girls' school years of the "cross-dressed beauty"). *Hanashi* 4:250–56.

Terazawa Takanobu. 1943. Ken'etsukei no tachiba kara (From the censors' standpoint). *Engei Gahō* 37(8):3.

Tō Jūrō. 1972. Shōjo kamen (*Shōjo* mask). In *Gendai Nihon gikyoku taikei* (Outline of modern Japanese drama), ed. San'ichi Shobō Henshūbu, 8:7–23. Tokyo: San'ichi Shobō.

Tōgō Minoru. 1945. Daitōa kensetsu to sakkon mondai (The construction of Greater East Asia and interracial marriages). *Shin Jawa* 2(1):30–34.

Toita Yasuji. 1956 (1950). *Engeki gojūnen* (Fifty years of theater). Tokyo: Jijitsūshinsha.

Tomioka Masakata. 1938. Dansei josō to josei dansō (Males in women's clothing, females in men's clothing). *Kaizō* 10:98–105.

Tsubouchi Hakase Kinen Engeki Hakubutsukan, ed. 1932. *Kokugeki yōran* (Survey of national [Japanese] theater). Tokyo: Azusa Shobō.

Tsubouchi Shōyō. 1921. *Ware pējentogeki* (Our pageants). Tokyo: Kokuhonsha.

Tsuganesawa Toshihiro. 1991. *Takarazuka senryaku* (Takarazuka's strategy). Kōdansha gendai shinsho 1050. Tokyo: Kōdansha.

Tsuji Misako. 1976. *Niji no fuantajia* (Rainbow fantasia). Tokyo: Shinromansha.

Tsumura Hidematsu. 1914a. Shakai keizai mondai to shite no joku (Female laborers as a social economic problem). *Ōsaka Mainichi Shinbun*, February 18.

———. 1914b. Shakai keizai mondai to shite no joku (Female laborers as a social economic problem). *Ōsaka Mainichi Shinbun*, February 19.

Tsurugi Miyuki katarogu (Tsurugi Miyuki catalogue). 1986. *Takarazuka Gurafu* 7:44–45.

Ueda Yoshitsugu. 1974. *Takarazuka sutā: Sono engi to bigaku* (Takarazuka stars: Their acting and aesthetics). Tokyo: Yomiuri Shinbunsha.

———. 1986 (1976). *Takarazuka ongaku gakkō* (The Takarazuka Music Academy). Tokyo: Yomiuri Raifu.

Uemoto Sutezō. 1941. Manshū ni okeru engeki seisaku ni tsuite (The production of theater in Manchuria). *Gendai Engeki* 4(3):48–50.

Ueno Chizuko. 1990 (1989). Rorikon to yaoizoku ni mirai wa aruka?! (Is there a future for gays and [males with] Lolita complexes?!). *Bessatsu Takarajima* 104:131–36.

Ukai Masaki. 1995. Uchimakumono sae kiyoi Takarazuka (Takarazuka, it's even pure behind the scenes). *Asahi Shinbun*, November 6.

Umehara Riko. 1991. *Silk Hat*. Hiratsuka: Umehara Riko.

———. 1994. *For Beginners: Takarazuka*. Tokyo: Gendai Shokan.

Untenshi ni charenji (Challenge for the driver). 1976. *Takarazuka Gurafu* 11:50–51.

Ushijima Yoshimoto. 1943. *Joshi no shinri* (Female psychology). Tokyo: Ganshodō.

Usumi Saijin. 1935. Joryū sakka seikatsu ura omote (The inside and out of the everyday lives of female novelists). *Hanashi* 4:42–43.

Utsu Hideo. 1941. Mōkyō o yuku (Travels to the edges of Mongolia). *Takarazuka Kageki Kyakuhonshū* 24(10):15–20.

Utsumi-sensei to onnayaku (Professor Utsumi and players of women's roles). 1967. *Takarazuka Gurafu* 1:53–55.

Waga pari yo (Our Paris!). 1927. *Takarazuka Shōjokageki Kyakuhonshū* 81:22–31.

Watanabe Tsuneo. 1990. Serufu rabu: Otoko to iu "yokuatsu" kara nogareru tame ni (Self-love: On escaping the "repression" called masculinity). *Bessatsu Takarajima* 107:80–90.

Watanabe Yasu. 1965. *Kabuki ni joyū o* (Actresses to Kabuki). Tokyo: Maki Shoten.

"Watashi" wa "boku" e ([The masculine] "I" is replacing [the feminine/neutral] "I"). 1932. *Ōsaka Mainichi Shinbun*, February 10.

Watashitachi no Rekishi o Tsuzuru Kai, ed. 1987. *Fujin zasshi kara mita 1930 nendai* (The 1930s as observed in women's magazines). Tokyo: Dōjidaisha.

Yabushita Tetsuji. 1990. Yume o ikiru hitobito (People who live in dreams). *Shingeki* 442:106–13.

Yagi Kimiko. 1989. Onna no fukusō (Women's clothing). In *Onna o yosōu*, ed. Komashaku Kimi, 80–115. Tokyo: Keiso Shobō.

Yamada Kōshi. 1968. Rittaiteki ni miryoku o saguru (Searching for charm in three dimensions). *Takarazuka Gurafu* 252:70–72.

Yamana Shōtarō. 1931. *Nihon jisatsu jōshiki* (A history of suicide and love suicide in Japan). Tokyo: Ōdōkan Shoten.

Yamane Kazuma. 1986. *Hentai shōjo moji no kenkyū* (A study of abnormal *shōjo* script). Tokyo: Kōdansha.

Yamawaki, Fusako. 1914. Joshi kyōiku ni tsuite (ge) (On education for girls and women [Part 2]). *Aikokufujin*, no. 301, July 15, p. 3.

Yasuda Tokutarō. 1935. Dōseiai no rekishikan (History of homosexuality). *Chūō Kōron* 3:146–52.

Yasui Shūhei. 1953. Otoko ga onna ni, onna ga otoko ni dōshite nareta ka (How did a male become a woman, and a female a man?). *Fujin Asahi* 3:84–85.

Yasukawa Hajime. 1989. Kansei riaritei to jendā (Sensory reality and gender). In *Jendā no shakaigaku* (Sociology of gender), ed. Ehara Yumiko et al., 196–232. Tokyo: Shinyōsha.

Yomiuri Shinbun. 1935. April 23.

Yoshida Genjirō. 1935. Musume no ren'ai, dōseiai to haha (Mothers and their daughter's love match and/or homosexuality). *Fujin Kōron* 3:156–60.

Yoshii Kinryō. 1940. Eiseijō kara mitaru kōshō mondai (The problem of prostitution viewed from the perspective of hygiene). *Kakusei* 30(1):38–39.

Yoshitake Teruko. 1986. *Nyonin Yoshiya Nobuko* (The woman Yoshiya Nobuko). Tokyo: Bunshun Bunkō.

Yoshiwara Ryūko. 1935. Gekkyu shochōki ni aru musume o motsu okāsama e (To mothers with pubertal daughters). *Fujin Kōron* 3:184–87.

Yoshiya Nobuko. 1950. Takarazuka kageki no sonzai (The existence of the Takarazuka Revue). *Fujin Kōron* 3:68–73.

———. 1963. Kobayashi Ichizō. In *Watakushi no mita hito* (The people I have seen), 27–30. Tokyo: Asahi Shinbunsha.

Yoshizawa Jin. 1966. Kō Nishiki no kako, genzai, mirai (Kō Nishiki's past, present, and future). *Takarazuka Gurafu* 229:51–53.

———. 1967. Gō Chigusa no kako, genzai, mirai (Gō Chigusa's past, present, and future). *Takarazuka Gurafu* 236:69–71.

Yoshizawa Norio and Ishiwata Toshio. 1979. *Gairaigo no gogen* (Etymology of loanwords). Tokyo: Kadokawa Shoten.

Yōsō danpatsu no shiiku na sugata (The chic look of Western dress and short hair [on women]). 1932. *Ōsaka Mainichi Shinbun*, August 21.

Yuki-gumi kōen o mite (A look at the Snow Troupe's performance). 1968. *Takarazuka Gurafu* 9:68–69.

Yuri Yukiko. 1985. Jendā (Gender). *Asahi Shinbun,* evening ed., July 2.

Za Modan (The modern). 1990. *Takarazuka kageki, Tsuki-gumi kōen* (Takarazuka Revue, Moon Troupe's performance). Takarazuka: Takarazuka Kagekidan.

Za Rebyūsukōpu (The revuescope). 1987. *Takarazuka kageki, Hana-gumi kōen* (Takarazuka Revue, Flower Troupe's performance). Takarazuka: Takarazuka Kagekidan.

Zuka gāru ga jishuku ([Takara]zuka girls practice self-discipline). 1940. *Kokumin Shinbun,* September 6.

Zuka musume danzen jishuku ([Takara]zuka daughters must practice self-discipline). 1940. *Kōbe Shinbun,* August 23.

ENGLISH AND OTHER SOURCES

Adams, Abigail. 1993. Dyke to Dyke: Ritual Reproduction at a U.S. Men's Military College. *Anthropology Today* 9(5):3–6.

Adorno, Theodor, and Max Horkheimer. 1972. *Dialectic of Enlightenment.* New York: Herder and Herder.

Ahmad, Aijaz. 1986. Jameson's Rhetoric of Otherness and the "National Allegory." *Social Text* 15:65–88.

Amadiume, Ifi. 1987. *Male Daughters, Female Husbands: Gender and Sex in an African Society.* London: Zed Books.

Anderson, Benedict. 1983. *Imagined Communities: Reflections on the Origin and Spread of Capitalism.* New York: Schocken Books.

Archer, William. 1888. *Masks or Faces? A Study in the Psychology of Acting.* London: Longman's, Green.

Arnott, P. 1969. *Theatres of Japan.* London: Macmillan.

Asami, Noboru. 1924. *Japanese Colonial Government.* New York: [Self-published].

Atkinson, Dennis. 1984. "Takarazuka: Japan's Premier Amusement Park and Modern Theater." Selected Papers in Asian Studies, new series no. 18. Western Conference of the Association for Asian Studies.

Atsumi, Reiko. 1988. Dilemmas and Accommodations of Married Japanese Women in White-Collar Employment. *Bulletin of Concerned Asian Scholars* 20(3):54–62.

Aziz, M. A. 1955. *Japan's Colonialism and Indonesia.* The Hague: Martinus Nijhoff.

Barthes, Roland. 1982 (1970). *Empire of Signs,* trans. Richard Howard. New York: Hill and Wang.

Batson, Benjamin. 1996. Phra Sarasas: Rebel with Many Causes. *Journal of Southeast Asian Studies* 27(1):150–65.

Bauman, Zygmunt. 1991. *Modernity and Ambivalence.* Cambridge: Polity Press.

Beasley, William. 1987. *Japanese Imperialism, 1894–1945.* Oxford: Clarendon Press.

Bell-Metereau Rebecca. 1985. *Hollywood Androgyny.* New York: Columbia University Press.

Benedict, Ruth. 1974 (1946). *The Chrysanthemum and the Sword*. New York: Meridian.

Bergstrom, Janet. 1991. Androids and Androgyny. In *Close Encounters: Film, Feminism, and Science Fiction*, ed. Constance Penley et al., 33–60. Minneapolis: University of Minnesota Press.

Berlin, Zeke. 1988. *Takarazuka: A History and Descriptive Analysis of the All-Female Japanese Performance Company*. Ann Arbor, Mich.: University Microfilms International.

Bernstein, Gail, ed. 1991. *Recreating Japanese Women, 1600–1945*. Berkeley: University of California Press.

Bérubé, Allan. 1990. *Coming Out under Fire: The History of Gay Men and Women in World War Two*. New York: Free Press.

Bhabha, Homi. 1983. The Other Question: The Stereotype and Colonial Discourse. *Screen* 24(6):18–36.

———. 1985. Signs Taken for Wonders: Questions of Ambivalence and Authority under a Tree Outside Delhi, May 1817. *Critical Inquiry* 12:144–65.

———. 1990. Interrogating Identity: The Postcolonial Prerogative. In *Anatomy of Racism*, ed. David Theo Goldberg, 183–209. Minneapolis: University of Minnesota Press.

———. 1991. "Race," Time, and the Revision of Modernity. *Oxford Literary Review* 13:193–219.

Blair, Juliet. 1981. Private Parts in Public Places: The Case of Actresses. In *Women and Space: Ground Rules and Social Maps*, ed. Shirley Ardener, 205–28. New York: St. Martin's Press.

Bollinger, Richmod. 1994. *La Donna È Mobile*. Wiesbaden, Germany: Harrassowitz Verlag.

Bourdieu, Pierre. 1984 (1979). *Distinction: A Social Critique of the Judgement of Taste*, trans. Richard Nice. Cambridge, Mass.: Harvard University Press.

Bowers, Faubion. 1989. From Japan, a Revue Dipped in Dazzle. *New York Times*, October 22.

Bratton, Jacquelin Susan. 1991. Introduction to Bratton et al. 1991:1–17.

Bratton, Jacquelin Susan, et al., eds. 1991. *Acts of Supremacy: The British Empire and the Stage, 1790–1930*. Manchester: Manchester University Press.

Brau, Lorie. 1990. The Women's Theatre of Takarazuka. *The Drama Review* 34(4):79–95.

Buck-Morss, Susan. 1991 (1989). *The Dialectics of Seeing: Walter Benjamin and the Arcades Project*. Cambridge, Mass.: MIT Press.

Buruma, Ian. 1985 (1984). *Behind the Mask: On Sexual Demons, Sacred Mothers, Transvestites, Gangsters, and Other Japanese Cultural Heroes*. New York: Meridian.

Butler, Judith. 1990. *Gender Trouble: Feminism and the Subversion of Identity*. New York: Routledge.

Carr, C. 1989. Noh Business Like Show Business. *Village Voice*, October 31, pp. 47–48.

Carrier, James. 1992. Occidentalism: The World Turned Upside-Down. *American Ethnologist* 19:195–212.

Case, Sue-Ellen. 1988. *Feminism and Theatre*. New York: Methuen.

Chen, Xiaomei. 1992. Occidentalism as Counterdiscourse: "He Shang" in Post-Mao China. *Critical Inquiry* 18:686–712.

Clifford, James. 1988. On *Orientalism*. In *The Predicament of Culture*, 255–76. Cambridge, Mass.: Harvard University Press.

Collier, Jane, and Sylvia Yanagisako. 1987. Toward a Unified Analysis of Gender and Kinship. In *Gender and Kinship: Essays toward a Unified Analysis*, ed. Jane Collier and Sylvia Yanagisako, 14–50. Stanford: Stanford University Press.

Comaroff, John, and Jean Comaroff. 1992. *Ethnography and the Historical Imagination*. Boulder, Colo.: Westview Press.

Corrigan, Philip, and Derek Sayer. 1985. *The Great Arch: English State Formation as Cultural Revolution*. London: Basil Blackwell.

Dana, Henry. 1943. *Drama in Wartime Russia*. New York: National Council of American-Soviet Friendship.

Davidson, Arnold. 1987. Sex and the Emergence of Sexuality. *Critical Inquiry* 14:16–48.

de Grazia, Victoria. 1981. *The Culture of Consent: Mass Organization of Leisure in Fascist Italy*. Cambridge: Cambridge University Press.

de Lauretis, Teresa. 1987. *Technologies of Gender*. Bloomington: Indiana University Press.

De Vos, George. 1973. *Socialization for Achievement: Essays on the Cultural Psychology of the Japanese*. Berkeley: University of California Press.

Devor, Holly. 1989. *Gender Blending: Confronting the Limits of Duality*. Bloomington: University of Indiana Press.

Doak, Kevin. 1994. *Dreams of Difference: The Japan Romantic School and the Crisis of Modernity*. Berkeley: University of California Press.

Dower, John. 1986. *War without Mercy: Race and Power in the Pacific War*. New York: Pantheon.

———. 1993. *Japan in War and Peace: Selected Essays*. New York: New Press.

Dream Girls. 1993. Directed by Kim Longinotto and Jano Williams. Color video and 16mm. Distributed by Women Make Movies, New York.

Duus, Peter, Ramon Myers, and Mark Peattie, eds. 1989. *The Japanese Informal Empire in China, 1895–1937*. Princeton: Princeton University Press.

———. 1996. *The Japanese Wartime Empire, 1931–1945*. Princeton: Princeton University Press.

Ernst, Earle. 1956. *The Kabuki Theatre*. New York: Grove Press.

Evans, David. 1993. *Sexual Citizenship: The Material Construction of Sexualities*. London: Routledge.

Evans-Pritchard, E. E. 1951. *Kinship and Marriage among the Nuer*. Oxford: Clarendon Press.

Faludi, Susan. 1994. The Naked Citadel. *New Yorker*, September 5, pp. 62–81.

Fawkes, Richard. 1978. *Fighting for a Laugh: Entertaining the British and American Armed Forces, 1939–1946*. London: Macdonald and Jane's Publishers.

Feuerwerker, Albert. 1989. Japanese Imperialism in China: A Commentary. In Duus, Myers, and Peattie 1989:431–38.

Fischer-Lichte, Erika. 1992 (1983). *The Semiotics of Theater*, trans. Jeremy Gaines and Doris Jones. Bloomington: Indiana University Press.

Fiske, John. 1989. *Understanding Popular Culture*. Boston: Unwin Hyman.

————. 1991. Popular Discrimination. In *Modernity and Mass Culture*, ed. James Naremore and Patrick Brantlinger, 103–16. Bloomington: Indiana University Press.

————. 1992. The Cultural Economy of Fandom. In Lewis 1992:30–49.

Foucault, Michel, ed. 1980 (1978). *Herculine Barbin; Being the Recently Discovered Memoirs of a Nineteenth-Century French Hermaphrodite*, trans. R. McDougall. New York: Pantheon Books.

Frow, John. 1995. *Cultural Studies and Cultural Value*. Oxford: Clarendon Press.

Frühstück, Sabine. 1996a. Good Sex, Pure Science, and Ambivalent Politics. Paper presented at the Association for Asian Studies, 48th Annual Meeting, Honolulu, April 12.

————. 1996b. Die Politik der Sexualwissenschaft: Zur Produktion und Popularisierung sexologischen Wissens in Japan 1900–1941 (The politics of sexology: The creation and popularization of the science of sexuality in Japan, 1900–1941). Ph.D. diss., University of Vienna, Austria.

Fukushima, Yukio, and Marcus Nornes, eds. 1991. *Media Wars: Then and Now*. Yamagata International Documentary Film Festival '91. Tokyo: Sōjinsha.

Furukawa, Makoto. 1994. The Changing Nature of Sexuality: The Three Codes Framing Homosexuality in Modern Japan, trans. Alice Lockyer. *U.S.-Japan Women's Journal* (English supplement), no. 7:98–127.

Garber, Marjorie. 1992. *Vested Interests: Cross-Dressing and Cultural Anxiety*. New York: Harper Perennial.

Gilman, Sander. 1985. *Difference and Pathology: Stereotypes of Sexuality, Race, and Madness*. Ithaca, N.Y.: Cornell University Press.

Gluck, Carol. 1985. *Japan's Modern Myths: Ideology in the Late Meiji Period*. Princeton: Princeton University Press.

Goodman, Grant, ed. 1991. *Japanese Cultural Policies in Southeast Asia During World War 2*. New York: St. Martin's Press.

Gordon, Andrew. 1991. *Labor and Imperial Democracy in Prewar Japan*. Berkeley: University of California Press.

Gough, Kathleen. 1971. Nuer Kinship: A Re-Examination. In *The Translation of Culture: Essays to E. E. Evans-Pritchard*, ed. Thomas Beidelman, 79–121. London: Tavistock Publications.

Hall, D. G. E. 1981. *A History of South-East Asia*. 4th ed. New York: St. Martin's Press.

Hardacre, Helen. 1990. Gender and the Millennium in Ōmotokyō, A Japanese New Religion. In *Japanese Civilization in the Modern World*, vol. 6, *Religion*, ed. Tadao Umesao, Helen Hardacre and Hirochika Nakamaki, 47–62. Senri Ethnological Studies 29. Osaka: National Museum of Ethnology.

Harootunian, H.D. 1990. Disciplinizing Native Knowledge and Producing Place: Yanagita Kunio, Origuchi Shinobu, Takata Yasuma. In Rimer 1990:99–127.

Hauser, William. 1991. Women and War: The Japanese Film Image. In Bernstein 1991:296–313.

Haworth, Abigail. 1995. Where the Girls Are. *Planet Wired Tokyo* (Internet).

Hayashida, Cullen. 1976. Identity, Race, and the Blood Ideology of Japan. Ph.D. diss., University of Washington.

Heilbrun, Carolyn. 1982 (1964). *Toward a Recognition of Androgyny*. New York: Norton.

Hicks, George. 1996. The "Comfort Women." In Duus, Myers, and Peattie 1996: 305–23.

Hirschfeld, Magnus. 1935. *Women East and West: Impressions of a Sex Expert*. London: William Heinemann (Medical Books).

Holden, Stephen. 1994. Film Review: The Men Are Women and Fans Love Them. *New York Times*, August 18.

Holder, Heidi. 1991. Melodrama, Realism, and Empire on the British Stage. In Bratton et al. 1991:129–49.

Horiuchi, Katsuaki. 1990. Trendsetters Must Be Wordsmiths, Too. *Japan Times*, March 20.

Hosokawa, Shuhei. 1994. East of Honolulu: Hawaiian Music in Japan from the 1920s to the 1940s. *Perfect Beat* 2(1):51–67.

Hunter, Janet. 1984. *Concise Dictionary of Modern Japanese History*. Berkeley: University of California Press.

Huyssen, Andreas. 1986. Mass Culture as Woman: Modernism's Other. In *After the Great Divide: Modernism, Mass Culture, Postmodernism*, 44–62. Bloomington: Indiana University Press.

Hyde, Janet, and B. G. Rosenberg. 1980 (1976). *Half the Human Experience: The Psychology of Women*. Lexington, Mass.: D. C. Heath.

Ichizo Kobayashi, Man of Genius. 1944. *The Ōsaka Mainichi and Tokyo Nichinichi*, July 26.

Ivy, Marilyn. 1995. *Discourses of the Vanishing: Modernity, Phantasm, Japan*. Chicago: University of Chicago Press.

Jackson, Laura. 1976. Bar Hostesses. In *Women in Changing Japan*, ed. Joyce Lebra, Joy Paulson, and Elizabeth Powers, 133–56. Stanford: Stanford University Press.

Jansen, Marius. 1984. Japanese Imperialism: Late Meiji Perspectives. In Myers and Peattie 1984:61–79.

Jed, Stephanie. 1989. *Chaste Thinking: The Rape of Lucretia and the Birth of Humanism*. Bloomington: Indiana University Press.

Jenkins, Henry. 1991. *Star Trek* Rerun, Reread, Rewritten: Fan Writing as Textual Poaching. In *Close Encounters: Film, Feminism, and Science Fiction*, ed. Constance Penley et al., 171–202. Minneapolis: University of Minnesota Press.

———. 1992a. "Strangers No More, We Sing": Filking and the Social Construction of the Science Fiction Fan Community. In Lewis 1992:208–36.

———. 1992b. *Textual Poachers: Television Fans and Participatory Culture*. London: Routledge.

Kaite, Berkeley. 1987. The Pornographer's Body Double: Transgression Is the

Law. In *Body Invaders: Panic Sex in America*, ed. Arthur Kroker and Marilouise Kroker, 150–68. New York: St. Martin's Press.

Kasza, Gregory. 1988. *The State and Mass Media in Japan, 1918–1945*. Berkeley: University of California Press.

Kato, Hidetoshi. 1989a. Japanese Popular Culture Reconsidered. In Powers and Kato 1989:301–18.

———. 1989b. Some Thoughts on Japanese Popular Culture. In Powers and Kato 1989:xvii–xviii.

Kershaw, Baz. 1992. *The Politics of Performance: Radical Theater as Cultural Intervention*. London: Routledge.

Kessler, Suzanne, and Wendy McKenna. 1985 (1978). *Gender: An Ethnomethodological Approach*. Chicago: University of Chicago Press.

Kiernander, Adrian. 1992. The Orient, the Feminine: The Use of Interculturalism by the Théâtre du Soleil. In *Gender in Performance: The Presentation of Difference in the Performing Arts*, ed. Laurence Senelick, 183–92. Hanover, N.H.: University Press of New England.

King, Anthony. 1995. The Times and Spaces of Modernity (or Who Needs Postmodernism?). In *Global Modernities*, ed. Mike Featherstone, Scott Lash, and Roland Robertson, 108–23. London: SAGE Publications.

Kipnis, Laura. 1986. "Refunctioning" Reconsidered: Towards a Left Popular Culture. In *High Theory/Low Culture: Analysing Popular Television and Film*, ed. Colin MacCabe, 11–36. New York: St. Martin's Press.

Kleinhans, Chuck. 1994. Taking Out the Trash: Camp and the Politics of Parody. In Meyer 1994a:182–201.

Komatsuzawa Hajime. 1991. *Momotaro's Sea Eagle*. In Fukushima and Nornes 1991:241–46.

Kuhn, Annette. 1985. *The Power of the Image: Essays on Representation and Sexuality*. London: Routledge and Kegan Paul.

Kurasawa, Aiko. 1991. Films as Propaganda Media on Java under the Japanese, 1942–45. In Goodman 1991:36–92.

Lavin, Maud. 1992. Photomontage, Mass Culture, Modernity. In *Montage and Modern Life, 1919–1942*, ed. Matthew Teitelbaum, 37–59. Cambridge, Mass.: MIT Press.

Lebra, Joyce, ed. 1975. *Japan's Greater East Asia Co-Prosperity Sphere in World War II*. Kuala Lumpur: Oxford University Press.

Lebra, Takie Sugiyama. 1976. *Japanese Patterns of Behavior*. Honolulu: University of Hawai'i Press.

———. 1985 (1984). *Japanese Women: Constraint and Fulfillment*. Honolulu: University of Hawai'i Press.

Leupp, Gary. 1995. *Male Colors: The Construction of Homosexuality in Tokugawa Japan*. Berkeley: University of California Press.

Lewis, Lisa, ed. 1992. *The Adoring Audience: Fan Culture and Popular Media*. New York: Routledge, Chapman, and Hall.

Lowe, Lisa. 1991. *Critical Terrains: French and British Orientalisms*. Ithaca, N.Y.: Cornell University Press.

Lukas, Paul. 1997. *Inconspicuous Consumption*. New York: Crown.

Mackrell, Judith. 1994. Weird, Man. *Independent*, July 13.

Maclean, Marie. 1988. *Narrative as Performance: The Baudelairean Experiment.* New York: Routledge.

Manners Important at Performances. 1993. *Ann Arbor News*, May 7.

Matsudaira, S. 1984. Hiiki Renchū (Theater Fan Clubs) in Osaka in the Early Nineteenth Century. *Modern Asian Studies* 18:699–709.

Matsumoto, Narao. 1938. Takarazuka Girls' Opera Popular. *Osaka Mainichi and Tokyo Nichinichi*, January 8.

———. 1939. Pick of 13 Zukettes Is Going to China to Cheer Up Nippon Soldiers at Front. *Osaka Mainichi and Tokyo Nichinichi*, August 9.

———. 1940. 'Zuka in August. *Osaka Mainichi and Tokyo Nichinichi*, August 10.

———. 1941a. Nippon Export Trade Is Theme for Revue. *Osaka Mainichi and Tokyo Nichinichi*, April 12.

———. 1941b. Takarazuka Revues Emergency Minded; Shows Are More Serious, Less Comic. *Osaka Mainichi and Tokyo Nichinichi*, February 22.

———. 1942. Hukuko Sayo Shines in Grand Zuka Opera. *Osaka Mainichi and Tokyo Nichinichi*, March 8.

———. 1943a. *Children of East Asia* in 18 Scenes Pleasing Takarazuka Fans in August. *Mainichi*, August 15.

———. 1943b. Nippon Navy's Growth, Activities Featured on Takarazuka Stage. *Mainichi*, May 9.

———. 1943c. Story World Is Linked with Realities in *Children of Sun* at Takarazuka. *Mainichi*, April 18.

———. 1943d. Thai Foreign Chief's Drama Adapted for June Takarazuka Feature Item. *Mainichi*, June 13.

———. 1944. 'Zuka Assimilates *Midsummer Night's Dream*. *Mainichi*, June 8.

McConachie, Bruce. 1985. "The Theatre of the Mob": Apocalyptic Melodrama and Preindustrial Riots in Antebellum New York. In McConachie and Friedman 1985b:17–46.

McConachie, Bruce, and Daniel Friedman. 1985a. Introduction to McConachie and Friedman 1985b:1–17.

———, eds. 1985b. *Theatre for Working-Class Audiences in the United States, 1830–1980*. Westport, Conn.: Greenwood Press.

Meigs, Anna. 1976. Male Pregnancy and the Reduction of Sexual Opposition in a New Guinea Highlands Society. *Ethnology* 15:393–407.

Melville, James. 1986. *Go Gently, Gaijin*. New York: Fawcett Crest.

Meyer, Moe, ed. 1994a. *The Politics and Poetics of Camp*. London: Routledge.

———. 1994b. Under the Sign of Wilde: An Archaeology of Posing. In Meyer 1994a:75–109.

Michener, James. 1954 (1953). *Sayonara*. New York: Random House.

Millot, Catherine. 1990 (1983). *Horsexe: Essay on Transsexuality*, trans. K. Hylton. New York: Autonomedia.

Mochizuki Mamor[u]. 1959. Cultural Aspects of Japanese Girl's Opera. In *Japanese Popular Culture*, ed. Hidetoshi Kato, 165–74. Tokyo: Charles E. Tuttle.

Mohanty, Satya. 1989. Us and Them: On the Philosophical Bases of Political Criticism. *Yale Journal of Criticism* 2(2):1–31.

Mook, Hubertus J. 1944. *The Netherlands Indies and Japan: Their Relations, 1940–1941*. London: George Allen and Unwin.

Moore, Sonia. 1988 (1960). *The Stanislavski System*. New York: Penguin.

Morimura, Yasumasa. 1996b. *The Sickness unto Beauty: Self-Portrait as Actress*. Yokohama: Yokohama Museum of Art.

Morisaki, Kazue. 1973. Two Languages, Two Souls. *Concerned Theater Japan* 2(3/4):153–65.

Mosse, George. 1985. *Nationalism and Sexuality: Middle-Class Morality and Sexual Norms in Modern Europe*. Madison: University of Wisconsin Press.

Myers, Ramon. 1989. Japanese Imperialism in Manchuria: The South Manchuria Railway Company, 1906–1933. In Duus, Myers, and Peattie 1989:101–32.

Myers, Ramon, and Mark Peattie, eds. 1984. *The Japanese Colonial Empire, 1895–1945*. Princeton: Princeton University Press.

Nagy, Margit. 1991. Middle-Class Working Women during the Interwar Years. In Bernstein 1991:199–216.

Nakamura, Kyoko. 1983. The Significance of Amaterasu in Japanese Religious History. In *The Book of the Goddess: Past and Present*, ed. Carl Olson, 176–89. New York: Crossroad.

Nakane, Chie. 1972 (1970). *Japanese Society*. Berkeley: University of California Press.

Nanda, Serena. 1990. *Neither Man Nor Woman: The Hijras of India*. Belmont, Calif.: Wadsworth.

New Order of Living. 1940. *Osaka Mainichi and Tokyo Nichinichi*, July 13.

Newton, Esther. 1972. *Mother Camp: Female Impersonators in America*. Englewood Cliffs, N.J.: Prentice-Hall.

Nochlin, Linda. 1985. The Paterson Strike Pageant of 1913. In McConachie and Friedman 1985b:87–95.

Nolte, Sharon. 1983. *Women, the State, and Repression in Imperial Japan*. Women in International Development Working Paper, no. 33. Lansing: Michigan State University.

———. 1987. *Liberalism in Modern Japan*. Berkeley: University of California Press.

Nolte, Sharon, and Sally Hastings. 1991. The Meiji State's Policy towards Women, 1890–1910. In Bernstein 1991:151–74.

Nornes, Markus. 1991. Dawn of Freedom. In Fukushima and Nornes 1991:257–63.

O'Connor, John. 1985. The Federal Theatre Project's Search for an Audience. In McConachie and Friedman 1985b:171–83.

Ollman, Leah. 1991. *Camera as Weapon: Worker Photography between the Wars*. San Diego: Museum of Photographic Arts.

Pacteau, Francette. 1986. The Impossible Referent: Representations of the Androgyne. In *Formations of Fantasy*, ed. Victor Burgin, James Donald, and Cora Kaplan, 62–84. New York: Methuen.

Parker, Andrew, Mary Russo, Doris Sommer, and Patricia Yaeger. 1992. Introduction to *Nationalisms and Sexualities*, ed. Andrew Parker, Mary Russo, Doris Sommer, and Patricia Yaeger, 1–18. New York: Routledge.

Pease, Donald. 1991. Toward a Sociology of Literary Knowledge: Greenblatt, Colonialism, and the New Historicism. In *Consequences of Theory*, ed. Jonathan Arac and Barbara Johnson, 108–53. Baltimore: Johns Hopkins University Press.

Peattie, Mark. 1984a. Introduction to Myers and Peattie 1984:3–52.

———. 1984b. Japanese Attitudes toward Colonialism, 1895–1945. In Myers and Peattie 1984:80–127.

———. 1988. *Nan'yō: The Rise and Fall of the Japanese in Micronesia, 1885–1945*. Pacific Islands Monograph Series, no. 4. Honolulu: University of Hawai'i Press.

Pflugfelder, Gregory. 1989. "Smashing" in Cross-Cultural Perspective: Japan and the United States. Department of History, Stanford University. Unpublished paper.

Pickering, Michael. 1991. Mock Blacks and Racial Mockery: The "Nigger" Minstrel and British Imperialism. In Bratton et al. 1991:179–236.

Pinguet, Maurice. 1993 (1984). *Voluntary Death in Japan*, trans. Rosemary Morris. Cambridge: Polity Press.

Pollack, Andrew. 1994. Japanese Graduates Finding Few Jobs. *New York Times*, June 25.

Porter Poole, Fitz John. 1984. Transforming "Natural" Women: Female Ritual Leaders and Gender Ideology among Bimin-Kuskusmin. In *Sexual Meanings: The Cultural Construction of Gender and Sexuality*, ed. Sherry Ortner and Harriet Whitehead, 116–65. New York: Cambridge University Press.

Powers, Richard, and Hidetoshi Kato, eds. 1989. *Handbook of Japanese Popular Culture*. New York: Greenwood Press.

Pribram, E. Deidre, ed. 1988a. *Female Spectators: Looking at Film and Television*. New York: Verso.

Pribram, E. Deidre. 1988b. Introduction to Pribram 1988a:1–11.

Radden, Viki. 1991. Japan: Trying to Get a Job. *Off Our Backs*, March 6, pp. 6–8.

Radway, Janice. 1984. *Reading the Romance: Women, Patriarchy, and Popular Literature*. Chapel Hill: University of North Carolina Press.

Raz, Jacob. 1983. *Audience and Actors: A Study of Their Interaction in the Japanese Traditional Theater*. Leiden: E. J. Brill.

Rea, Kenneth. 1994. Girls Will Be Boys. *Times* (London), July 9.

Renov, Michael. 1991. Warring Images: Stereotype and American Representations of the Japanese, 1941–1991. In Fukushima and Nornes 1991:86–114.

Reynolds, E. Bruce. 1991. Imperial Japan's Cultural Program in Thailand. In *Japanese Cultural Policies in Southeast Asia During World War 2*, ed. Grant Goodman, 93–116. New York: St. Martin's Press.

Rich, Adrienne. 1976. *Of Woman Born: Motherhood as Experience and Institution*. New York: Norton.

Rich, B. Ruby. 1983. *Maedchen in Uniform*: From Repressive Tolerance to Erotic Liberation. *Jump Cut* 24/25:44–50.

Rigby, Brian. 1991. *Popular Culture in Modern France: A Study of Cultural Discourse*. London: Routledge.

Rimer, J. Thomas. 1974. *Toward a Modern Japanese Theater: Kishida Kunio*. Princeton: Princeton University Press.

Roberts, JoAnn. 1988. *Art and Illusion: A Guide to Crossdressing*. 2d ed. King of Prussia, Pa.: Creative Design Services.

Roberts, S. H. 1929. *A History of French Colonial Policy, 1870–1925*. London: P. S. King and Son.

Robertson, Jennifer. 1984. Sexy Rice: Plant Gender, Farm Manuals, and Grass-Roots Nativism. *Monumenta Nipponica* 39:233–260.

———. 1987. Redressing Gender Roles: The Takarazuka Revue. Paper presented at the Association for Asian Studies 39th Annual Meeting, Boston, April 11.

———. 1989. Gender-Bending in Paradise: Doing "Female" and "Male" in Japan. *Genders* 5:188–207.

———. 1991a. The Shingaku Woman: Straight from the Heart. In Bernstein 1991:88–107.

———. 1991b. Theatrical Resistance, Theaters of Restraint: The Takarazuka Revue and the "State Theater" Movement. *Anthropological Quarterly* 64(4):165–77.

———. 1992a. Doing and Undoing "Female" and "Male" in Japan: The Takarazuka Revue. In *Japanese Social Organization*, ed. Takie S. Lebra, 165–93. Honolulu: University of Hawai'i Press.

———. 1992b. The "Magic If": Conflicting Performances of Gender in the Takarazuka Revue of Japan. In *Gender in Performance: The Presentation of Difference in the Performing Arts*, ed. Laurence Senelick, 46–67. Hanover, N.H.: University Press of New England.

———. 1992c. The Politics of Androgyny in Japan: Sexuality and Subversion in the Theater and Beyond. *American Ethnologist* 19:419–42.

———. 1994 (1991). *Native and Newcomer: Making and Remaking a Japanese City*. Berkeley: University of California Press.

———. 1995. Mon Japon: The Revue Theater as a Technology of Japanese Imperialism. *American Ethnologist* 22:970–96.

———. 1997a. Beauty and Blood: Body Politics and "Race Reform" in Imperial Japan. Paper presented at the Wissenschaftskolleg zu Berlin, May 6.

———. 1997b. Empire of Nostalgia: Rethinking "Internationalization" in Japan Today. *Theory, Culture, and Society* 14(4):97–122.

———. Forthcoming. Dying to Tell: Sexuality and Suicide in Imperial Japan. In *Signs: Journal of Women in Culture and Society*.

Robinson, Ronald. 1991. Introduction: Railway Imperialism. In *Railway Imperialism*, ed. Clarence Davis and Kenneth Wilburn, Jr., 1–6. Contributions in Comparative Colonial Studies, no. 26. New York: Greenwood Press.

Roden, Donald. 1990. Taishō Culture and the Problem of Gender Ambivalence. In *Culture and Identity: Japanese Intellectuals during the Interwar Years*, ed. J. Thomas Rimer, 37–55. Princeton: Princeton University Press.

Roscoe, Will. 1991. *The Zuni Man-Woman*. Albuquerque: University of New Mexico Press.

Said, Edward. 1979 (1978). *Orientalism*. New York: Vintage Books.

Sarasas, Phra. 1940. *Whom the Gods Deny*. London: Heath Cranton.

Schalow, Paul. 1990. Introduction to *The Great Mirror of Male Love* by Ihara Saikaku, trans. Paul Schalow, 1–46. Stanford: Stanford University Press.

Schechner, Richard. 1964. Stanislavski at School. *Tulane Drama Review* 9(2): 199–211.

———. 1988. *Performance Theory*. New York: Routledge.

Schnapp, Jeffrey. 1993. 18BL: Fascist Mass Spectacle. *Representations*, no. 43 (Summer):89–125.

Schodt, Frederik. 1985. *Manga! Manga! The World of Japanese Comics*. New York: Kodansha.

Seidensticker, Edward. 1983. *Low City, High City*. New York: Alfred A. Knopf.

———. 1990. *Tokyo Rising*. New York: Alfred A. Knopf.

Seward, Jack. 1968. *Hara-Kiri: Japanese Ritual Suicide*. Rutland, Vt.: Charles E. Tuttle.

Sexual Revolution in the Making. 1996. *Japan Times Weekly*, international ed., June 24–30, p. 7.

Shephard, Ben. 1986. Shobiz Imperialism: The Case of Peter Lobengula. In *Imperialism and Popular Culture*, ed. John Mackenzie, 94–112. Manchester: Manchester University Press.

Shiach, Morag. 1989. *Discourse on Popular Culture: Class, Gender, and History in Cultural Analysis, 1730 to the Present*. Stanford: Stanford University Press.

Shillony, Ben-Ami. 1991 (1981). *Politics and Culture in Wartime Japan*. Oxford: Clarendon Press.

Shively, Donald. 1970. *Bakufu* versus *kabuki*. In *Studies in the Institutional History of Early Modern Japan*, ed. John Hall and Marius Jansen, 231–61. Princeton: Princeton University Press.

Sievers, Sharon. 1983. *Flowers in Salt: The Beginnings of Feminist Consciousness in Modern Japan*. Stanford: Stanford University Press.

Silverberg, Miriam. 1990. *Changing Song: The Marxist Manifestos of Nakano Shigeharu*. Princeton: Princeton University Press.

———. 1991. The Modern Girl as Militant. In Bernstein 1991:239–66.

———. 1992. Constructing the Japanese Ethnography of Modernity. *Journal of Asian Studies* 51(1):30–54.

———. 1993. Constructing a New Cultural History of Prewar Japan. In *Japan in the World*, ed. Masao Miyoshi and H. D. Harootunian, 115–43. Durham, N.C.: Duke University Press.

Singer, A. 1973. Marriage Payments and the Exchange of People. *Man*, n.s., 8(1):80–92.

Singer, Jane. 1996. The Dream World of Takarazuka. *Japan Quarterly* 40(2):162–81.

Sischy, Ingrid. 1992. Onward and Upward with the Arts: Selling Dreams. *New Yorker*, September 28, pp. 84–103.

Smith-Rosenberg, Carroll. 1985. *Disorderly Conduct: Visions of Gender in Victorian America*. New York: Oxford University Press.

Stimpson, Catharine. 1989 (1974). The Androgyne and the Homosexual. In

Where the Meanings Are: Feminism and Cultural Spaces, 54–61. New York: Routledge.

Stoler, Ann. 1989. Making Empire Respectable: The Politics of Race and Sexual Morality in 20th-Century Colonial Cultures. *American Ethnologist* 16:634–660.

Stourac, Richard, and Kathleen McCreery. 1986. *Theatre as a Weapon: Workers' Theatre in the Soviet Union, Germany, and Britain, 1917–1934*. London: Routledge and Kegan Paul.

Summerfield, Peggy. 1986. Patriotism and Empire: Music-Hall Entertainment, 1870–1914. In *Imperialism and Popular Culture*, ed. John Mackenzie, 17–48. Manchester: Manchester University Press.

Takarazuka. 1989. Takarazuka: Takarazuka Kagekidan.

Takarazuka to Add Troupe. 1994. *Daily Yomiuri*, October 26.

Takarazuka to Get New Tokyo Theater. 1996. *Japan Times*, October 23.

Tanaka, Stefan. 1993. *Japan's Orient: Rendering Pasts into History*. Berkeley: University of California Press.

Taylor, Diane. 1991. Transculturating Transculturation. In *Interculturalism and Performance*, ed. Bonnie Marranca and Gautam Dasgupta, 60–74. New York: PAJ Publications.

Taylor, Helen. 1989. *Scarlett's Women: Gone with the Wind and Its Female Fans*. New Brunswick, N.J.: Rutgers University Press.

Theweleit, Klaus. 1989 (1978). *Male Fantasies*. Vol. 2, *Male Bodies: Psychoanalyzing the White Terror*, trans. Erica Carter and Chris Turner. Minneapolis: University of Minnesota Press.

Thompson, John. 1984. *Studies in the Theory of Ideology*. Cambridge: Polity Press.

3.4% of Women Feel Equal at Work. 1994. *Japan Times*, June 14.

Touwen-Bouwsma, Elly. 1994. Japanese Minority Policy: The Eurasians on Java and the Dilemma of Ethnic Loyalty. Netherlands State Institute for War Documentation. Unpublished paper.

Treat, John. 1993. Yoshimoto Banana Writes Home: *Shōjo* Culture and the Nostalgic Subject. *Journal of Japanese Studies* 19:353–87.

Tsuchiya, Hiroko. 1985. "Let Them Be Amused": The Industrial Drama Movement, 1910–1929. In McConachie and Friedman 1985b:97–110.

Ueno, Toshiya. 1991. The Other and the Machine. In Fukushima and Nornes 1991:61–85.

Vance, Carol. 1985. Pleasure and Danger: Toward a Politics of Sexuality. In *Pleasure and Danger: Exploring Female Sexuality*, ed. Carol Vance, 1–27. Boston: Routledge and Kegan Paul.

Vicinus, Martha. 1989. Distance and Desire: English Boarding School Friendships, 1870–1920. In *Hidden from History: Reclaiming the Gay and Lesbian Past*, ed. Martin Duberman, Martha Vicinus, and George Chauncey, 212–29. New York: New American Library.

Watanabe, Tsuneo, and Jun'ichi Iwata. 1989 (1987). *The Love of the Samurai: A Thousand Years of Japanese Homosexuality*, trans. D. R. Roberts. London: GMP.

Watson, Sophie, ed. 1990. *Playing the State: Australian Feminist Interventions*. New York: Verso.

Westney, Eleanor. 1987. *Imitation and Innovation: The Transfer of Western Organizational Patterns to Meiji Japan*. Cambridge, Mass.: Harvard University Press.

What Will Become of Girls' Revue in Japan? 1940. *Osaka Mainichi and Tokyo Nichinichi*, March 20.

White, Anne. 1990. *De-Stalinization and the House of Culture: Declining State Control Over Leisure in the USSR, Poland, and Hungary, 1953–1989*. London: Routledge.

Whitehead, Harriet. 1984. The Bow and the Burden Strap: A New Look at Institutionalized Homosexuality in Native North American. In *Sexual Meanings: The Cultural Construction of Gender and Sexuality*, ed. Sherry Ortner and Harriet Whitehead, 80–115. New York: Cambridge University Press.

Williams, Walter. 1986. *The Spirit and the Flesh: Sexual Diversity in American Indian Culture*. Boston: Beacon Press.

Willis, Ronald. 1964. The American Lab Theatre. *Tulane Drama Review* 9(1): 112–16.

Wolff, Janet. 1981. *The Social Production of Art*. London: Macmillan.

Women's Work Conditions Improve but Barriers Remain. 1990. *Japan Times*, March 19.

Yano, Christine. 1995. Shaping the Tears of a Nation: An Ethnography of Emotion in Japanese Popular Song. Ph.D. diss., University of Hawai'i at Manoa.

Young, Robert. 1995. *Colonial Desire: Hybridity in Theory, Culture, and Race*. London: Routledge.

Zortman, Bruce. 1984. *Hitler's Theater: Ideological Drama in Nazi Germany*. El Paso, Tex.: Firestein Books.

Index

Page numbers in italics refer to illustrations.

Acting, as process of assimilation, 94–95
Acting methods: in Kabuki, 53–55; in
  Takarazuka, 12–14, 59–61, 94–95
Actors: banning of female, 7, 51, 96, 122,
  217–18n9; double standards for female, 52–53; in Edo period, 54; fan
  support needed by, 164–65, 181; female, 7–8; private vs. public roles
  of, 15–16, 175–76; prostitution associated with, 8, 168, 218n9; types of
  roles for, 10. *See also* Takarasiennes;
  specific men's and women's roles
*Advance, Naval Ensign! (Susume kaigun-
  hata),* 128–29
Ageism, in workplace, 66, 145
Aihōkai (Love Takarazuka Club), 171,
  234n16
Akiyama, Satoko, 49, 205
Allied (American) Occupation, xii,
  114–15
Amakasu, Tadahiko, 210
American Federal Theater Project, 105,
  228n15, 233n13
American Laboratory Theater (United
  States), 218n16
Androgyny *(andorojenii)*: anima vs.
  animus in, 222n4; as asexual, 48,
  87; assimilation and, 96–97; as big
  business, 205–7; in clothing, 49;
  defined, 47, 49; as deviant, 56–57;
  in Edo period, 51–52; gender transformations in, 53–54, 55, 58–59, 85,
  223n8; hybridity associated with,
  91–92, 207; in Japan, 87–88, 145; in
  Kabuki, 47, 48, 53–55; as loanword,
  48–49; by men, 202; of Modern Girls,
  65; of *nimaime,* 56; of *onnagata,* 53–55;
  of *otokoyaku,* 78–79; physiological, 49–
  51, 87; popular culture and, 205–7,
  215, 235n13; postwar, 73–77; *ryōsei*
  vs. *chūsei* in, 49–51, 222n2, 224n17;
  sexologists on, 49–50; sexual politics
  of, 48, 88, 145; in Takarazuka revues,
  74–77, 78–81, 87–88

Androgyny (Andorojenii), 78, 212
Animations, 205, 228n14, 235n13
Anju, Mira, 82
Ano hata o ute (Dawn of Freedom), 103
Aoki, Ryōichi, 125
Aoyagi, Yūbi, 170
Arasoi wa koko ni mo (Battle Is Also Here),
  133, 154, 230–31n41
Archer, William, 94, 227n8
Ariake no wakare (Parting at Dawn),
  225n33
Aristotle, 17, 218n16
Asaji, Saki, 166, 167, 223n11
Asakusa district (Tokyo), 6
*Asakusa Kurenaidan (Scarlet Gang of Asa-
  kusa)* (Kawabata), 234n1
Asami, Rei, 1, 3, 4, 84–85
Asano, Michiko, 49, 205, 223n8, 235n12
Asexuality, 48, 81–82, 87
Ashihara, Kuniko, 73, 165, 166, 225n32
Assimilation: androgyny and, 96–97,
  204; in capitalism, 207; of colonial
  subjects vs. *otokoyaku,* 95–96; cultural
  politics of, 93; in French colonial
  theory, 226–27n5; hybridity and,
  91–96; in Indonesia, 104; in Japanization, 95–96, 104; masculine females
  and, 96; mass, 115; of national cultural identity, 92–93, 132–35; New
  Half and, 204, 214; sexual politics
  of, 94; in Takarazuka Revue, 94–97;
  whiteface as, 190–91. *See also* Colonialism; Japanization
Atarashii onna (New Woman), 133, 134,
  156, 213–14, 223n12, 231n44
Atarashiki hata (New Flag), 120
Audiences: class of, 126; cultivation of
  wartime, 124; etiquette for, 126–27,
  140–42, 232n3; female, 140–42, 153;
  female to male ratios in, 147, 153;
  sizes of, 115; wartime, 125–26;
  Western vs. Japanese, 126, 141–42,
  232n3. *See also* Fans; Spectatorship
Autographs, 179, 180

Indexer: Amy Harper
Compositor: Integrated Composition Systems
Text: 10/13 Palatino
Display: Palatino
Printer and binder: Malloy Lithographing